LUTHER'S WORKS

American Edition

VOLUME 52

Published by Concordia Publishing House

and Fortress Press in 56 volumes.

LUTHER'S WORKS

VOLUME 52

Sermons

II

EDITED BY

HANS J. HILLERBRAND

GENERAL EDITOR

HELMUT T. LEHMANN

FORTRESS PRESS/PHILADELPHIA

Library of Congress Catalog Card Number 55-9893

ISBN 0-8006-0352-4

3214C74   Printed in United States of America   1-352

GENERAL EDITORS'
PREFACE

The first editions of Luther's collected works appeared in the sixteenth century, and so did the first efforts to make him "speak English." In America serious attempts in these directions were made for the first time in the nineteenth century. The Saint Louis edition of Luther was the first endeavor on American soil to publish a collected edition of his works, and the Henkel Press in Newmarket, Virginia, was the first to publish some of Luther's writings in an English translation. During the first decade of the twentieth century, J. N. Lenker produced translations of Luther's sermons and commentaries in thirteen volumes. A few years later the first of the six volumes in the Philadelphia (or Holman) edition of the Works of Martin Luther appeared. But a growing recognition of the need for more of Luther's works in English has resulted in this American edition of Luther's works.

The edition is intended primarily for the reader whose knowledge of late medieval Latin and sixteenth-century German is too small to permit him to work with Luther in the original languages. Those who can will continue to read Luther in his original words as these have been assembled in the monumental Weimar edition (D. Martin Luthers Werke. Kritische Gesamtausgabe; Weimar, 1883–   ). Its texts and helps have formed a basis for this edition, though in certain places we have felt constrained to depart from its readings and findings. We have tried throughout to translate Luther as he thought translating should be done. That is, we have striven for faithfulness on the basis of the best lexicographical materials available. But where literal accuracy and clarity have conflicted, it is clarity that we have preferred, so that sometimes paraphrase seemed more faithful than literal fidelity. We have proceeded in a similar way in the matter of Bible versions, translating Luther's translations. Where this could be done by the use of an existing English version—King James, Douay, or Revised Standard—we have done so. Where it could not, we have supplied our own. To indicate this in each specific instance would have been pedantic; to adopt a uniform procedure would have been artificial—especially in view of Luther's own inconsistency in this regard. In each volume the translator will be responsible primarily for matters of text and language, while the responsibility of the editor will extend principally to the historical and theological matters reflected in the introductions and notes.

Although the edition as planned will include fifty-five volumes, Luther's writings are not being translated in their entirety. Nor should they be. As he was the first to insist, much of what he wrote and said was not that important. Thus the edition is a selection of works that have proved their importance for the faith, life, and history of the Christian church. The first thirty volumes contain Luther's expositions of various biblical books, while the remaining volumes include what are usually called his "Reformation writings" and other occasional pieces. The final volume of the set will be an index volume; in addition to an index of quotations, proper names, and topics, and a list of corrections and changes, it will contain a glossary of many of the technical terms that recur in Luther's works and that cannot be defined each time they appear. Obviously Luther cannot be forced into any neat set of rubrics. He can provide his reader with bits of autobiography or with political observations as he expounds a psalm, and he can speak tenderly about the meaning of the faith in the midst of polemics against his opponents. It is the hope of publishers, editors, and translators that through this edition the message of Luther's faith will speak more clearly to the modern church.

J. P.
H. T. L.

CONTENTS

IDB   — *The Interpreter's Dictionary of the Bible,*
         edited by George A. Buttrick
         (New York and Nashville, 1962).

LW   — American Edition of *Luther's Works*
         (Philadelphia and St. Louis, 1955–   ).

MPL   — *Patrologiae, Series Latina,*
         edited by J. P. Migne
         (Paris, 1844–1904).

O.D.C.C.   — *The Oxford Dictionary of the Christian Church,*
         edited by F. L. Cross
         (2nd ed., London, 1958).

WA   — *D. Martin Luthers Werke.* Kritische Gesamtausgabe
         (Weimar, 1883–   ).

INTRODUCTION TO VOLUME 52

Martin Luther, whose verdicts on his own writings oscillated between the extremes of exuberant commendation and devastating stricture, observed on one occasion that the "postil is the very best book which I ever wrote"[1]—and the historian is inclined to concur with this judgment. There is a striking freshness about this *Church Postil* (*Kirchenpostille*) or *Wartburg Postil*, as it is variously called, which deservedly ranks among the very best of Luther's writings in terms of clarity of exposition and incisiveness of thought.[2] It epitomizes Luther's genius.

Luther wrote the *Postil* during his "exile" on the Wartburg between 1521 (the first sermon was completed in June) and 1522 (the last sermon was completed around the middle of February). The background of Luther's turning to the task is worth noting. The period of the storm and stress of the indulgence controversy had come to an end. Luther and his fellow reformers had made their initial pronouncements about the need for ecclesiastical change and religious reorientation. One of their persistent pronouncements pertained to the centrality of Scripture as the source of religious authority.

Luther's major preoccupation during his ten months on the Wartburg, after having been removed from the turbulence of the events leading to his ecclesiastical excommunication and political censure, was with two practical ramifications of this scriptural emphasis. He set out to translate the New Testament into German and to write the *Church Postil*. The translation sought to make the New Testament writings generally accessible in the vernacular, while

---

[1] See *WA* 23, 278.
[2] A detailed exposition of the historical and technical details of the *Postil* is offered by Gottfried G. Krodel in *LW* 48, 237–45. The term *postil* came into usage in the early part of the sixteenth century. It was derived from the Latin *postilla*, "exposition," which in turn grew out of the standard phrase *post illa verba sacrae scripturae*, "according to these words of Sacred Scripture," with which the sermonic exposition customarily began.

the *Postil* was to provide homiletical material to be used by ministers in the exposition of the gospel. Both efforts were meant to be immensely practical. The common people were to be enabled to read the gospel themselves and the clergy were to be given the means to propagate this gospel from their pulpits.

The very essence of Luther's conception of his reformative task found expression here. The appeal to the man-on-the-street, or to those who in turn might influence common people directly, namely, the clergy, constituted the marrow of his strategy of reform. The need for a practical guide for preaching was real indeed. Preaching, while increasingly popular in the later Middle Ages, was hardly widespread in the early sixteenth century. Given the theological preeminence of the mass, preaching had a secondary place, though the establishment of specific preaching posts in the late fifteenth century increased the prevalence of homiletical activity. Luther echoed the new emphasis; his stress lacked innovative revolutionary quality, but constituted an intensification of previous practice. The call for the preaching of the gospel—as against the propagation of what Luther and his comrades-in-arms called "man-made" doctrines —meant that the clergy had to be supplied with practical help for the execution of this mandate.

The *Postil* does not contain actual sermons, preached by Luther, but sermon guides, homilies written by him for the use of other ministers.[3] One suspects, all the same, that many of the "sermons" in the *Postil* were undoubtedly soon echoed (verbatim or otherwise) a thousandfold from Lutheran pulpits throughout Germany.

The *Wartburg Postil*, to which we have made reference thus far, is itself complex and part of a larger series of publications. Luther's goal was to have available homiletical expositions of all the gospel and epistle lessons for the church year. The *Wartburg Postil* made a beginning, in that it covered the Sundays of Advent and Christmas. The two parts of this postil are known, specifically,

---

[3] For a summary essay on the characteristics of Luther's preaching see Harold J. Grimm, "The Human Element in Luther's Sermons," *Archiv für Reformationsgeschichte* 49 (1958), 50–60. Other useful studies include: Gerhard Ebeling, *Evangelische Evangelienauslegung: Untersuchungen zu Luthers Hermeneutik* (Munich, 1942); Hermann Werdermann, *Luthers Wittenberger Gemeinde, widerhergestellt aus seinen Predigten* (Gütersloh, 1929); Emanuel Hirsch, "Luthers Predigtweise," *Luther* 25 (1954), 1–23; Paul Althaus, "Luther auf der Kanzel," *Luther* 3 (1921), 17–34.

as the *Christmas Postil* and *Advent Postil*, written by Luther in that order. The *Lenten Postil*, covering the Sundays between Epiphany and Easter, was published in 1525. In later years the gaps left by the three publications were filled. Stephan Roth published the *Summer Postil* and the *Festival Postil* in 1527. These were followed one year later by a second series of sermons on the "winter" lessons, also published by Roth, for which Luther, somewhat reluctantly, provided a preface. Later editions included a series of sermons on the church year, written by Luther between 1531 and 1535, when ill health prevented his public preaching.

The citations in the text are primarily to scriptural passages; other citations are few and far between. Luther's situation on the Wartburg—without access to books and a library—offers a practical explanation for this paucity of citations, as does his obvious desire to remain aloof from any reliance, however cursory, on man-made doctrines.

The sermons convey the full range of Luther's creativity which finds expression even in the English translation. Luther's denunciation of the ecclesiastical establishment is clear; the Catholic church, pope, bishops, clergy, monks, and universities, come under his biting attack. Also very much in evidence is Luther's ability to concentrate on the important issues. Although the free flow of exposition is somewhat restricted by the need to stay close to the biblical text, Luther's treatment is wide and comprehensive enough to permit him to state his main theological affirmations with emphasis, if also with a certain redundancy. He himself noted in later years that he had been "immoderately verbose."[4] Luther writes about the nature of faith, about human merit, about the joyfulness and spontaneity of the Christian profession; the "theology of the cross" is given extensive elaboration. In short, Luther's own epilogue, in which he stated that he hoped that in the *Postil* "the Christian life may have been so fully depicted that more than enough has been said to the Christian about what is necessary for salvation," is altogether appropriate.

One particular element in Luther's homilies on the various gospel texts deserves, regrettably, special mention. By stressing the

---

[4] *WA TR* 1, 488.

traditional Christian notions concerning the relationship between Jesus and his Jewish environment, Luther echoes the traditional antisemitism of Christian theology.[5] By putting Jesus' life into stark relief, Christian theology sought to intensify the mystery of the incarnation: precisely in the Jewish rejection of Jesus' messianic claim was this mystery to be most splendidly expressed. Consequently, the tendency to speak negatively about the Jews, to denounce and deride, has been real. While the motifs of Christian antisemitism through the centuries are varied and complex, its reality has always been somber. The reader will note in several passages in this volume that the line between authentic Christian affirmation and cultural antisemitism is thin as a razor's edge. Luther's comments must thus be put into that traditional setting. To those of us in the twentieth century who have seen our Jewish brethren suffer through the inferno of the Holocaust, the proper understanding of Luther's words—as well as our acknowledgment of our distance from them—becomes doubly important. Part of the problem lies in the vocabulary: the word "Jew" has a historical, theological, and contemporary meaning, and strictures of a historical or theological sort turn at once into contemporary observations as well. Accordingly, I have deemed it appropriate to use the word "Israelite" instead of the more standard word "Jew" whenever Luther used the word *Juden*. By the use of the archaic and historical term the proper focus of some of Luther's remarks will be better observed—and a painful misunderstanding obviated.

Our volume includes selections from the *Christmas Postil*, specifically the "sermons" on the gospel lessons for Christmas Eve, the Early Christmas Service, the Main Christmas Service, St. Stephen's Day, the Sunday after Christmas, New Year's Day, and the Festival of the Epiphany. The translation of these selections is based on the text of the *Kirchenpostille* as published in WA 10[I, 1], 58–95, 128–141, 180–247, 270–289, 379–448, 504–519, 555–728. The basis for the WA text, in turn, is the first edition of the *Kirchen-*

---

[5] On Luther and the Jews the reader may consult the editorial remarks by Franklin Sherman in *LW* 47, 123–136. Perceptive comments are also found in Aarne Siirala, "Luther and the Jews," *Lutheran World* 11 (1964), 337–357. A comprehensive monograph on the topic remains a desideratum. A survey of recent research is found in Bernhard Lohse, "Die Lutherforschung im deutschen Sprachbereich seit 1966," *Luther-Jahrbuch* 38 (1971), 116 ff.

postille as published by Johann Grunenberg in Wittenberg in 1522. An earlier English translation of the expositions included in this volume was made by John Nicholas Lenker in volume 10 of the Standard Edition of Luther's Works: *Luther's Church Postil, Gospels: Advent, Christmas and Epiphany Sermons,* volume 1 (Minneapolis: Lutherans in All Lands Co., 1905).

I wish to thank my research assistants, Ms. Shelley Baranowski and Ms. Laura Fishman, for various helps and kindnesses in the preparation of the manuscript. Mr. John Kleiner, of Fortress Press, very carefully examined the translations provided by Messrs. Kunstmann and Hebart. I stand in all their debt.

H.J.H.

LUTHER'S WORKS

VOLUME 52

DEDICATION TO
COUNT MANSFELD

May the grace and the peace of God be with my noble and high-born Lord, Count Albrecht of Mansfeld and Schraplau and Helderungen, etc.[1] This is the prayer of Martin Luther.

When the saintly King David wished to appoint the heir to his royal throne, he commanded that after his death his youngest son should inherit the realm, in order that the kingdom of Israel should remain one and undivided [I Kings 1:30 ff.]. Should this youngest son's family die out, then the family of the son next to the youngest son should take their place. In this manner he made Solomon, his youngest son, king in preference to all the others, and the throne remained in the family of Solomon until King Joash. At that time the bloodthirsty Queen Athaliah, Solomon's family having died out with her son, Ahaziah, destroyed the whole family of David. There remained but one spark, Joash, miraculously preserved by God from the family of Nathan, Solomon's youngest brother [II Kings 11:1–3]. This was for the sake of Christ who had been promised to David as one who should descend from his flesh and blood.

Now it is true, this command could be regarded as not con-forming to the law of Moses which gives to the first son dominion over his brothers in addition to a double portion of the inheritance. However, it did conform to it since David's first son, Amnon, had already been slain by his brother, Absalom, and the reason for such a command was that David saw how his children pressed to inherit the realm. Moreover, and this was much more important, it was done in order to bring about a prefiguration of Christ who, as the true Solomon, is the youngest and the smallest among all the chil-dren of God. He himself says in Matthew 11[:11] that among those born of women there did not arise a greater one than John the

---

[1] On Count Albrecht of Mansfeld, Luther's territorial lord, see LW 49, 103, n. 6.

3

Baptist; nevertheless the smallest in the kingdom of heaven is greater than he. This smallest one is none other than Christ. No one has ever been humbled so deeply, no one has made himself smaller than did Christ, and for this reason, too, he alone may say: "Learn of me, I am meek and lowly in heart." Such words no saints have ever said or been able to say, nor could they compare themselves to his perfect lowliness and meekness. All of them remain pupils of this teacher, so that even St. Paul, when he says to the Corinthians [I Cor. 11:1], "Follow me," immediately names the proper teacher by adding, "even as I follow after Christ." Paul does not want to proffer himself as example, but rather Christ within himself and himself in Christ. For that reason, too, Christ is elevated and has been seated as king above all his brothers, namely, us and all Christians, as Psalm 45[:7] declares: "Your God has anointed you (i.e., consecrated you as king) above all your companions." Thus is also fulfilled in him that which was prefigured in Solomon, and not merely fulfilled, but set up for us as an example that we should see everywhere the chief article of evangelical teaching which is, in the words of Christ: "Whoever humbles himself, shall be exalted," and "Whoever among you wishes to be greatest, let him be the least." The whole gospel, is nothing more than an account of the least son of God and of his "lessening" as Paul says, I Corinthians 2[:2]: "Among you I have not permitted myself to imagine I know anything except Jesus Christ and him crucified."

The reason, Your Grace, for writing the above is that I had determined to dedicate this book to the ruler of my native country. People should not consider it strange that I, contrary to custom, do not begin with the oldest member, but with the youngest of both branches of the family, but this is what the character of his book demands: in it only the lowliest and the youngest are constantly considered. I have adapted the preface to the situation and, to the extent it could be done, I have avoided dissonance. For I did not want the teaching of the gospel to float in the midair of words, but wanted to show at least a bit of it in practice. For the big shots in this world, who live in pleasant settings and in the reputation of their high and mightiness, need to be reminded occasionally, in accordance with the gospel, of their disrepute and smallness before God, even though they must and need only recognize those above

4

all else. Moreover, I should have acted a long time ago as one of your subjects toward you, Your Grace. But the gospel is plain and says, no matter what seems right and good to men, that "The last are the first, and the first are the last." And my detractors are not to be given opportunity nor reason to assume that I primarily strive after my own glory and that of my family. The gospel earnestly teaches one should not seek his own first, but, as stated, one should humble and despise himself.

In order that this preface conform in every respect to the gospel, therefore, the writer, too, is a despised and damned person. By the grace of God I am under sentence of excommunication by the pope and in greatest disfavor; in addition his followers curse and hate me greatly. So I hope it should be all right for me to treat this despised, little, poor book of the gospel concerning the least and most despised child of God, and to forget about the high, big, and long books of the tiara-crowned king in Rome, even if it should be a bit above me, inasmuch as all universities, convents, and monasteries are tied to the tiara and disregard the youngest and littlest book, the gospel. Yet necessity demands and compels that someone consider the book of the uncrowned and despised son of God, whatever the outcome! It cannot be entirely bad.

Your Grace has seen the bull of excommunication issued in Rome and the opinion rendered by the faculty at Paris.[2] Without a doubt, the two documents were published with a special divine intention, so that the world should know how potently truth can disgrace and blind her enemies through the very deeds and words of these enemies. I do not wish to make utter fools of them and to cause them to cover themselves with shame, but I am satisfied if, for the sake of truth, the proverb, which utters a truth that is quite close to the gospel, is vindicated: "The wise ones are the fools." It is the gospel's intention to bring to the light of day and to prove that the wise are fools and the fools wise, and that those who are defamed as heretics are Christians and that those who boastingly call

---

[2] The bull excommunicating Luther, *It Is Right that the Roman Pontiff* (*Decet Romanum Pontificem*), was issued on January 3, 1521; cf. *LW* 31, xix–xx. On April 15, 1521, the University of Paris published its *Conclusion of the Paris Theologians regarding the Lutheran Doctrine* (*Determinatio theologorum Parisiensium super doctrina Lutheriana*) which condemned Luther's teachings; cf. *LW* 48, 258, n. 7.

themselves Christians are heretics. This I say, My Lord, because I believe you must have gotten acrid smoke into your eyes about me. You may have heard from the learned and clever followers of the pope that I am a disgrace and a dishonor to Your Grace's realm, that is, a poor, despised religious "Cinderella." These holy people try to look so painstakingly for reasons to slander and to defame that, because of me, they do not permit the good innocent people of Sangerhausen to remain unmaligned (and all this, because their city borders on my birthplace!).[3] Yet it is still undecided whether Kunz Schmid or the "gray sparrow" is a terrible heretic or a cat.[4] John Huss, Jerome of Prague, and many more have been burned in Germany, but to this very day they have not been refuted.[5] A current prophecy concerning the Antichrist asserts that he is going to burn the Christians with fire. This prophecy must be fulfilled. For this reason I pray Your Grace to think again of the gospel, which reverses everything and proceeds contrary to reason. What they call dishonor is honor. What they call honor is dishonor. They who do the burning, should be burned at the stake, and they who are burned, should occupy the judge's bench, where they will indeed sit on the Last Day. At that time what the prophet declares in Psalm 18[:26] will be most clearly revealed: "With those who are perverse God, too, is perverse." Because they act contrary to reason and judge unfairly, he acts the same way and judges contrary to reason.

So I commend Your Grace and your entire realm and all those who love the gospel to God's mercy. May he mercifully protect them against the teachings of men and preserve them correctly and firmly with his teaching in the free Christian faith. Amen.

---

[3] Augustine Alveld, a Franciscan opponent of Luther, had claimed in a treatise which he published in 1520 that Sangerhausen had been a center of the Bohemian heresy in the fifteenth century. Cf. *WA* 10$^{I, 1}$, 7, n. 1.

[4] Kunz Schmid is a reference to a flagellant and spiritualistic preacher-prophet who had gathered a group of followers in Thuringia and was executed in Sangerhausen either in 1369 or 1414. The "gray sparrow" is almost certainly a reference to Alveld (see above, n. 1), who had described Schmid as a Beghard and claimed that the Bohemian heresy had been planted in Sangerhausen by Schmid; from there it spread to Eisleben, the town where Luther was born. In this way Alveld felt he was able to document the fact that Luther had been infected by the Bohemian heresy from his earliest days.

[5] John Huss (*ca.* 1369–1415), Bohemian reformer, and Jerome of Prague (d. 1416), his friend and disciple, were condemned as heretics by the Council of Constance (1414–18) and burned at the stake.

THE GOSPEL FOR CHRISTMAS
EVE, LUKE 2[:1–14]

It is written in Haggai 2[:6, 21] that God says: "I will move the heavens and the earth when he will come whom all people desire." This has been fulfilled today. For the heavens, that is, the angels who are in heaven and who were praising God with their song, and the earth, that is, the people on earth, were moved. Thus everybody started out and was traveling, I submit, into one town here and into another town there throughout the land, as the Gospel says, and yet it was not a bloody upheaval, but a peaceful one, brought about by God, who is a God of peace. The meaning is not that all countries everywhere on earth were in motion in that manner, but only those that were subject to the Romans. This "earth" is to signify only the area of the Roman Empire which occupied not even half of the earth's surface. Furthermore, no land was moved as much as was the Jewish land which was divided in an orderly fashion among the tribes of Israel, although at that time the tribe of Judah was the most populous in the land, since the ten tribes of Israel that had been taken to Assyria had stayed away.

St. Luke says that this registration was the very first one. In Matthew 17[:24–27] and in other places, we find that it was continued, so that they demanded the tribute money from Christ, too, and that they tried to set a trap for him by means of the tribute money (Matt. 22[:17–21]); furthermore, on the day of his passion they leveled against him the accusation that he had forbidden the payment of this tribute money. For the Israelites paid it unwillingly, and they could scarcely tolerate this sort of registration and imperial decree. They claimed to be God's people and to be free of the emperor, and they engaged in disputations as to whether they were obligated to pay the tribute money; yet they had to and they were powerless to uphold their claims. For this reason they would gladly have entangled Christ in the disputation and handed him over to

7

the Romans. Therefore this registration was nothing but a common provision in all countries to the effect that every person annually was to give one penny. The officials who collected and exacted this and other duties and taxes were called *publicani*, which is translated into German as "manifest sinners," but this translation is incorrect.

Notice the certainty in the statement of the evangelist that the birth of Christ took place at the time of Emperor Augustus and when Cyrenius was governor of the Roman Empire in Syria of which the Jewish land was a part, as Austria is a part of Germany. It came to pass during this very first registration. The tribute money had never been paid before the time when Christ was to be born. In this manner he has indicated how his realm should not be in any way secular and that he should not rule as a secular ruler over a secular dominion, but that he would subject himself and his parents to the secular powers. Just because he comes at the time of the first registration, he permits no doubt to remain about this; for if he had wanted to raise doubts, then he could have been born later during a different registration. Then one might have said that it had happened accidentally and by chance, and without design. Similarly, too, if he had not wanted to be a subject, he could have been born at an earlier time prior to this registration. Since, however, all his works are nothing but precious teaching, there is no other possible explanation than that, following God's counsel and purpose, he does not want to exercise worldly rule, but wants to be a subject. This is the first blow against the papal system and that of the pope's followers, whose system tallies with Christ's kingdom as night does with day!

The Gospel is so clear that there is little need of learned interpretation. It is only necessary to ponder it well, to contemplate it, and to take it completely into your heart. None will derive more benefit from it than they whose hearts hold still and who divest themselves of material considerations and concentrate diligently on it. This lesson is just like the sun: in a placid pond it can be seen clearly and warms the water powerfully, but in a rushing current it cannot be seen as well nor can it warm up the water as much. So if you wish to be illumined and warmed here, to see God's mercy and wondrous deeds, so that your heart is filled with fire and light and becomes reverent and joyous, then go to where you may be still and impress the picture deep into your heart. You will find no end of wondrous deeds. However, in order to start out the simple people and to give them incentive, let me show them a little how to go about it; later on they may go into it a bit more thoroughly.

In the first place, notice how ordinarily and simply things take place on earth, and yet they are held in such high respect in heaven! This is what takes place on earth: there is a poor, young woman, Mary, in Nazareth. Nobody pays any attention to her, and she is considered to be one of the least significant inhabitants of the town. Nobody realizes the great wonder she is carrying. She is silent, does not put on airs, and considers herself the lowliest person in town. She starts out on the journey with Joseph, her husband. Maybe they have no hired woman or man, but Joseph is master and servant and she lady and maid in the house, and so they left the house unattended or in the care of other people. Let us assume Mary had a donkey to sit on, although the Gospel account does not mention this and it is likely that she walked on foot with Joseph. Think how disrespectfully she was treated on the way in the inns, and yet she deserved to be carried in a gilded coach and with the greatest pomp. How many wives and daughters of great lords were living at that time in splendid circumstances and in great honor, while here this woman, the mother of God, journeys across country on foot, in the midst of winter, in the last stages of pregnancy! Oh, what injustice! It was certainly more than a day's journey from Nazareth in Galilee to Bethlehem in the land of Judah; they certainly had to bypass Jerusalem or to pass through it, for Bethlehem lies to the south of Jerusalem, and Nazareth to the north.

Then when they came to Bethlehem, they were the most insignificant, the most despised people, as the evangelist indicates. They were obliged to make room for everybody, until they were shown into a stable and had to be satisfied to share with the animals a common hostel, a common table, a common room and bed! At the same time many a rogue occupied the seat of honor in the inn and was treated as a gentleman. Nobody notices or understands what God performs in the stable. He permits the big houses and the expensive rooms to remain empty; he permits them to eat, to drink, and to be of good cheer, but this solace and this treasure is hidden

9

from them. Oh, what a dark night must have been over Bethlehem at that time that they did not see such a light! Thus God indicates that he pays no attention at all to what the world is or has or can do, and on the other hand the world proves that it knows nothing at all of, and pays no attention to, what God is or has or does. Behold, this is the first symbol wherewith Christ puts to shame the world and indicates that all of its doing, knowledge, and being are contemptible to us, that its greatest wisdom is in reality foolishness, that its best performance is wrongdoing, and that its greatest good is evil. What did Bethlehem really have, when it had not Christ? What do those have now, who at that time were well off? And what do Mary and Joseph lack now, even though at that time they had no place to sleep comfortably during the night?

Some have explained the word "inn" [*diversorium*, Luke 2:7] in this text as if it meant "a public vaulted-over passage," through which everybody walks and where ordinary donkeys stand;[1] they are of the opinion that Mary did not receive lodging. This explanation is incorrect. The evangelist wants to indicate that Joseph and Mary had to retreat into the stable because they had no room in the inn and in the quarters where the guests customarily stay. All the guests were taken care of in the inn with respect to quarters, bed, and board, except that these poor people were forced to crawl into a stable at the rear where the animals were customarily kept. This word *diversorium*, for which Luke writes *katalyma*, designates a room for guests, and this is proved by Christ's words in Luke 22[:11] when he sent his disciples to prepare the evening meal and said: "Go and say to the householder: 'The master says to you, Where is the *katalyma*, i.e., the guesthouse, where I can eat my paschal lamb with my disciples?'" The same applies here, too; Joseph and Mary found no room in the *katalyma*, in the guesthouse, only in the stable, in the courtyard of that householder, who was not worthy to put up and to honor such a guest properly. They had no money or prestige, and so they had to stay in the stable. How mad is the world and how blind are you, man!

But the birth itself was even more pitiful: nobody took pity on this young woman who was about to give birth for the first time;

---

[1] E.g., Bonaventure, *Meditations on the Life of Christ* (*Meditationes vitae Christi*), chap. 7.

10

nobody took to heart the heaviness of her body; and nobody cared that she was in strange surroundings and did not have any of the things which a woman in childbirth needs. Rather, she was there without anything ready, without light, without fire, in the middle of the night, alone in the darkness. Nobody offered her any of the services which one naturally renders to pregnant women. Everyone was drunk and roistering in the inn, a throng of guests from everywhere, and nobody bothered about this woman. I suspect she did not expect to give birth so soon; otherwise she might have remained in Nazareth. Consider now what sort of cloths she may have used to wrap him in; perhaps her veil or whatever she did not need to cover her own body. The people of Aix-la-Chapelle claim to know that she wrapped him up in Joseph's pants, but that has the ring of a fairy tale and sounds frivolous.[2] These are fables of which, I am sure, there are many more all over the world. That Christ is born in the cold of winter, in a strange land, on a journey across country, under circumstances so miserable and so poor—surely all this adds up to inconvenience.

Then there are some who express opinions concerning how this birth took place, claiming Mary was delivered of her child while she was praying, in great joy, before she became aware of it, without any pains. I do not condemn these devotional considerations— perhaps they were devised for the benefit of simple-minded folk— but we must stay with the Gospel text which says she gave birth to him, and with the article of the creed which says "born of the Virgin Mary." There is no deception here, but, as the words indicate, it was a real birth. Now we know, do we not, what the meaning of "to bear" is and how it happens. The birth happened to her exactly as to other women, consciously with her mind functioning normally and with the parts of her body helping along, as is proper at the time of birth, in order that she should be his normal natural mother and he her natural normal son. For this reason her body did not abandon its natural functions which belong to childbirth, except that she gave birth without sin, without shame, without pain, and without injury, just as she had conceived without sin. The curse of Eve, which reads: "In pain you shall bear your children" [Gen.

---

[2] In Aix-la-Chapelle, certain relics were publicly exhibited in 1486, including what were alleged to be a slip of Mary and pants of Joseph.

3:16], did not apply to her. In other respects things happened to her exactly as they happen to any woman giving birth. For grace does not destroy or impede nature and nature's works; indeed, grace improves and promotes them. In the same way she nurtured him in a natural fashion with milk from her breasts; undoubtedly this was not done with milk from another woman, or by means of another part of her body. No, she gave him her breasts which God had filled in a supernatural manner with milk, without injury and uncleanness as we sing concerning her: *ubere de coelo pleno*.[3]

I am talking about this so that we may have a foundation for our faith and that we let Christ be a natural human being, in every respect exactly as we are. Nor must we put him in a separate category as far as nature is concerned except where sin and grace are involved. In him and his mother nature was pure in all members and in all the functions of the members. No female body or one of its organs ever attained its natural function without sin, except in this virgin. Here, for one time, God honored nature and its function. The more we draw Christ down into nature and into the flesh, the more consolation accrues for us. Therefore whatever is not contrary to grace should in no way be subtracted from his and his mother's nature. The text clearly states and declares that she bore him, and that "he is born" is also proclaimed by the angels.

How could God have demonstrated his goodness more powerfully than by stepping down so deep into flesh and blood, that he does not despise that which is kept secret by nature, but honors nature to the highest degree exactly where it was brought into shame to the highest degree in Adam and Eve? Thus from now on even that is godly, proper, and clean which in all men is the opposite of godly, and most shameful and unclean. Indeed, these are wondrous works of God! How could he have presented to us a more forceful, a more powerful and purer example of chastity than this birth? How completely do all desires and thoughts, no matter how strong they may be, topple down, when we merely look at this birth and ponder how God's exalted majesty with all earnestness, with boundless love and kindness goes to work and has to do in the

---

[3] The reference is to a response that was spoken after one of the lections for the Matins service on The Circumcision of Our Lord (January 1), as found in the *Breviarium Romanum*.

female flesh and blood of this virgin. No woman ever gives to a man such pure thoughts as does this virgin, and likewise, no man to a woman as does this child. Pure chastity wells forth from this birth, no matter how we regard it, if only we recognize in it the work of God.

But what is taking place in heaven because of this birth? Even as it is disregarded on earth, it is highly honored in heaven, and indeed a thousand times more. Suppose an angel from heaven praised you and your works, would you not consider it greater than the praise and honor of all the world? You would feel you could not bear enough humbleness and contempt for it. Now, what sort of honor is it that all the angels in heaven cannot contain themselves for joy, that they burst forth giving poor shepherds in the field a chance to hear them, that they preach, praise, sing, and pour out their joy beyond measure? Can the joy and honor of all the people of Bethlehem, indeed that of all kings and lords on the earth, be compared to this joy and honor? It is nothing but filth and abomination, of which nobody likes to think when he contemplates this joy and honor! Behold, how richly God honors those who are despised and apt to be despised of men! Here you see where his eyes are turned: into the depths and low places, as it is written: "He sits above the Cherubim and looks into the depth or the abyss." Then, too, the angels could not find any princes or potentates, but only unlearned lay people and the lowliest of all the folk on earth. Could they not have addressed the high priests and the learned men of Jerusalem? After all, they talk a lot about God and the angels. No, poor shepherds, who were nothing on earth, had to be worthy to receive such great grace and honor in heaven. How completely does God spurn that which is high! And we only strive madly and frantically after vain heights, lest we be honored in heaven; again and again we step out of God's horizon, so that he might not see us in the depths, the only place where he looks.

Let this be enough of an incentive for contemplation on the part of simple people. Let each one strive by himself! All words are pure fire, they warm the heart, provided a person keeps them there, as we read in Jeremiah 23[:29]: "My words are like fire." As we see, it is the nature of the divine words to teach us to understand God and his works; their aim is to show us that this life is nothing. Since he does not live in accordance with this life and does not own goods, honor, and power of this temporal life, he has no regard for them and he does not speak of them, but teaches only the reverse, and acts "foolishly": he looks at that from which the world turns away, teaches those things from which the world flees, picks up what the world casts aside. And although we do not like going along with such actions of God and do not wish to give up goods, honor, and life in this manner, yet that is how it must be. For it cannot be changed; God teaches and acts in no other manner. We must take our direction from him; he will not take his direction from us. Also, whoever disregards his word, his deed—the nativity—and his consolation, certainly has no good sign of salvation in him. How could God have demonstrated more pleasantly that he is gracious to all those who are lowly and despised on earth than by this lowly birth, from which the angels derive joy and which he reveals to none but the poor shepherds?

Now let us see what sort of mysteries, hidden things, are presented to us in this story. Generally speaking, there are two matters which are expressed in all mysteries—the gospel and the faith, i.e., what one is to preach, and what one is to believe, and who are to be the preachers and who are to be the hearers. Let us have a look at these two matters.

The First Matter

The first matter is the faith which is truly to be perceived in all the words of God. This faith does not merely consist in believing that this story is true, as it is written. For that does not avail anything, because everyone, even the damned, believe that. Concerning faith, Scripture and God's word do not teach that it is a natural work, without grace. Rather the faith that is the right one, rich in grace, demanded by God's word and deed, is that you firmly believe Christ is born for you and that his birth is yours, and come to pass for your benefit. For the Gospel teaches that Christ was born for our sake and that he did everything and suffered all things for our sake, just as the angel says here: "I announce to you a great joy which will come to all people; for to you is born this day a

14

Savior who is Christ the Lord" [Luke 2:10–11]. From these words you see clearly that he was born for us.

He does not simply say: "Christ is born," but: "*for you* is he born." Again, he does not say: "I announce a joy," but: "*to you* do I announce a great joy." Again, this joy will not remain in Christ, but is for all people. A damned or a wicked man does not have this faith, nor can he have it. For the right foundation of all salvation which unites Christ and the believing heart in this manner is that everything they have individually becomes something they hold in common. What is it that they have?

Christ has a pure, innocent, holy birth. Man has an impure, sinful, damned birth, as David says in Psalm 51[:5]: "Behold, in sin am I fashioned in the womb, and in sin did my mother conceive me." There is no remedy for this except through the pure birth of Christ. Now the birth of Christ cannot be distributed physically, even as that would not be of any help either. For this reason it is distributed spiritually, by means of the word, to everyone, as the angel says, so that all who firmly believe that it is given to them in this manner shall not be harmed by their impure birth; this is the manner and means to become cleansed from the stain of the birth we have from miserable Adam. Christ willed to be born so that we might be born in different manner, as he says in John 3[:3–6]. This happens through that faith, as James 1[:18] says: "He has born us of his own will through his word of truth, so that we begin to be his new creation." In this manner Christ takes to himself our birth and absorbs it in his birth; he presents us with his birth so that we become pure and new in it, as if it were our own, so that every Christian might rejoice in this birth of Christ and glory in it no less than if he, too, like Christ, had been born bodily of Mary. Whoever does not believe this or has doubts about it, is not a Christian.

This is the great joy, of which the angel speaks, this is the consolation and the superabundant goodness of God, that man (if he has this faith) may boast of such treasure as that Mary is his real mother, Christ his brother, and God his father. For these things are, all of them, true and they come to pass, provided we believe them; this is the chief part and chief good in all the gospels, before one derives from them teaching concerning good works. Christ, above all things, must become ours and we his, before we undertake good works. That happens in no other way than through such faith; it teaches the right understanding of the gospels and it seizes hold on them in the right place. That makes for the right knowledge of Christ; from it the conscience becomes happy, free, and contented; from it grow love and praise of God, because it is he who has given us freely such superabundant goods in Christ. Then there follows a mind right willing to do, to refrain from doing, and to suffer everything that is pleasing to God, be it a matter of living or dying, as I have said many times. This is the meaning of Isaiah 9[:6]: "To us a child is born, and to us a son is given." To us, to us, born to us and given to us. Therefore see to it that you derive from the Gospel not only enjoyment of the story as such, for that does not last long. Nor should you derive from it only an example, for that does not hold up without faith. But see to it that you make his birth your own, and that you make an exchange with him, so that you rid yourself of your birth and receive, instead, his. This happens, if you have this faith. By this token you sit assuredly in the Virgin Mary's lap and are her dear child. This faith you have to practice and to pray for as long as you live; you can never strengthen it enough. That is our foundation and our inheritance; on it the good works are to be built.

Now when Christ has thus become your own [in the manner described], and when you through him have become cleansed in such faith, then you have received your inheritance and the chief goods, without any merit of your own, as you see, but solely because of God's love who gives to you as your own his son's possessions and works. Now there follows the example of good works, that you also do to your neighbor as you see that Christ has done for you. Here we learn what good works are in themselves. For tell me, what are Christ's good works? Is it not true that, in every case, they are good for the reason that they took place for your benefit, for God's sake who commanded him to perform such works for your benefit? Thus Christ was obedient to his father in this, that he lived and served us. Because you are full and rich, you have no other commandment according to which you serve and obey Christ, except that you direct all your works so that they are good and useful to your neighbor, exactly as Christ's works are good and useful to you. For this reason he said while eating the evening meal: "This is my commandment that you love each other as I have loved you" [John 13:34]. You see here that he has loved us and that he has done all his works for us. The purpose is that we, in turn, do likewise, not to him—he is not in need of it—but to our neighbor. That is his commandment; that is our obedience; and so faith brings about that Christ is ours, even as his love brings about that we are his. He loves, and we believe, and those are the ingredients of the cake. Again, our neighbor believes and is expecting our love. We, then, should love him, too, and not let him look and wait for us in vain. The one is the same as the other: Christ helps us, so we help our neighbor, and all are satisfied.

From this you should yourself note how far afield they have gone who have tied good works to stone, wood, clothing, food, and drink. What does it avail your neighbor if you should build a church out of pure gold? What benefit does he derive from the ringing of big bells and many bells? What benefit does he derive from the great display of pomp and pretense in the churches by means of vestments, reliquaries, statues, and vessels made of silver? What benefit does he derive from the burning of many candles and much incense? What benefit does he derive from the making of lots of noise, murmuring, the singing of vigils and masses? Do you think God will permit himself to be paid off by means of the ringing of bells, the smoke of candles, the display of gold and other nonsense? None of these has he commanded to you. But [he has commanded] that if you see that your neighbor errs, sins, is in need, and suffers in his body, possessions, or soul, then and there you should get busy, let everything else go, and help him with all you are and have. When you can do no more, then you should help him with words and with prayer. For that is what Christ has done for you and he has given you an example that you should do likewise. Behold, these are the two things that a Christian should practice. The one is directed toward Christ, that he draw Christ unto himself and through faith make him his own, that he be clothed with Christ's riches and boldly trust in him. The second is directed toward his neighbor, that he get down to his level and also let him have disposition of his possessions. Whoever does not

17

practice these two things is not benefited, no matter whether he kills himself fasting or becomes a martyr, permits himself to be burned at the stake, and performs all miracles, as St. Paul teaches in I Corinthians 13[:1–3].

[The Second Matter]

The second mystery or hidden teaching is that in the church nothing other than the gospel shall be preached. Now the gospel teaches only the two previous things, Christ and his example, two kinds of good works: one kind belonging to Christ, by means of which we in faith, attain salvation, the other kind belonging to us, by means of which our neighbor is helped. Whoever teaches differently from the gospel, he misleads, and whoever does not teach the gospel in accordance with these two parts, he misleads even more and is worse than he who teaches without the gospel, because he desecrates and corrupts the word of God, as St. Paul complains about some [II Cor. 2:17; 4:2]. Now nature by itself could not have discovered such teaching, nor can the intelligence, reason, and wisdom of all men devise it. For who would fathom from his own resources that faith in Christ unites us with Christ and makes us owners of all the possessions of Christ? And who would imagine that no works are good except those which pertain to our neighbor or are, at least, aimed in that direction? Nature teaches no more than to act according to the wording of the commandments. Hence nature operates in terms of its own works so that this one assumes he fulfills the commandments by making endowments, and that one, by means of fasting, and another, with vestments, and a fourth, by making a pilgrimage—one by doing one thing and another by doing still another—and yet these are nothing more than self-devised, futile works, which afford help to nobody. At the present time, unfortunately, the whole deluded world is going astray on account of human teaching and works, so that faith and love have vanished together with the gospel. Hence the gospel and its interpretation are an entirely supernatural sermon and light, setting forth only Christ.

This is brought out in the first place in this, that it was not one human being who announced to another this birth of Christ, but it was an angel who came from heaven and announced to the shepherds this birth of Christ. No human being knew a thing about it. In the second place, midnight, at which time Christ was born, has a meaning, namely, that all the world is in darkness at his advent and that reason is unable to recognize Christ. There must be a revelation from heaven. In the third place, the light which shone around the shepherds is meant to teach that there is needed here a light entirely different from any natural reason. St. Luke speaks here of *gloria dei*, the glory of God shone about them. He calls this light a *gloria* or honor of God. Why does he do this? In order to touch on the mystery and to indicate the nature of the gospel. Since the gospel is a heavenly light, teaching nothing but Christ in whom God's grace is given us and our doing is summarily rejected, it raises up only the honor of God so that henceforth nobody can boast of a single capability, but is obliged to give honor to God and to leave the glory to him, so that it is purely through his love and goodness that we are saved through Christ. Behold God's glory and God's honor are the light in the gospel which comes from heaven and shines around us through the apostles and their successors who preach the gospel; for the angel represented all the preachers of the gospel, and the shepherds represented all hearers, as we shall see. For this reason the gospel is unable to permit any other teaching in addition to it. For man's teaching is this earth's light and is man's glory. It raises up man's glory and praise and makes souls arrogantly rely on their own works, whereas the gospel teaches them to rely on Christ and on God's mercy and kindness, to glory and to be bold in Christ.

Likewise, in the fourth place, there is a significance to the names "Judea" and "Bethlehem," where Christ wanted to be born. "Judea" in German means "confession" or "giving of thanks," as when we confess and praise God and thank him that all our goods are gifts from him. Such a "confessor" and "praiser" is called *Judeus*. The king of such "Jews" is Christ, as his inscription reads: *Jhesus nazarenus rex iudeorum*. Thus, we too, say in German of a grateful or of an ungrateful person: he acknowledges it, he does not acknowledge it, etc. In this manner it is indicated that no teaching makes such confession, except the gospel which teaches Christ.

Likewise *Beth* means "house," *lehem* means "food" or "bread"; "Bethlehem" means "house of bread." The town bears this name

19

because, situated in a good, fertile area, it abounded in grain; therefore, like the surrounding towns, it was regarded as a grain depot, just as we call such a town a lardpit. In former times it was called "Ephrathah", i.e., "fertile." The rationale behind both names is the same: it had fertile, grain producing soil. The meaning of this is that without the gospel there is nothing but desert on earth and no confession of God and no thanksgiving. But where the gospel and Christ are, there is Bethlehem abounding in grain, and grateful Judea; there everybody has enough in Christ and there is nothing but thanksgiving for God's mercies. But the doctrines of men thank only themselves, and yet they permit arid land and deadly hunger to remain. No heart is ever satisfied unless it hears Christ preaching properly in the gospel; when this happens, a person comes to Bethlehem and finds him; then he also comes and stays in Judea and thanks his God eternally; then he is satisfied; then, too, God is praised and confessed. Apart from the gospel there is nothing but ingratitude and we do nothing but die of hunger.

But the angel demonstrates the gospel most clearly with his words. To show that nothing else should be preached in Christendom, he takes over the office and the word that are appropriate to the gospel and says: *Evangeliso*. He does not say "I preach to you," but "I am speaking a gospel to you." I am an evangelist and my word is a gospel. Thus, as is explained earlier in the *Advent Postil*,[4] gospel signifies a good, joyous message, and that shall be the sermon in the New Testament. And whereof does the gospel speak? Listen! He says: "A great joy do I announce to you; my gospel tells of a great joy" [cf. Luke 2:10]. Where is it? Listen again: "For you is born a Savior, Christ the Lord, at Bethlehem in the town of David" [cf. Luke 2:11]. See there what the gospel is: a joyous sermon concerning Christ, our Savior. He who preaches him properly, preaches the gospel and nothing but joy. What greater joy may a heart know than that Christ is given him as his very own? He does not just say: "Christ is born," but he appropriates Christ's birth for us and says: "Your Savior." Thus the gospel does not merely teach the story and accounts of Christ, but personalizes them and gives them to all who believe in it, which is also

---

[4] Cf. WA 7, 473, 504, 505.

(as mentioned above) the right and real nature of the gospel. What good would it do me, if he were born a thousand times and if this were sung to me every day with the loveliest airs, if I should not hear that there was something in it for me and that it should be my own? When that voice sounds, no matter how furtively and imperfectly, my heart listens with joy, and the voice reaches through all the way and sounds splendidly. If there were something else to preach, then the evangelical angel and angelic evangelist would have touched on it.

Then he says: "This will be a sign for you: you will find the child wrapped up and laid in a manger" [Luke 2:12]. The cloths are nothing but Holy Scripture, in which Christian truth lies wrapped up. Here one finds faith described. For the entire Old Testament contains nothing but Christ as he is preached in the gospel. Therefore we see how the apostles adduce testimony from the Bible and how in this manner they prove everything that is to be preached and to be believed concerning Christ. Thus Paul says in Romans 3[:21] that faith in Christ, by means of which we are justified, is manifested through the law and the prophets; and Christ himself, after his resurrection, opens unto them the Scriptures and shows how they talk of him. Likewise on Mount Tabor, Matthew 16[17:3], when he was transfigured, there stood two men, Moses and Elijah, with him (i.e., the law and the prophets) as his two witnesses, his sign, pointing to him. For this reason, I take it, the angel says that the cloths are the sign by which one would know him. For there exists no other witness on earth to Christian truth but Holy Scripture. Similarly, Christ's indivisible coat signifies the Scripture of the New Testament which was apportioned and gambled away during his passion. This signifies how the pope, the Antichrist, would not deny the gospels, but would tear them apart and play tricks with them by means of false interpretations, with the result that one could no longer find Christ in them. For the four soldiers who crucified the Lord were prefigurations of all bishops and teachers in the four parts of the world who tear apart the gospel and kill Christ and faith in him with their teachings of men, something the pope together with his papists fulfilled a long time ago.

21

Thus we see that the law and the prophets, too, cannot be preached or recognized properly, unless we see Christ wrapped up in the Scriptures. It is true that it does not seem that Christ is in them. The Israelites, we know, do not see Christ in them. They are inconspicuous, unimportant cloths, simple words, and they seem to speak of unimportant external matters, so that of itself nothing striking is discernible, but the New Testament, the gospel, must explain, reveal, and illumine, as has been pointed out. First the gospel must be heard, and one must believe the appearance of the angel and his voice. Had the shepherds not heard from the angels that Christ was lying there, they might have looked at him a thousand and another thousand times and yet they would not have found out from that that the child was Christ. Thus St. Paul says in II Corinthians 4 [3:14–16]: "The law remains dark and covered up for the Jews until they are converted to Christ." For Christ must first be heard in the gospel and then one sees how beautifully the entire Old Testament is attuned solely to him and makes sense so sweetly that man must give himself up captive in faith; then he realizes how true are the words which Christ says in John 5[:46]: "Moses has written of me; if you believed him you would also believe me." For this reason let us beware of all teachings which do not teach Christ. What more do you want to know? What more do you need? If you know Christ to the extent (as has been said above) that through him you walk in faith toward God and in love toward your neighbor and if you do to your neighbor as he has done to you, that is indeed the whole Bible condensed into the shortest span, so that there is no more need of words or books, but only that you live and do accordingly.

He lies in the manger. Look at this so that you may be certain that only Christ is to be preached in all the world. What else is the manger than the gathering of the Christian people in church to listen to the sermon? We are the animals that go with this manger. There Christ is placed before us, and with this food we are to feed our souls, that is, lead them to the sermon. He who goes to listen to a sermon, goes to this manger, but the sermons must deal with Christ. For not all mangers hold Christ and not all sermons teach the faith. Notice there was only one manger in Bethlehem in which this treasure lay, and it was, in addition, an unused, despised manger which at other times contained no fodder. Thus the preaching of the gospel is free of all other things; it has Christ and teaches only him. Should it, however, teach something else, then it has already ceased being Christ's little manger, and has become the manger of cavalry horses, filled with the physical fodder of temporal teaching. But so that you can see how Christ wrapped up in the cloths signifies faith in the Old Testament, let me cite a few examples.

We read in Matthew 8[:4], where Christ cleanses the leper, that he says to him: "Go now, show yourself to the priest and offer up your offering, as commanded by Moses, for a testimony to them." Here you are told that the law of Moses was given to the Israelites to be a testimony or sign, as the angel also declares in this passage, namely, a sign that the law means something else than merely what the words say. What other meaning? Christ is the priest; all men are spiritual lepers because of unbelief. But when we believe in him, he touches us with his hand, he gives us and attributes to us his works. Thereby we become clean and healthy, without any merit of our own, and we are "to show ourselves" to him, that is, to be grateful and acknowledge that we have become righteous [frum], not through our doing, but through his grace. In this way we are set right with God. Now we are to offer up our gift, that is, we are to share what is ours with our neighbor and do good to him as Christ has done to us. This is the meaning of serving Christ and bringing your gift to the real priest, for it is done for his sake and to show love and praise for him. Do you see how beautifully both Christ and faith are wrapped up in the simple passage of Scripture and the metaphor? You comprehend now that Moses in the law has only given a testimony and a signification of Christ. In this manner one must understand all of the Old Testament and one must let these the cloths be signs which point to Christ, so that one can recognize him.

Another example: the fact that the Sabbath was so strictly regulated and that one could not perform any work on that day, indicates that there shall be in us not our works, but the works of Christ, for, as said before, it is not our doing, but what Christ has done, which redeems us. Now there are two kinds of works, as indicated above. In the one category those works which Christ has done personally, without us. These are the chief works, and faith is involved here. The second category are the works which he works in us and which we do toward our neighbor in love. The former may be called works of the evening and the latter works of the morning. Thus, "evening and morning become one day," as it is written in Genesis 1[:5 *et passim*]. For the Bible begins the day in the evening and brings it to a conclusion in the morning; that is, evening together with the night is the first half, and morning together with the day is the second half of an entire natural day. Now as the first half is dark and the second light, just so the first works of Christ's are ours in faith and are hidden, but the others, the works of love, are to come out into the light of day and to be revealed to the neighbor publicly. See, thus is the whole sabbath celebrated and sanctified! And don't you see how well Christ lies here in his swaddling cloth? How well does the Old Testament show forth faith and love in Christ and in his Christians. Now baby diapers are commonly of two kinds, one for the outside, coarse, woollen material, the other for the inside, linen, softer material. The woolen, coarse outside material is the metaphor which is now narrated from the law. But the linen material is the sayings of the prophets, set forth without metaphors, as the one in Isaiah 7[:14]: "Behold, a virgin shall be pregnant and bear a son; his name shall be called Emmanuel," and similar ones which likewise would not be understood as being about Christ, if the gospel did not indicate them and point out Christ in them.

So have we indicated the two, faith and the gospel, that they and nothing else should be preached in Christendom. Now let us see who are to be the preachers and the pupils. The preachers are to be angels, i.e., messengers of God, and they are to lead a heavenly life, dealing all the time with the word of God, so that they never preach human doctrines. It is a most unseemly thing, to be God's messenger and not to promulgate his message. *Angelus* means "messenger" and here Luke calls him *angelus domini*, "messenger of God." There is also more significance attached to the message than to the messenger's life: if he leads a bad life, he hurts himself, but if he delivers a falsified message as God's message, he seduces and harms everyone who listens to him, and he creates idolatry among the people, so that they honor lies as truth, men as

God, and worship the devil instead of God. For this reason there is no more gruesome plague, misery, or misfortune on earth than a preacher who does not preach God's word. Unfortunately the whole world is full of this kind nowadays. Yet they are of the opinion they are performing well and are pious people, although their true nature is that they murder souls, blaspheme, set up idolatry, so that they would fare far better, if they had been robbers all the time and murderers and the very worst criminals—at least they would know that they were evildoers. But, as it is, they go about under the name and appearance of priest, bishop, pope, clergyman and in reality they are ravening wolves in sheep's clothing. It would be a boon, if nobody listened to their sermons.

The pupils are shepherds, poor folk out in the fields. Here Christ keeps the promise made in Matthew 11[:5]: "The poor have the gospel preached to them," and in Matthew 5[:3]: "Blessed are the poor, for theirs is the kingdom of heaven." Here there are no learned people, no wealthy people, no powerful people; for such people do not accept the gospel. The gospel is a heavenly treasure which refuses to tolerate another treasure alongside it; it cannot get along with another earthly guest in the heart. Therefore whoever loves the one, must let go the other, as Christ says in Matthew 6[:24]: "You cannot serve God and mammon at the same time." The shepherds indicate this in that they are found in the field under the sky, and not in houses; thus they do not cling or cleave to temporal goods. In addition, they are in the field at night, despised and not recognized by the world which sleeps during the night and likes to strut and be seen during the day. But the poor shepherds are up and working during the night. They represent all the lowly ones who lead a poor, despised, unostentatious life on earth and live under the open sky, subject to God. They are ready to receive the gospel. The fact that they are shepherds means that nobody should listen to the gospel for his own benefit solely, but each one should tell someone who has no knowledge of it; for whoever believes for himself, that one has enough and he must see to it from then on how he might bring others also to such a faith and knowledge, so that one person is the shepherd of the other, and pastures him and takes care of him on this earth in the darkness of his life. The first thing the angel does

25

is to frighten the shepherds. For nature is initially aghast when it hears the gospel message that all our doing is nothing and is damned in the sight of God, and nature is loath to give up its opinion and impudence.

Now each and everyone should measure himself against the gospel and should see how near or how far away from Christ he is and how he stands in the matter of faith and love. There are many who become inflamed with unreal devotion when they hear of such poverty of the Christ-child. They are almost filled with wrath against the citizens of Bethlehem; they condemn their blindness and ingratitude and are of the opinion, that had they been there, they would have rendered outstanding service to the Lord and his mother and they would not have stood for such miserable treatment. But they do not look around themselves to see how many of their immediate neighbors there are who could use their help and whom they are neglecting and leaving exactly as they are. Who is there on earth who is not surrounded by poor, miserable, ailing, erring, or sinful people? Why then does he not perform his deeds of love right here? Why does he not do to them as Christ has done to him? It is a plain lie and deception for you to think you would have done a lot of good for Christ, if you do not do it for these people. Had you been at Bethlehem, you would have paid just as little attention to him as did the others. Of course, now, because his identity has been revealed, you want to serve. If he were to come now and lie down in the manger and have you informed that it is he about whom you now know so much, then you might do something, but prior to that you would not have done it! If somebody had told the rich man in the gospel, so that he would have known for sure, what an important person poor Lazarus would be later on, he would not have left him lying and rotting there [Luke 16:19–31]. Similarly, if at the present time your neighbor were that which he is slated to be later on and if he were lying before you, then in all likelihood, you would take care of him. But since this is not so, you disregard everything and you do not recognize your Lord in your neighbor. You do not do to him as he has done to you. For this reason God lets you become blind, lets you be deceived by the pope and false preachers, so that you spend money for wood and stone, paper and wax and in this manner lose the means whereby you might have been able to help your neighbor.

Finally we must explain the song of the angels which we use daily in the mass: *Gloria in excelsis deo*, etc. They enumerate three things in this song: honor, peace, and good pleasure or good will. Honor they give to God, peace to the earth, and good pleasure to men. Good will or good pleasure might be understood as the divine good will and good pleasure which God has toward men through Christ. But we prefer to leave it as the good will which men have from this birth, the sense which is given by the words which read *anthropis eudokia, hominibus beneplacitum* [Luke 2:14]. The first item is the honor of God. This is where one should begin, in order that in all things the glory and the honor be given to God, i.e., to him who does, gives, and has all things, so that nobody may attribute anything to himself or assume anything. For the honor is due nobody except God alone; it cannot be shared with anybody or become common property. Adam has stolen the honor through the persuasion of the evil spirit and has usurped it to himself, so that all men, because of it, are in disgrace with God; and to this day it is so deeply rooted in all men that no vice is so deep-seated in them as is striving after honor. Nobody wants to be or to have nothing; everybody is well pleased with himself, and this is the source of all misery, hostility, and war on earth. Christ has restored honor once more to God by teaching us that all that is ours is nothing in the sight of God but plain wrath and disgrace. Therefore, we may not in any way glorify ourselves nor please ourselves in what is ours, but must be in fear and shame as if we were in direst peril and disgrace, so that, as a consequence, our honor and self-satisfaction are thrust down and become absolutely nothing, and we become glad that we are rid of them in this manner so that we may be found and saved in Christ, as we have said.

The second item is peace on earth. For just as there must be absence of peace where there is not honor of God—as Solomon says: *inter superbos*, "among the overbearing there is always bickering" (Prov. 13:10)—in the same manner, where there is honor of God, there must be peace. Why should they bicker, if they know that nothing is their own, but that everything they are, have, and can do belongs to God? They let him be in charge and are satisfied that they have a gracious God. He who knows that all his possessions are nothing in the sight of God does not pay too much attention to them and directs his thoughts to something else that is important in the sight of God, and that is Christ. The result is that where there are true Christians there cannot be feuding, bickering, hostility. As Isaiah 11[:9] announces and says: "They shall not kill or harm one another on my holy mountain" (i.e., in Christendom). The reason for this follows: "For the earth is full of the knowledge of God," that is, because they recognize God, that everything is his and our things are nothing, therefore they may indeed have peace among themselves. Just as this same Isaiah says in chapter 2[:4]: "They shall change their swords into plowshares and their spears into sickles. In the future they shall not lift up the swords against each other or prepare themselves for combat." For this reason our Lord Christ is called a King of Peace and is prefigured in King Solomon, whose name means "rich in peace." He creates peace inwardly toward God in our conscience through faith in him, and outwardly toward man through love. This occurs as we go through life, so that through him there is peace everywhere on earth.

The third item is the good will of men. Good will here does not refer to that which brings forth good works, but to the good pleasure and peaceful heart which permit man to be pleased with everything that happens to him, be it good or bad. For the angels knew very well that the peace of which they sing does not extend farther than among those who truly believe in Christ; these certainly have peace with each other. But the world and the devil take no rest and they grant no peace to them: they persecute them to death, as Christ says, in John 16[:33]: "In me you shall have peace, in the world you will have tribulation." For this reason the angels were not satisfied to sing of peace on earth; they also sang of the good will of men, i.e., that they should be pleased with everything and praise and thank God, considering God's ways and dealings with them to be right and good. They do not grumble but live most patiently and with acquiescence in God's will. Indeed, because they know that God does and works everything, the same God whom they have received through Christ in faith as a gracious father, they glorify him and rejoice when they are persecuted. As

28

St. Paul says in Romans 5[:3]: "We glory and rejoice in persecutions." Everything that happens to them they consider to be the best, because of the abundance of the happy conscience they have in Christ. Behold, it is such a good will, good pleasure, good construction on all things, whether they are good or bad, that are what the angels have in mind here in their song. For where good will does not exist, peace does not remain for long. In the absence of good will the worst construction is placed on all things, evil is always enlarged, and misfortune is doubled. As a result men are not pleased with God's dealing with them; they want it to be different; and what is written in Psalm 18[:26] is fulfilled: "With the merciful thou wilt show thyself merciful; with the perfect man thou wilt show thyself perfect; with the pure thou wilt show thyself pure"; that is, whoever has the pleasure in all things which God has, in him God will also have pleasure, even as with the perverse God will also show himself perverse. Just as God and all his works are not pleasing to him, so, on the other hand, God and all those on God's side are not pleased with him. Concerning good will Paul says in I Corinthians 3 [cf. Rom. 15.2, I Cor. 9:22]: "Endeavor to please everyone." How is this brought about? If all things seem good to you and please you, you, in turn, will please everyone. It is a simple rule: If you do not wish to please anybody, be pleasant with nobody; if you do wish to please everybody, then be pleased by everybody, with this limitation, however, that you do not forsake God's word over it, for there all pleasing and displeasing stop. But what may be yielded without infringement of God's word, should be yielded, in order that you may please everybody. If you consider it good before God, then you have this good will of which the angels sing.

From this song we may learn what sort of creatures the angels are. Disregard the fantastic notions of the worldly-wise teachers concerning them; here the angels are pictured so well that they cannot be pictured any better. Even their hearts and thoughts may be discovered here. In the first place, by joyfully proclaiming in their song the honor of God, they indicate that they are full of light and fire. They recognize that all things are God's and only God's; they do not attribute anything to themselves, but with great fervor they bring honor to him to whom it belongs. Hence, if you wish to think of a humble, pure, obedient, joyful heart that praises God, then think of the angels. This is their first concern in their conduct in God's sight.

The second is their love toward us, exactly as we are taught in the passage above. Here you see what favorable and great friends of ours they are, for they are willing to favor us no less than themselves; they rejoice over our salvation as if it were their own, so that they give us in their song a comforting inducement to regard them as one would his best friends. This is the right understanding concerning angels, not understanding them with respect to their essence, a topic treated by the sophisticated teachers without success, but with respect to their innermost heart, disposition, and mind. When I do not know what they are but know what their highest desire is and in what they are constantly engaged, then I see into their heart! Let this suffice concerning this Gospel. What Mary, Joseph, and Nazareth signify will be explained in connection with the Gospel from Luke 1.[5]

The Armor of This Gospel

In this Gospel is found the basis of the article of the creed where we say: "I believe in Jesus Christ who is born of the Virgin Mary." Although this statement is assuredly based on several passages of Scripture, yet nowhere is it set forth as clearly and abundantly as here. St. Mark says no more than that Christ has a mother, likewise St. John; neither says anything concerning the birth. St. Matthew says that he was born at Bethlehem of Mary. That is all he says, except that he gloriously proclaims Mary's virginity (as we shall hear in due time). But Luke describes the birth clearly and in detail. It was also told in ages past in the patriarchs and in the prophets, as when God says to Abraham, Genesis 22[:18]: "In your seed shall all the nations of the earth be blessed." And again, when he says to David, Psalm 89[:4–5] and Psalm 132[:11]: "God has sworn an oath to David in truth and he will not fail him: 'Out of the fruit of your body will I create a king on your throne.'" But these are obscure statements compared with this Gospel.

---

[5] Cf. Luther's Sermon for the Annunciation, Luke 1:26–38, in WA 12, 457–62.

Then, again, his birth also is signified [or: is anticipated] in many figures, as in the rod of Aaron which blossomed in a supernatural manner, even though it was only a dry stick of wood (Numbers 17[:8]). Similarly Mary, without natural and physical blood, semen, power, and works, nevertheless gave birth in a supernatural manner to a true, natural son, and was a natural mother, just as the rod, also, bore natural almonds and yet remained an ordinary rod.

Again, the birth is prefigured in the fleece of Gideon, Judges 7 [6:37–38] which became moist from the dew of heaven while the ground remained dry. There are many more. It is, however, not necessary to enumerate them at this time. These prefigurations are not contrary to faith, rather they adorn faith. For something must, first of all, be believed and established before I can believe that a prefiguration is of service.

This article possesses much importance and we must never permit it to be taken away in time of tribulation; the evil spirit does not attack anything so violently as our faith. For this reason we must be prepared and know where in Holy Scripture this faith is set forth, so that we can point whatever attacks our faith to these places. If that is done, the attack is withstood, for the evil spirit cannot stand up against the word of God.

There are also many ethical teachings in this lesson, for example, concerning humility, patience, poverty, and many others, but they have been sufficiently mentioned. Furthermore they are not points of controversy inasmuch as they are good works and fruits of faith.

THE GOSPEL FOR THE
EARLY CHRISTMAS SERVICE,
LUKE 2[:15-20]

This Gospel can be understood quite easily from the interpretation of the preceding one; for it contains an example and carrying out of the teaching which is contained in the previous lesson in that the shepherds did and found what the angels had told them. So the content of the present lesson deals with the consequences and fruits of the word of God and the signs by which we recognize whether the word of God is in us and has been effective.

The first and chief item is faith. If these shepherds had not believed the angel, they would not have gone to Bethlehem nor would they have done any of the things which are related of them in the Gospel. But if anybody should say: Of course, I, too, surely would believe if the message were brought to me by an angel from heaven, then such a person deceives himself. For whoever does not accept the word on its own account, is never inclined to accept it on account of any preacher, even if all the angels were preaching to him. And whoever accepts it on account of a preacher, he believes neither the word, nor in God through the word, but believes the preacher and in the preacher. If such is the case, faith does not last long. But whoever believes the word pays no attention to the one who proclaims it. He does not honor the word because of him who preaches it, but, on the contrary, he honors him who preaches because of the word; he never elevates the preacher above the word, and even if the preacher should perish or, as a renegade, preach a different message, he rather gives up the person preaching than the word. He abides with what he has heard—no matter who the preacher might be, no matter whether he is coming or going, and no matter what happens.

This is also the real difference between godly faith and human faith: human faith clings to a person; it believes, trusts and honors the word on account of him who speaks it. But godly faith clings to the word, which is God himself; it believes, trusts and honors the word not on account of him who has spoken it, but feels that here is such a certainty of truth that nobody can ever tear it away from it, even if the very same preacher should try it. The Samaritans prove this, John 4[:42]: initially they heard of Christ from the pagan woman, having left town and come to Christ on her word. Now, having heard him with their own ears, they said to the woman: "We do not believe any longer on account of what you have said; for now we recognize that this is the Savior of the world." Again, all those who believed Christ on account of his person and his miracles deserted him when he was crucified. That is the way it is now and has always been. The word itself, disregarding the person, must satisfy the heart, must embrace and capture the man so that he, like one who is imprisoned in it, feels how true and right it is, even if all the world, all angels, all the princes of hell had a different message, indeed, even if God himself had a different message. For God at times tests his elect and pretends to want something other than he previously indicated, as happened to Abraham when he was ordered to sacrifice his son, Isaac, and to Jacob, when he struggled with the angel, and to David when he was driven away by Absolom, his son, etc.

This faith persists, in both life and death, even as in hell and heaven, and nothing can overthrow it; for it rests on the word alone, without regard to any person. These shepherds also had such a faith; for they agree and they adhere to the word so much that they forget the angels who told it to them. They do not say: "Let us go and see the story which the angels have told us," but "which the Lord has told us." The angels are quickly forgotten, and only the word of God remains. Likewise Luke says that Mary kept and pondered the words in her heart and that, without a doubt, she was not troubled by the lowly estate of the shepherds, but considered everything the word of God. She was not the only one who did this; all the others who heard the account from the shepherds and were filled with wonder also did the same, as the text says. All clung only to the word. Although it is a peculiarity of the Hebrew language that, when talking about an action it expresses it by referring to the word as Luke does here (because the action is comprehended in words and thus made known), yet God also arranged that there be described the faith which clings to the word and acquiesces in the word which expresses the action. For if Christ's life and suffering were not comprehended in the word to which faith might cling, they would have availed nothing, for all those who were eyewitnesses received no benefit from their experience, or only very little.

The second item is the single-mindedness of the spirit. It is the nature of the Christian faith to make the hearts one, so that they are of one mind and of one will, as Psalm 68[:6] says in this regard: "God the Lord, Christ, our God makes harmonious inhabitants in the house," and Psalm 133[:1] states: "Ah, how beautiful and joyful it is that brothers dwell with one another in unity." St. Paul speaks of the unity of the spirit in many places: Romans 12[:16], I Corinthians 12[:4–31], and Ephesians 5[4:3], and he says: Be ever diligent to be of one mind, of one will. Such unity is not possible outside of the realm of faith. As the saying goes, "Each one likes his own ways best, and so the country with fools is blessed." Experience teaches us how the religious orders, the estates, and the sects are divided among themselves. Each believes that his order, his estate, his ways, his works, his undertaking is best and the right road to heaven, and looks down upon the others, taking no interest in them. We observe this nowadays among the priests, monks, bishops, and the entire clergy. But those who have a right faith know that the one important thing is faith; on this they all are in accord. Thus there is no disunity among them and no division because of some external order, action, or work. Externals make no difference to them, no matter how varied they may be. Thus in this story the shepherds are of one mind, of one will; they voice one opinion among themselves, they speak one and the same words when they say, "Let us go," etc.

The third item is humility. The shepherds acknowledge themselves as human beings. For this reason the evangelist adds the words: "the men, the shepherds," etc. For faith teaches immediately that whatever is human is nothing in the sight of God. For this reason they despise themselves and consider themselves to be nothing, and this is true and real humility and self-knowledge.

34

Humility means that they are not interested in all those things which are high and mighty in the world and that they associate with lowly, poor, despised people. As St. Paul teaches and says in Romans 12[:16]: "Do not be haughty, but associate with those who are lowly." And as Psalm 15[:4] also says: "The just despises the despiser and honors those who fear God." From all of this, then, comes peace; for whoever considers all external and big things to be nothing, gives them up easily and does not fight with anybody on account of them. He feels within himself, in the faith of his heart, something that is better. No doubt one also finds concord, peace, and humility among murderers and public sinners, as also among those who put on a show of virtue. However, this is a unity of the flesh, not of the spirit, as when Pilate and Herod became united with one another and practiced peace and humility with one another [Luke 23:13]. The Israelites did the same thing as Psalm 2[:2] says. "The kings and princes of this earth have become united among themselves against the Christ." In the same manner, too, the pope, monks, and priests are united, whenever they direct their activities against God, whereas at other times they are split into factions. For this reason this is called concord, humility, and peace of the spirit, because it is related to and deals with spiritual things, that is to say, with Christ.

The fourth item is love of one's neighbor and renunciation of self. The shepherds demonstrate this by leaving their sheep and by proceeding, not to the high and mighty lords in Jerusalem, not to the town councillors at Bethlehem, but to the lowly people in the stable. They present themselves to the lowly and are ready and willing to serve and to do what was expected of them. Had they not had faith, they would not have left their sheep, as they did, and they would not have left their property lying around, especially as the angels had not commanded them to do so. For they did this out of their own free will and following their own counsel, as the text says. They talked about it among themselves and they came in haste, even though the angel did not command, admonish, or advise them to do so. All he did was to indicate what they would find; he left it up to their free will whether they wanted to go and to look. Love operates in exactly the same manner. Love needs no command; it does everything of its own accord, does not tarry, but hurries, and considers it sufficient that the direction is pointed out. Love does not need—and will not tolerate—someone to goad it along. Oh, much could be said on this topic. Thus a Christian should move freely in love. A Christian should forget himself and that which is his; he should think only of his neighbor and be concerned about him, as St. Paul says in Ephesians 5 [Phil. 2:4]: "Let no one consider what is his, but that which is the others"; and Galatians 5 [6:2]: "Let each one bear the other's burden and thus you will fulfill the law of Christ." But these days the pope with his bishops and priests has filled the world with laws and restraints, and there is nothing in all the world but sheer compulsion and intimidation; voluntary orders or estates no longer exist, in accordance with the prophecy that love would be extinguished and the world corrupted with the doctrines of men.

The fifth item is joy which expresses itself in words so that we like to talk and hear about what faith has received in the heart. Thus the shepherds chatter with one another happily and amicably concerning what they had heard and believed. They use many words as if they were chattering aimlessly. It is not enough for them to say, "Let us go to Bethlehem and see what has happened there." No, they add to this and say: "which God has done and has made known to us." Is it not superfluous talk when they say: "that has happened there, which God has done"? They could have said it briefly in this fashion: Therefore let us see the deed which God has done there. But the joy of the spirit flows over, as it were, with happy words, and yet there is not too much said, indeed, all too little; they are unable to say it as much as they really would like to, as Psalm 45[:1] reads: "My heart gulps forth a good word," as if the psalmist wanted to say: I should like to say it right out, but I cannot. It is greater than I can express, so that my word is scarcely more than a gulp. This accounts for the expression found in Psalm 50 [35:28] and in several other places: "My tongue shall gulp forth your righteousness," i.e., it will talk, sing, and speak while I jump for joy. And Psalm 119[:171] says: "My lips will gush forth your praise," just as a boiling pot seethes and gushes.

The sixth item is that they follow through with action; for, as St. Paul says in I Corinthians 3 [4:20]: "God's kingdom does not consist in words but in deeds." Accordingly the shepherds here do not merely say: "Let us go and see," but they actually go. Indeed, they do more than what they express in their words; for the text says: "They came with haste." This is a great deal more than ordinary walking, as they had agreed to do. Thus faith and love always do more than they say and their works are in every respect alive, active, and overflowing. Thus a Christian should be sparing with his words but rich in his deeds, as he certainly will be, if he is a true Christian. If he does not act in this manner, then he is as yet not a true Christian.

The seventh item is that they freely confess and publicly proclaim the word that was told them concerning the child. This is the greatest work in the Christian life, and for it one must be willing to risk life and limb and goods and reputation. For the evil spirit does not attack someone very vigorously if he has the right faith and lives rightly but privately and only for himself. But if someone is willing to go out and to spread the word, to confess, to preach, to praise for the benefit of others, that he does not tolerate. Therefore Luke reports that they not only came and saw, but that they also proclaimed—not only to Mary and Joseph but also to everyone— the news concerning the child and the message they had heard on the field. Do you not think that there were many people who considered them fools and bereft of their senses because they dared, as uncouth and unschooled lay people to speak of the angels' song and message? How would they be received today, should they tell the pope, the bishops, and scholars such a story? Or even a less important one? But the shepherds, filled with faith and joy, were happy for the sake of God to be considered foolish in the sight of men. A Christian does the same; for God's word must be considered foolishness and error in this world.

The eighth item is Christian liberty which is not tied to any work. On the contrary, all works are the same to a Christian, no matter what they are. For these shepherds do not run away into the desert, they do not don monk's garb, they do not shave their heads, neither do they change their clothing, schedule, food, drink, nor any external work. They return to their place in the fields to serve God there! For being a Christian does not consist in external conduct, neither does it change any one according to the external position; rather it changes him according to the inner disposition, that is to say, it provides a different heart, a different disposition, will, and mind which do the works which another person does without such a disposition and will. For a Christian knows that it all depends upon faith; for this reason he walks, stands, eats, drinks, dresses, works, and lives as any ordinary person in his calling, so that one does not become aware of his Christianity, as Christ says in Luke 17[:20–21]: "The kingdom of God does not come in an external manner and one cannot say, 'Lo, here and there,' but the kingdom of God is within you." Against this liberty the pope and the spiritual estate fight with their laws and their choice of clothing, food, prayers, localities, and persons. They catch themselves and everybody else with such soul snares, with which they have filled the world, just as St. Anthony saw in a vision.[1] For they are of the opinion that salvation depends on their person and work. They call other people worldly, whereas they themselves in all likelihood are worldly seven times over, inasmuch as their doings are entirely human works concerning which God has commanded nothing.

The ninth and last item is praise and thanksgiving rendered to God. For we are unable to give to God anything, in return for his goodness and grace, except praise and thanksgiving, which, moreover, proceed from the heart and have no great need of organ music, bells, and rote recitation. Faith teaches such praise and thanksgiving; as it is written concerning the shepherds that they returned to their flocks with praise and thanksgiving and were well satisfied, even though they did not become wealthier, were not awarded higher honors, did not eat and drink better, were not obliged to carry on a better trade. See, in this Gospel you have a picture of true Christian life, especially as pertains to its external aspects: on the outside, it shines forth not at all or at most a little bit in the sight of the people so that, indeed, most people see it as error and foolishness; but on the inside it is sheer light, joy, and bliss. Thus we see what the apostle has in mind when he enumerates the fruits of the spirit in Galatians 5[:22]: "The fruits of the spirit (that is, the works of faith) are love, joy, peace, kindness, being able to get along, patience, confidence, mercy, chastity."

---

[1] Cf. *On the Lives of the Fathers* (*De Vitis Patrum*), III (*MPL* 73, 785).

No person, canonical hour, food, garment, location, or any self-selected human work of this kind, as we see them swarming about in the life of the papists, is enumerated.

But what it means to find Christ in such poverty and what his baby diapers and the manger signify, these things have been stated in the previous Gospel.[2] We saw that his poverty teaches how we are to find him in our neighbor, in the lowliest and the neediest, and that his diapers are Holy Scripture. Thus in our active life we are to stick with the needy, while in our studies and in our contemplative life we are to stay only with God's word, so that Christ alone is in both respects the man who is everywhere before us. The books of Aristotle and those of the pope and of any other man should be avoided or they should be read in such a way that we do not seek in them information concerning the edification of the soul, but we should use them to improve our temporal life, to learn a trade or civil law. It was not without intention that Luke writes: "They found Mary and Joseph and the babe in the manger," mentioning Mary before Joseph and both of them before the infant. As we said above, Mary is the Christian church and Joseph the servant of the church, and this is exactly what the position of the bishops and priests should be when they preach the gospel. The church comes before the prelates of the church, as Christ, too, says in Luke 21 [22:26]: "He who wishes to be the greatest among you, must be the least." Nowadays this has been reversed, and one need not be astonished about it because they have rejected the gospel and exalted the babblings of men. The Christian church, on the contrary, keeps all the words of God in her heart and ponders them, compares one with the other and with Holy Scripture. Therefore he who wants to find Christ, must first find the church. How would one know Christ and faith in him if one did not know where they are who believe in him? He who would know something concerning Christ, must neither trust in himself nor build his bridge into heaven by means of his own reason, but he should go to the church; he should attend it and ask his questions there.

The church is not wood and stone but the assembly of people who believe in Christ. With this church one should be connected

---

[2] Cf. above, pp. 21 ff.

and see how the people believe, live, and teach. They certainly have Christ in their midst, for outside the Christian church there is no truth, no Christ, no salvation. It follows that the pope or a bishop erroneously claims that he alone should be believed, posing as master; for all of them are in error and may be in error. Their teaching should rather be subject to the assembly of believers. What they teach, should be subject to the judgment and verdict of the congregation; to this judgment one should defer, so that Mary may be found ahead of Joseph and the Church preferred to the preachers. For it is not Joseph but Mary who keeps these words in her heart, who ponders them and keeps them or compares them. The apostle taught the same thing in I Corinthians 14[:29–30] when he says: "One or two are to interpret scripture, the other shall sit in judgment, and whenever a revelation comes to him who sits, then the former must be silent." But nowadays the pope and his followers have become tyrants; they have reversed this Christian, divine, apostolic order and have introduced an altogether heathen-ish and Pythagorean order, so that they are able to talk, babble, and act foolishly according to their own whims. Nobody is permitted to judge or interrupt them, or to command them to be silent. In this manner, too, they have quenched the spirit, so that one finds among them neither Mary, nor Joseph, nor Christ, but only the rats, mice, adders, and serpents of their poisonous teachings and hypocrisy.

This is not really a Gospel of strife, for, although it teaches Christian conduct and works, it does not set forth the articles of faith in plain language, even though there might be enough in its allegories, as has been shown; but allegorical passages must not be used in polemics. We need plain utterances which clearly set forth the articles of faith.

THE GOSPEL FOR THE
MAIN CHRISTMAS SERVICE,
JOHN 2[:1-14]

This is the most important Gospel of all, but it is not—contrary to the opinion of some—obscure or difficult. For here is most clearly established the foundation for the noble article of the divinity of Christ which all Christians should know and can understand fully. Nothing is too esoteric for faith. Therefore we shall, to the best of our ability, expound the Gospel's meaning; and not hide it from the common people, frightening them away with fabricated subtleties, as do the scholastics. There is no need for many clever, hairsplitting considerations, but only for simple and plain attention to the words of the text.

In the first place, we should know that everything taught and written by the apostles comes from the Old Testament. For in the Old Testament all is prophesied which was to be fulfilled in Christ and to be preached, as St. Paul says in Romans 1[:2]: "God promised the gospel concerning his Son Christ through the prophets in Holy Scripture." Thus their preaching is based on the Old Testament, and there is no word in the New Testament that does not look back into the Old Testament where it was first told. We have noted in the Epistle how the divinity of Christ is confirmed by the apostle from the Old Testament passages.[1] For the New Testament is nothing but a revelation of the Old; it is as if somebody had a sealed letter and later on broke it open. In like manner the Old Testament is a last will and testament of Christ; after his death he had it unsealed and read through the gospel and preached everywhere. This is signified in Revelation 5[:1-5] where the Lamb of God alone opens the book with the seven seals which,

---

[1] Cf. WA 10I, 1, 142 ff.

otherwise, nobody could open up, neither in heaven, nor the earth, nor under the earth.

In order that this Gospel might become clearer and brighter, we must go back to the Old Testament, to the passages on which this Gospel is based. That means going back to Moses, to the first chapter and beginning of Genesis; there we read: "In the beginning God created heaven and earth. The earth was without form and void, and darkness was upon the abyss, and the Spirit of God hovered upon the water. Then God said, 'Let there be light,' and there was light," etc. In this manner Moses continues to narrate how all creatures were created in the same manner as was the light, namely, through the speaking or the word of God. For instance, God said, "Let there be a heaven," and he said, "Let there be a sun, a moon, and stars," etc. From Moses' text one clearly draws the conclusion, that God has a word with which he spoke before there existed any creatures. This word assuredly cannot be a creature, inasmuch as all creatures are created through the speaking of this same divine word, as the Mosaic text sets forth clearly, powerfully, and convincingly when it says: "God said, 'Let there be light', and there was light." The word, clearly, must exist before the light, since the light comes into being through the word, and it existed prior to all creatures which also came into being through the word.

Let us continue. If the word existed before all creatures, and if all creatures came into being and were created by it, then it must be a being other than a creature. It did not come into being nor was it created like the creatures; hence it must be eternal and cannot have had a beginning, for when all things had their beginning, it was already in existence. It cannot be categorized under "time" or under "creature," but it is above "time" and "creature." As a matter of fact, "time" and "creature" come into being and have their beginning through it. It is undeniable that whatever is not temporal must be eternal, and whatever has no beginning cannot be temporal, and whatever is not a creature, must be God. For outside of God and creature there is nothing. Thus we conclude on the basis of this text of Moses that the word of God, which was in the beginning and through which the creatures came into being, must be an eternal God and cannot be a creature.

Furthermore, the word and he who utters it cannot be one and the same person. For it is impossible for the speaker himself to be the word. What sort of speaker would that be who, himself, was the word? He would have to be a mute, or the word would have to become audible without the speaker and to speak itself. Now here the text states strongly and clearly, with unambiguous words: "God said." Thus God and his word must be two. Had he written: "There was an utterance," or "There has been an utterance," then it would not be so obvious that there were present two, the word and him who spoke it. But since he expresses it thus: "God said," and since he mentions the speaker and the word spoken by him, he compels you mightily to agree that two different things are present and that the speaker is not the word and, also, that the word is the speaker; but rather [he compels] you to agree that the word comes from the speaker and that it has its nature not from itself, but from the speaker and that, on the other hand, the speaker does not come from the word nor derive his nature from it, but from himself. Thus Moses concludes that there are two persons in the godhead from eternity prior to all creatures, the one derives his nature from the other and the other derives his nature from nobody but himself.

On the other hand, the Bible contends and teaches firmly that there is only one god, as Moses writes at the outset: "In the beginning God created heaven and earth" [Gen. 1:1], and in Deuteronomy 6[:4]: "Hear, Israel, your God is only one God." See, in this manner the Bible employs simple words that are easily grasped and teaches important things so clearly that everybody can easily understand them and so cogently that nobody can argue against them. Who can fail to grasp from these words of Moses that there must be two persons in the godhead and yet only one godhead, unless he would deny the clear text of the Bible? Or who is so subtle that he would argue against these words? He must admit that the word is something different from God who speaks it and he must certainly confess that it existed prior to all creatures and that the creatures were made through it. Thus he must certainly admit that the word is God, for outside of the creatures there is nothing but God. So he must also confess that there is only one God. Therefore this Scripture passage forces us to conclude that these two persons are one complete God, that each one is the one, true, complete, natural God, who has created all things, and that the speaker has his nature not from the word, but that the word has its nature from the speaker—although the word is in every respect eternal and in eternity distinct from all creation.

The heretical Arians wanted to obscure this clear passage and to bore a hole into heaven, inasmuch as they could not ignore it.[2] They said that this word of God is, to be sure, a god, but it is a created and not a natural god; all things were made through it, but it, too, had first been made; then, through it, all the other things were made. All this they propounded out of their own dreams and without any scriptural basis because they forsook the simple word of Scripture and followed their own imagination. For this reason I have said: he who wants to proceed safely and avoid error, should beware of the many subtle and hairsplitting words or fictions, and stay with the simple, powerful, clear words of Scripture. Then he will stand firm. We shall also see how John anticipated these same heretics and refuted their evasions and fabrications. Thus we have in Moses the true gold mine from which everything is taken that is written in the New Testament concerning the divinity of Christ. Here you see the source of St. John's Gospel and where its foundation lies; and this knowledge helps you to understand it easily. From the same source flows the verse in Psalm 33: "The heavens are made by the word of God" [v. 6]; also Solomon, in Proverbs 8[:22–32], where he speaks of the wisdom of God and describes with many beautiful words how it existed with God before all things, has taken his thoughts from this chapter of Moses; and all prophets have worked this mine assiduously and dug up its treasure. Concerning the Holy Spirit, however, there are other statements, again in the writings of this same Moses. When, for instance, he says: "The Spirit of God hovers over the waters" [Gen. 1:2], then the Spirit of God must also be something different from him who breathes him into existence, and yet he must exist prior to all created beings. Similarly, when he states that God blessed the creatures, that he regarded them and had pleasure in them, this blessing and kindly regard indicates the Holy Spirit; for this reason

---

2 The Arians were a fourth and fifth century movement within the church whose adherents denied the true divinity of Christ; cf. *O.D.C.C.*, pp. 80–81.

the Bible assigns to him life and kindness. However, these statements have as yet not been developed as well as those which refer to the Son, and for this reason they do not as yet shine brightly. The precious metal still lies half buried in the mire. The passage can be easily believed, if human reason is captured so that it believes in the existence of two persons. But if someone had the time and compared the New Testament statements concerning the Holy Spirit and this Mosaic text, he would discover light, satisfaction, and joy.

Now we must open wide our hearts and minds, so that we do not regard such statements as ordinary, perishable words of a human being; rather we must regard his words to be as great as the greatness of him who speaks them. The word he speaks within himself and which remains within him, is never separated from him. Hence, following the apostle's thought, we must think that God carries on a dialogue with himself and that he utters a word from himself; however his word is not merely an exhalation or a noise, but it carries with it the whole essence of the divine nature and, as we said above in the Epistle where we dealt with brightness of his glory and image, divine nature is formed to accompany the image and it becomes the very image itself.[3] The brilliance also radiates the glory so that it merges with the glory. Accordingly, in this passage too, God of himself speaks his word so that the godhead follows the word and remains with its nature in the word and is there in its essence. Behold, here we see the source of the apostle's words when he calls Christ an image of the divine essence and a brightness of divine glory: he derives them from this text of Moses who teaches here that God speaks a word concerning himself which cannot be anything else but an image which represents him. For every word is a sign with a meaning. Here the meaning is naturally in the sign or in the word, which is not the case with other signs, and for this reason he calls it correctly an essential image or sign of his nature.

Human speech also indicates something about this; for through it the heart of man can be known. As the common saying has it: I have his heart or his intention, when he has only spoken

---

[3] Cf. WA 10[I, 1], 155 ff.

his words. This is so because the intention of the heart follows the word and from the word, the heart is known as if it were in the word. This is the reason why, taught by experience, the pagans said: *Qualis quisque est, talia loquitur*, "A man's speech is just like his life." Or: *oratio est character animi*, "Speech is the image of the heart."[4] If the heart is pure, it speaks pure words. If it is impure, then it speaks impure words. With this the gospel agrees, for Christ says: "Out of the abundance of the heart the mouth speaks" [Matt. 12:34]. And again: "How can you speak good words, inasmuch as you are evil?" Likewise St. John the Baptist says in John 3[:31]: "Whoever is of the earth, speaks of the earth." Similarly the German proverb says: The mouth flows over with what fills the heart. Thus all the world fully agrees that no image of the heart is so nearly like it and true to it as are the words of the mouth. The bird is known by its song, for it sings as its beak allows exactly as if the heart were essentially in the word.

That is exactly as it is with God. His word is so much like himself, that the godhead is wholly in it, and he who has the word has the whole godhead. But this comparison, admittedly has its limitation. The human word does not carry with itself the essence or the nature of the heart; but it is only able to signify or to act as a sign, just as a wooden or gold statue does not carry with it the essence of the human being whom it portrays. But here, in God, the word brings not only the sign and representation, but also the whole being and it is as full of God as he whose image or word it is. If human words expressed a pure heart or the intention of the heart or if the meaning of the heart were words, the comparison would be perfect. But that is impossible. Therefore this word of God is above all words and there is none like it among all creatures.

No doubt there have been very learned discussions about the inner word of the heart of man, which remains within man, since man was created after the image of God.[5] But the discussion has remained deep and obscure, and will probably remain so; even the discussants do not understand it. So we shall not bother about it either and proceed to the Gospel which is, of itself, clear and obvious.

---

[4] Seneca, *Epistles* 114, 2.
[5] Thomas Aquinas, *Summa theologiae*, I, ques. 12 ff.

"In the beginning was the word" [John 1:1].

What sort of beginning does he have in mind, other than the one of which Moses says: "In the beginning God created heaven and earth"? This was the beginning of creation; apart from this there was no other beginning, for God did not begin to be—he is eternal. Thus it follows that the word, too, is eternal, because it did not begin in the beginning, but already was in the beginning, as John says here. It did not begin; rather, when all things had their beginning, it *was* already, and its existence did not begin, but was present. How carefully the evangelist speaks! He does not say: In the beginning the word came into being, but he says: it was there and did not come into being. Its being has a different origin, different from either "becoming" or "beginning." This is the intent of the words "in the beginning." Had he been created before the world, as the Arians claim, he would not have existed in the beginning, but would himself have been the beginning. But John declares firmly and clearly: In the beginning was the word, and he was not the beginning. Whence come such words of John? From Moses, as it is written in Genesis 1[:3]: "God said, 'Let there be light.'" From that text the words of John are obviously derived: "In the beginning was the word." For if God spoke, there had to be a word. And if he spoke it in the beginning, when creation began, the word was in existence already in the beginning and did not begin with creation.

But why does he not say: Before the beginning was the word? That would have been clearer than the text before us. As St. Paul frequently says: "before the creation of the world," etc. [cf. Eph. 1:4]. The answer is: that to be in the beginning or before the beginning is exactly the same. One follows from the other. Thus St. John, as an evangelist, wanted to agree with Moses' text, and to explain it and indicate its source. This would not have been the case had he written "before the beginning"; for Moses says nothing about what is prior to the beginning, but he describes the word in the beginning, so that he could describe all the better the creation that was made through the word. For the same reason he also calls him "word," even though he could have used the terms "light," "life," or some other term, as he does further on; because Moses

47

speaks of a "word." Now "not begin" and "to be in the beginning" are exactly the same as "to be before the beginning."

But if the word had been "in the beginning" and not "before the beginning," it must have begun to be before the beginning, then the beginning would have been before the beginning, and this would be a contradiction and would be the same as saying that the beginning was not the beginning. Therefore, the expression "In the beginning was the word" is superb; it indicates that the word had no beginning and that, of necessity, it had existed eternally prior to the beginning.

"And the word was with God" [John 1:1].

Where else should it be? Apart from God it was truly nothing. Moses says this, too, when he writes: "God said, 'Let there be light.' " If he was to speak, the word surely would have to be with him. But here he clearly distinguishes the persons; the word is a different person from God with whom it was. This statement of John cannot be interpreted as meaning that God was alone, for it says that something had been with God, namely, his word. If there had been present only one thing, how could he say: "The word was with God." To have something with him is not the same as being alone or by himself. One should mark well that the evangelist insists on the little word "with"; for he uses it once more, and expresses clearly the difference between the persons, in order to counteract natural reason and future heretics. For while natural reason easily grasps that there is only one God, and many statements of the Bible substantiate this—and it is, of course, true—natural reason argues most violently against the notion that more than one person should be the same God.

That is why there arose the heretic, Sabellius, who says that Father, Son, and Holy Ghost are only one person.[6] Again Arius, although he admitted that the word was with God, would not concede that it was true God.[7] The former proclaims and teaches

---

[6] Sabellius was an early third century theologian who attempted to sustain monotheism by describing the Father, Son, and Holy Spirit as a succession of different modes or phases of the one God. The formulation of the Council of Nicaea in A.D. 325 excluded Sabellianism.

[7] Arius (*ca.* 250–*ca.* 336) taught that the Son of God was not eternal but a creation of God and, therefore, not God by nature. This doctrine was condemned by the Council of Nicaea, but it continued to spread; cf. above, p. 44, n. 2.

too great a simplicity within God; the latter teaches too great a multiplicity. Sabellius mingles the persons, one into the other; Arius divides the essence into separate parts. The true Christian faith, however, goes down the middle, teaching and confessing the individuality of the persons and the indivisibility of the nature. The Father is a person distinct from the Son, but he is not a different god. It is to be expected that natural reason does not comprehend this. Faith alone must comprehend it; natural reason creates heresy and error, while faith teaches the truth and clings to it; for it clings to Scripture, which neither deceives nor lies.

"*And God was the word*" [John 1:1].

Since there is only one God, it must be true that God himself is this word which existed in the beginning before all creatures. Some have wanted to turn this statement around and interpret it as follows: And the word was God, in which they followed their own subtle speculations. We, however, do not permit ourselves to be driven away from the text, as if John had not known how he should arrange his words. What he means is clear. There is no other God but the one, and this same God is in his whole essence that same word, of which John speaks, and there is nothing in the divine nature which is not in the word. Once and for all it is clearly expressed how in truth this word is God, so that not only "The word is God" is true, but also "God is the word."

This passage, which vigorously argues against Arius who teaches that the word is not God, seems just as vigorously to support Sabellius. For it sounds as if it mingled the persons, one into the other, and as if in this manner it were revoking or explaining away the previous passage where John separates the different persons and says: "The word was with God." But the evangelist has intentionally arranged his words in this manner, in order to refute all heretics. Here he runs Arius into the ground and attributes to the word the true, natural divinity by saying: "And God was the word," just as if he were saying: I do not simply say, "the word is God," for such phrasing might be understood to mean that the word is only said to be divine and is not so essentially (as you, Arius, say); but I say: "And God was the word." This statement can only be understood to mean that something which everybody calls God and esteems as such, is the word. On the other hand, lest

Sabellius and human reasoning believe that I side with them and mingle the persons, and revoke what I have said about this matter, now, therefore, I shall say it once more.

"The same was in the beginning with God" [John 1:2].

The word was with God, with God, and yet God was the word. See, this is the way in which the evangelist fights on both fronts, so that both propositions are true: God is the word, and the word is with God. It is one nature of divine essence and yet not one person only; and each person is full and complete God in the beginning and eternally. These are the statements upon which our faith is founded to which we, too, must cling. For it is, indeed, much too difficult for human reasoning to accept that there should be three persons and that each one is in every respect the one complete God, and yet that there are not three gods but only one. Our scholastics have belabored this matter back and forth with much subtlety, in order to render it comprehensible.[8] But if you do not wish to fall into the net of the evil foe, forget about their clever distinctions, their obscuring explanations, and their subtleness, and cling to these divine words; press into them and stay within them as does a rabbit in a cleft in the rock. If you amble forth and rely on human babbling, the foe will surely trap you and catch you in the end, so that you do not know where reason, faith, God, or you, yourself, remain.

Believe me—as one who has tried this and to whom this has happened—I am not talking through my hat when I say: Scripture has not been given us without purpose. If human reasoning had been able to chart the right course, there would not have been need of Scripture. Let Arius and Sabellius be horrible examples: had they remained with Holy Scripture and had they sent reason packing, they would not have caused such great damage. And our scholastics might also be Christians, provided they stopped their tomfoolery and their subtleties and remained with Holy Scripture.

"All things were made through him" [John 1:3].

Has this not been said clearly enough? Who will be surprised, if stubborn people refuse to be convinced of their error, no matter

---

8 Cf. Thomas Aquinas, *Summa theologiae*, I, ques. 39 ff.

how clearly and plainly the truth is told them. Thus the Arians evade this clear and explicit passage; they claim that all things were made by the word, but the word had been made before, and thereafter all things were made by it, whereas the passage plainly reads: "all things were made by him." There is no doubt, he was not made and is not to be included among the created things; for he who names everything, excludes nothing. This is the way St. Paul in Hebrews 2[:8] interprets the statement in Psalm 8[:6]: "Thou hast cast all things under his feet." By subjecting all things to him, St. Paul says, he has omitted nothing which is not subject to him. And I Corinthians 15[:27] states: "He has subjected everything to him except, undoubtedly, him who has subjected everything to him!" Hence here, too, "all things are made through him" must be understood to except him through whom all things were made, and apart from whom there was nothing that was made. This passage, too, he derives from Moses, Genesis 1[:3, 6, 7, etc.], where all the creatures whom God has made are enumerated, and where every time he says: "God said . . . and it was so" he shows they were all made through the word. St. John enlarges this passage and clarifies himself by saying:

"And without him nothing was made that was made" [John 1:3].

If nothing was made without him, then much less was he himself made, without whom nothing was made. This was written that the Arian heresy should never cause any controversy, although it did. Even without commentaries it is clear that this word is God and the real creator of all that is created, since without him nothing was made that was made. Some are doubtful about this text because of the arrangement of the words. They add the words "that was made" to the text that follows, in this manner: "that what was made was life in him." This is St. Augustine's interpretation.[9] Others—and I include myself—believe these words belong to the previous text just as I have put it: "And without him nothing was made that was made." The text means to say that of the things which have been made, not one was made without him, in order that it be clearly stated that all things were made through him and

---

[9] Augustine's position on this point is contained in the *glossa ordinaria* and this may be the source of Luther's comments; cf. WA 10ᴵ, 1, 195, n. 2.

that he, in turn, was not made, so that straightaway and firmly it be made clear that he is true God, although not of himself, but of the Father. For that reason he uses the expressions "made through him" and "begotten of the Father."

"In him was the life" [John 1:4].

Concerning this statement there is generally much esoteric speculation and difficult reasoning. It pertains to the twofold existence of created things, for which the Platonic philosophers are famous. They hold that all creation has its being, first, in its own nature and kind, as it is created; and second, in the eternal divine providence, in that God decided by himself to create all things. As he lives, so all things are living in him, and this existence of the creature within God, they say, is nobler than the existence of the creature within his own kind and nature. In God things live which in themselves do not live, as stones, earth, water, etc. Therefore St. Augustine says that this word is an image of all creation and like a treasure chamber full of such images called "ideas" (which is Greek for images), according to which the created things were made, every one according to its image.[10] It is with this in mind that John is said to have stated: "in him was life." They attach this text to the preceding one in this manner: that which was made was life in him, that is to say, whatever was created, before it was created, had been alive before in him.

I do not reject this. But I am of the opinion, that it goes too far and is a contrived interpretation of this passage. For John speaks very simply and plainly and does not mean to lead us into such hairsplitting and subtle speculation. Nor am I aware that the Bible anywhere speaks in this manner of the created beings. True, the Bible says that all things are known beforehand, elected, and ready and living in the presence of God, as if this had come to pass already, as Christ in Luke 20[:38] says of Abraham, Isaac, and Jacob: "God is not a god of the dead, but of the living, for they all live unto him." But we do not find this sort of statement: in him live all things. This statement also implies something more about the life of the creatures in him, which was before the world. In the

---

[10] Augustine, *On the Gospel of John* (*In Ioannis evangelium*), Tractate 1, 16 (*MPL* 35, 1387).

most simple manner it signifies that he is the fountain and the origin of life, that everything that lives has life of him and through him and in him, and that without him there is no life, as he himself says in John 14[:6]: "I am the way, the truth, and the life," and again in John 11[:25]: "I am the resurrection and the life." This is the reason why John in I John 1[:1] calls him the word of life and especially speaks of the life which men have from him, i.e., eternal life. It was for this very life he set out to write his Gospel. The whole text, too, proves this. John himself explains what sort of life he is talking about when he says: "The life was the light of men" [John 1:4]; here he undoubtedly shows that he is talking about the life and the light which Christ gives to men through himself. For this reason, too, he introduces John the Baptist as a witness to such light. Now it is certainly clear that John the Baptist preached Christ not in terms of esoteric speculation, as some do, but simply and in plain language, stating that Christ is light and life for the salvation of all men.

Therefore one should know that John, as the histories tell us, wrote his Gospel because Cerinthus, the heretic, arose at that time and taught that Christ had not existed before his mother Mary, thus making of him a mere man or creature.[11] In order to oppose this heretic, John begins his Gospel in such an exalted tone and continues in the same vein so that in almost every single letter he preaches the deity of Christ, which is done by no other evangelist. He does this so diligently that he introduces Christ in John 3 [2:4] as one acting strangely to his mother and talking harshly with her, as if she were anyone but his mother. He said to her: "Woman, what have I to do with you?" Was not this a strange, harsh word from a son to his mother? Likewise he said on the cross: "Woman, look, this is your son" [John 19:26]. All this was done, in order to demonstrate beyond a shadow of doubt against Cerinthus that Christ is true God. Yet he chooses his words in such a manner that he opposes not only Cerinthus but also Arius, Sabellius, and all other heretics.

We read, too, that the same St. John at one time recognized

---

11 Cerinthus (ca. 100) was a Gnostic who taught that Jesus was a man upon whom the Christ descended in baptism. Irenaeus (ca. 130–ca. 200) attempted to refute Cerinthus in his treatise *Against Heresies*; cf. *Against Heresies*, III, 11.

Cerinthus in a public bathhouse and said to his followers: "Let us quickly flee from here, lest we be destroyed with this person."[12] And when he reached the outside, the bathhouse collapsed and destroyed this enemy of truth. Therefore he sharpens and points all his words against the error of Cerinthus and says, Christ was not only before his mother, he was, in fact, in the beginning the word of which Moses writes in the first beginning, and all things were made by him, and he was with God and God was the word and it was in the beginning with God. Thus he strikes Cerinthus with real thunderbolts.

So we are of the opinion that the meaning of the evangelist in this passage is simple and straightforward: he who does not acknowledge Christ to be true God and does not believe in him as true God, as I have described him so far, and denies that he was the word and in the beginning with God and that all things were made through him, but wants to consider him to be merely a creature which had a beginning in time and first came into being after his mother (as Cerinthus teaches), that man is lost eternally and may not have eternal life. For there is no life outside of this word and Son of God. Only in him is life. Christ the man separate from and without God, would be useless, as he himself says in John 6[:63]: "The flesh is of no avail." "But my flesh is a true food and my blood is a true drink" [John 6:55]. Why say: "The flesh is of no avail," and yet: "My flesh is the true food?" The reason is that I am not mere flesh nor merely a human being, but I am God's Son. So my flesh is food, not because it is flesh, but because it is my flesh. This means that whoever believes that I, who am a human being, have flesh and blood like other human beings, but also that I am the Son of God and God, that man derives from me true nourishment and will live. But he who believes that I am only human, to him the flesh is of no use; for it is not my flesh or God's flesh. He says the same thing in John 8[:24]: "If you do not believe that I am he, then you must die in your sins." And again: "If the Son makes you free, you will be free indeed" [John 8:36]. Our passage, "In him was life," has the same meaning. He is the word of God from the beginning, and God himself must be our life, food, light, and salvation. Therefore we cannot say that it is Christ's humanity that

---

[12] Irenaeus, *Against Heresies*, III, 3.

brings us life: rather the life is in the word which dwells in the flesh and brings us to life through the flesh.

This interpretation is uncomplicated and helpful. Thus St. Paul is in the habit of calling the gospel teaching *doctrinam pietatis*, doctrine of piety, a teaching which makes man rich in grace. The other interpretation, entertained also by the pagans, that all creatures live in God, does indeed produce babblers of subtleties, and is obscure and difficult; it teaches nothing concerning grace nor does it produce men rich in grace. Scripture accordingly disavows it as being clever. Just as we interpret Christ's statement, "I am the life," so should we interpret this. There is nothing here about a philosophical interpretation of the life of creatures in God; rather these words speak only of how God lives in us and makes us partakers of his life, and how we live through him and from him and in him. For it cannot be denied, that through him natural life exists, which even unbelievers have from him, as St. Paul says in Acts 17[:28]: "In him we live and move and have our being and are of his kind." Indeed, natural life is a part of eternal life and its beginning, but it ends through death because it does not acknowledge nor honor him from whom it comes. Sin cuts it off, so that it must die eternally. On the other hand, those who believe in him, and acknowledge him from whom they have their being never die. Their natural life will be stretched out into life eternal, so that they never taste death, as he says in John 8[:52]: "He who keeps my words, will never taste death," and in John 11[:25]: "He who believes in me, even if he dies, will live." These and similar matters are understood well, if one rightly learns to know Christ, how he slew death and brought us life.

However, the fact that the evangelist says: "in him *was* life," rather than "in him *is* life," as if he were talking about something past, we must not connect with the time before creation or the time of the beginning. For he does not say: "in the beginning life was in him," as he just said of the word that it was in the beginning with God. Rather we should associate these words with the time of the life or sojourn of Christ on earth, when the word of God revealed itself to men and among men; for the evangelist proposes to write of Christ and his life, and in his writing he has asserted all that we need for life. He talks here in the same manner as he does concerning St. John the Baptist: "There was a man sent from God" [John 1:6]; and again: "He was not the light," etc. [John 1:8]; and again as he spoke later concerning the word: "The Word became flesh and dwelt among us" [John 1:14]; and again: "He came into the world"; and again: "He came to his own and they did not receive him" [John 1:11]; and the like. In this manner Christ also says of John the Baptist in John 5[:35]: "He was a burning and a shining light." In the same manner as he says here: "In him was life," so he himself also says in John 9[:5]: "As long as I am in the world, I am the light of the world." He speaks in this manner simply referring to the journey of Christ on earth which is now a thing of the past; for, as I have pointed out at the start, this Gospel is not as difficult as some people think.[13] They have made it difficult by searching for high and mysterious and strained things. He wrote it for ordinary Christians, no matter how unsophisticated, and his words are formulated so that they can be understood quite easily. Whoever disregards the life and sojourn of Christ and would prefer to look for him in another manner, now that he sits on his heavenly throne, would be mistaken. He must seek him as he was and walked on earth, and he will find life. Here he came to be our life, light, and salvation. Here on earth everything took place that we are to believe of him, and so it is said most appropriately: "In him was life." This does not mean that now he is not our life, but it means that he is not now doing what he did at that time. That this is the correct interpretation, is born out by his statement that St. John the Baptist came to give testimony concerning this light and life, so that all should believe in him through his testimony. It is certainly clear that John came solely to give testimony concerning Christ. He was a forerunner of Christ and yet he said nothing at all of the life of the creature in God according to the philosophical interpretation noted above. All statements and preaching were about Christ's sojourn on earth, whereby he became the life and light of men. The text continues:

"And the life was the light of men" [John 1:4].

Just as they managed to pull the word "life" away from its evangelical meaning, so they have also done to the word "light."

---

13 Cf. above, p. 46.

They speculate pointedly and "profoundly" about how the Word of God, according to its divinity, is a light which illuminates in a natural manner and which has always illuminated the reasoning powers of men, even those of the pagans. In this way they emphasize the light of reason and base it on this passage. But all these are still only human, Platonic, and philosophical thoughts which lead us away from Christ into ourselves, whereas the evangelist wants to lead us away from ourselves into Christ. He does not want to treat of the divine, almighty, eternal Word of God nor talk of it except in terms of the flesh and blood which sojourned here on earth. He does not want to disperse us into the creatures which are created through him, so that we should run after him and seek him there and speculate as do the followers of Plato. On the contrary, he wants to gather us together out of these farfetched high flown thoughts into Christ, as if he were saying: Why do you wander away and why do you do your looking in distant places? Behold, in Christ, the man, is everything; he has made everything; in him is life; he is the Word by whom all things were made. Remain in him, and you will find all of this. He is the life and light of all men. He who wants to show him to you at some other place is leading you astray; for he has presented himself in this flesh and blood and in them he wants to be sought and found. Follow the testimony of John the Baptist; he, too, does not show you any other life or light except this man who is God himself. Thus this light must be understood to be the true light of grace in Christ, and not the natural light which sinners, Israelites, pagans, and devils, the worst enemies of the light, also have.

Let nobody accuse me that my interpretation of this passage differs from that of St. Augustine who understood this passage to deal with the natural light.[14] I do not reject this interpretation for I know full well that the light of reason is everywhere kindled by the divine light and, as I have said of the natural life, that it is part and beginning of the true life, provided it comes to the right understanding. The light of reason, too, is a part and beginning of the true light provided it recognizes and honors him by whom it is kindled. However, it does not do this by itself, but remains within

---

[14] Augustine, *On the Gospel of John* (*In Ioannis evangelium*), Tractate 1, 18 (*MPL* 35, 1388).

itself and becomes corrupt, and also corrupts all things along with itself; and for this reason it will be extinguished and perish. The light of grace does not destroy the natural light. It is entirely clear, according to the light of nature, that three and two equal five, even as it is clear that one should do good and avoid evil. The light of grace does not extinguish this. But the natural light cannot reach so far that it could determine which things are good and which are bad. The same thing happens to the natural light as happened to the man who wanted to go to Rome and went in the opposite direction. He knew very well that he who wants to go to Rome should take the right road, but he did not know which one that was. Natural light does the same thing: it does not follow the right road to God, it does not know it and is not acquainted with it, although it knows sufficiently that one must follow the right road. Thus reason always prefers the evil instead of the good; it would never do this if it realized with a clear vision that only the good would be chosen. But this interpretation is not appropriate in connection with this Gospel passage, since only the light of grace is being preached here. Furthermore, St. Augustine was only a human being; we are not compelled to follow his interpretation, for the text clearly indicates that the evangelist is speaking of the light concerning which John the Baptist had been testifying, and this light is indeed the light of grace, Christ himself.

Since we have the opportunity, we shall characterize more fully the false natural light which causes so much misery and unhappiness. The natural light is like the other members and faculties of man. Nobody doubts that man with all his faculties was created by the eternal Word of God, as were all other things, and that he is God's creature. Nevertheless there is nothing good in him; this means (as Moses says in Genesis 6[:5]), that all his thoughts and senses with all faculties are continually inclined to evil. Thus although the flesh is truly God's creation it is not inclined to chastity but to unchastity; although the heart is truly God's creation, it is not inclined to humility, to love of neighbor, but to pride and to self-love. It also acts according to this inclination, unless it is forcibly prevented from doing so. The same also holds true for the natural light; although by nature it is enlightened enough to know that only good should be done, it is so corrupt that it never succeeds in choosing the good; rather it calls good whatever pleases it, settles for it, and does not hesitate to conclude that what it has chosen as good must be done. Thus it carries on and always follows the evil instead of the good.

We can prove this with examples. Reason knows very well that one should be godly and serve God; it can chatter a lot about this and opines that it can teach the whole world. Very well, this is true and well put, but when reason is called on to act and to show how and in what way we should become godly or serve God, then it can do nothing; it is as blind as a bat and says that we must fast, pray, sing, and do the works of the law. It continues to fool around in this manner with works, until it has gone so far astray and thinks we serve God by building churches, ringing bells, burning incense, reciting by rote, singing, wearing hoods, having tonsures, burning candles, and by other countless foolish acts of which the world is full, indeed more than full. Reason parades around with such great and blind error and yet always remains "the clear light": one must be godly and serve God. Now when Christ, the light of grace, appears, he, too, teaches one must be godly and serve God. He does not extinguish this natural light, but he opposes the manner and the means that reason uses to teach how one should become godly and serve God. He says: To become godly is not to perform works but first to believe in God, without any works, and afterward to do works; without faith no work is good.

Then the battle begins. Reason rages against grace and cries out against its light; reason accuses it of saying that it forbids good works. It does not want its way and manner of becoming godly to be rejected. It continues to rave that one must be godly and serve God. Thus the light of grace is made to appear foolish, indeed, to be error and heresy, which must be persecuted and banished. Behold, this is the virtue of the natural light that it does nothing else but rave against the true light and that it glories in the claim always to be godly. It forever clamors: good works, good works. However, it will not and cannot permit itself to be taught what being godly is and what good works are; rather, whatever reason believes and puts forth, that is supposed to be good and right. Behold, there you have in brief the cause and origin of all idolatry, of all heresy, of all hypocrisy, of all error; this is what all the prophets deplored and why they were killed, and against this all Scripture takes a stand. All of this comes from the stiff-necked, self-willed pride and delusion of natural reason which is puffed up because it knows that we must be godly and serve God; moreover, it does not want to listen to or tolerate any teacher. It is of the opinion that it is sufficiently informed and that it can find out on its own what it means to be godly and to serve God and how one should do it. This sort of arrogance divine truth cannot and must not suffer from reason; for it is the greatest error and is against God's honor. In this way controversy and misery arise.

Accordingly, it is clear, I believe, that John is not talking here of the false light, nor of the bright natural light which correctly asserts that we must be godly; for this is already here, and Christ did not come in order to bring it, in order to blind the false, self-willed pride and to dim it and to place the light of his grace, faith, in its stead. This is also the import of the words themselves when he says: "the life was a light of men" [John 1:4]. If it is a light of men, then it must be a light different from that which is in man. Since man already has the natural light within him, whatever enlightens man enlightens natural light within man and brings another light in addition to the light that is within man. He does not say that it is the light of animals without reason, but one of man who is a rational being. For no man exists in whom there is not the natural light of reason; this is the sole ground for calling him human and for his having human worth. If the evangelist had wanted this light to be understood as the natural light of reason, he should have said: the life was a light of darkness, as Moses writes in Genesis 1[:2] that there was darkness upon the waters. Therefore, this light must be understood as the one which is revealed to the world in Christ on earth.

Look also at the sequence of the words. John places the life before the light. He does not say that the light was the life of men, but "the life was the light of men," for the reason that in Christ are reality and truth, and not just the appearance of these things, as in man. For just as Luke says of Christ's external life in his last chapter [24:19]: "He was a man, mighty in deeds and words"; and in Acts 1[:1]: "Jesus began to do and to teach," so that the works precede the teaching for otherwise words without works are

60

hypocrisy; as John says of John the Baptist in John 5[:35] that he is the lamp that burns and sheds light, for shedding light without burning is fallacious—so here, too, in order that Christ may be recognized as the true, genuine light, he says, first, that everything was life in him, and then he says that the same life is the light of men.

It follows from this that man has no light other than Christ, God's son, in his human nature. He who believes that Christ is true God and that in him is life, is enlightened by this light, and quickened by it. The light sustains him so that he is where Christ is; for just as the godhead is eternal life, so this life also is an eternal light; just as this divine life cannot die, so this light cannot go out, and so, too, faith in such light cannot perish.

We must also especially notice that he attributes life to Christ as the eternal Word, and not to Christ as the human being. He says: "In him (notice: in the Word) was the life." For although it is true that he died as a human being, still he remained alive all the time, for life would not and could not die; for this reason, too, death was overcome and swallowed up in life in such a manner that his human nature, too, came immediately to life again. This same life is the light of men. Whoever acknowledges and believes in such a life in Christ, passes through death, and yet never dies, as has been pointed out above. The light of such life sustains him so that death does not touch him, and, even though the body must die and decay, the soul does not experience this death, because it is in this light and through it completely embraced in the life of Christ. But whoever does not believe this remains in darkness and death; even if his body remained alive (beginning with the Last Day, we know, it will remain alive throughout eternity), still his soul tastes and feels death and thus dies eternally.

From this we perceive the damage that is intended by Cerinthus and all who believe and teach Christ to be solely a human being and not true God. For his human nature would avail nothing if the divine nature were not within it; yet, on the other hand, God will not and cannot be found except through and in his humanity which, as Isaiah 11[:10] says, he has set up as a sure banner wherewith he gathers all his children from all the nations. Behold, if you believe that in Christ there is such a life which remained even when he died and overcame death, then the light shines for you and also remains for you the light and the life, even at the time of death. It follows that such a life and light cannot possibly be created; for no creature is able to overcome death, neither in itself nor in another.

Behold, this interpretation of the light is easy and becoming, and it certainly contributes to our soul's salvation. But those who make it into a natural light of reason are far from it; for that does not improve anybody. Indeed, it only leads far away from Christ into created beings and into false reason. We must enter right into Christ and not look at the lights which emanate from him; rather we must look at his light whence these lights emanate. We must not follow the stream flowing from the source away from the source, but direct our course solely and directly to the source. The text continues:

> "And the light shines into the darkness, and the darkness did not comprehend it" [John 1:5].

About this passage, too, there have been complicated speculations. It has been interpreted to mean that reason has a natural light, as mentioned above, and that it is kindled by God, and yet it does not recognize, comprehend, or sense him or the light from which it is kindled; therefore it is in darkness and does not see the light from which it has all its light and vision. Oh, that this interpretation might be eradicated from my heart where it is so deeply rooted! It is not that this interpretation is wrong or incorrect in itself, but that at this point in the Gospel it does not fit and is out of place. It does not permit the blessed, comforting words of the Gospel to remain simple and pure in their true meaning. Why, I ask, do they speak only of reason, saying that it is kindled by the divine light? Why do they not also say this of natural life? For natural life is quickened by the divine life in exactly the same manner as the light of reason is illuminated by the divine light. Hence, in all fairness, they should also say that life quickens the dead, and the dead do not comprehend it, as they say that the light illumines dark reason and reason does not comprehend it. Again, I might also say: The eternal will makes the unwilling willing, and the unwilling do not comprehend it. We could deal in the same manner with all our other natural gifts and powers. How is it that reason and its light enter into such speculation? Platonic philosophers first led St. Augustine to this interpretation of this text with their unprofitable and silly babbling. Their interpretation glistens so nicely that they were called the divine philosophers. Augustine in turn pulled all of us after him.[15]

What more can their babbling yield than this, that reason is illumined by God who is an incomprehensible light? Life, too, is given in like manner by God who is the incomprehensible life, and all our power is made powerful by God who is an incomprehensible power. As near as he is to the light of reason with his incomprehensible light, so near is he to life with his incomprehensible life, and to power with his incomprehensible power; as Paul says in Acts 17[:28]: "In him we live, move, and have our being," and as Jeremiah 23[:24, 23] says: "I fill heaven and earth. How should I then be a God who is far away and not closeby?" We have heard, above, in the Epistle that he upholds all things through the word of his power [Heb. 1:3].[16] Thus he is not only near to the light of reason, illumining it, but to all creatures, and he flows, pours, and illumines and works in them and fills all things. Accordingly, we are not to think that St. John is talking about these matters here; he is simply addressing mankind and explaining what sort of light they have in Christ outside of and above nature.

In addition, it is blind and awkward talk to say of the natural light that the darkness does not comprehend it. What other meaning is there but that reason is illumined and kindled by the divine light and yet remains dark and receives no light? Whence comes their natural light? Darkness cannot be where a light is kindled, even if there is darkness because of the lack of the light of grace. But they are not talking about the light of grace; they must not talk either of the same darkness. Hence it is contradictory to say that the light is to illuminate the darkness and that the darkness is not to comprehend it or is to remain dark; it is similarly contradictory to say that life is imparted to a dead person and that the dead person is not to comprehend life or to become aware of it and remains dead. Should one, however, say we do not comprehend

---

[15] Augustine, *op. cit.*, Tractate 1, 19 (*MPL* 35, 1388).
[16] Cf. WA 10[I, 1], 158 ff.

him who gives light and life, I would listen! Which angel comprehends him? Which saint comprehends him who gives him grace?
He remains hidden and uncomprehended. But this does not mean,
as the evangelist puts it here, that the lights are not comprehended
by the darkness, but, as the words read, this means: The light
shines in the dark places, but the dark places remain dark and are
not illuminated thereby; they let the light shine on them and yet
they do not see, just as the sun shines for the blind and yet they do
not perceive it. Look at the number of words I have to pour out, in
order to do away with this strange interpretation of our text!

Therefore let us cling to the simple interpretation which the
text furnishes freely and easily. All who are illumined by natural
reason comprehend the light and are illumined, each one according
to his measure. But this light of grace which is given to men in
addition to the natural light shines in the darkness, i.e., among the
blind people of this world who are without grace, but they do not
accept it. On the contrary, they persecute it; this is the meaning of
his words in John 3[:19]: "This condemns the world, that the light
has come into the world, and men loved the darkness more than
the light." Behold, in this manner Christ, before he was proclaimed
by John the Baptist, sojourned among the people on earth, but
nobody paid attention to him. Yet he was the life and the light of
men. He lived and shined, too, but there was nothing but darkness,
and this darkness sensed him not. All the people were worldly
blind and in darkness. Had they recognized him for what he was,
they would have given him the glory due him, as St. Paul says in I
Corinthians 2[18]: "Had they recognized the wisdom of God, they
would not have crucified the King of Glory." In such a manner,
too, Christ, even before his birth, from the beginning and until the
end, has always been life and light, and he shines at all times in all
creatures in the Holy Scriptures through his holy people, prophets
and preachers, with works and words, and he has never ceased to
shine. But there is darkness wherever he sheds his light, and the
darkness does not comprehend him. It is quite possible that St.
John directed these words also against his adversary Cerinthus. He
saw the plain Scripture and the truth which enlightened Cerinthus
whose dense darkness did not comprehend them. That is the way it
goes all the time, even today. Scripture may be shown to the blind

teachers so that they can grasp it, and it remains true that the light shines in the darkness and the darkness does not comprehend it.

One should notice in particular that the evangelist says: "the light shines" (*phanei*), that is, it is manifest or visible to the eyes in the darkness, but he who receives nothing more of it remains in darkness, just as the sun shines for the blind person, but he, nevertheless, does not see any more because of it, so this light, in exactly the same way, shines in the darkness but the darkness, nevertheless, does not become brighter because of it. In the believers, however, it does not only shine; it also renders them full of light and makes them see and lives in them, so that the text might well read: the life is the light of men, and again: the light without life is a shining of darkness. For this reason no amount of shining is of use to the unbelievers. No matter how clearly one shows and presents them the truth, they remain in darkness. So let us understand these passages of the evangelist as common attributes and names of Christ: by means of them, as in a preface and introduction to his Gospel, he wanted to indicate what was to be written about Christ in the whole Gospel, namely that he is true God and man, who has created all things, and that he was given to men to be life and light, although only a few of those to whom he is revealed receive him. It is such and nothing else which make up the content of the Gospel. St. Paul, in Romans 1[:1–6], also writes in this manner a preface and introduction to his epistle. Now follows the real beginning of the Gospel:

"There was a man sent by God, whose name was John" [John 1:6].

Mark and Luke also begin their gospels with John the Baptist, and it is fitting to begin with him, as Christ himself says in Matthew 11[:12]: "Since the days of John the kingdom of heaven has suffered violence." And in Acts 1[:22] St. Peter says that Christ began after John's baptism, in which he was also ordained and called to be a teacher, as John the Baptist shows when he says in John 1:[32–34, cf. Matt. 3:16]: "I saw the Holy Spirit descend like a dove and I heard the voice of the Father, 'This is my beloved Son, with whom I am well pleased.'" Then Christ was made a teacher, and his ministry began. Then the gospel had its beginning through Christ himself; for no one except Christ himself was to begin the exalted, blessed, comforting mission of the word. Because of this John had to come first and prepare the people for the preaching so that they might receive the light and the life. For, as we have heard, Christ is everywhere the light which shines in the darkness and is not comprehended; he was particularly present among the Israelites in his human nature and through his human nature he physically appeared among them and yet he was not recognized. For this reason only did his forerunner John come to this place, preaching concerning him, in order that he should be known and accepted. Therefore this passage follows the previous one nicely and fittingly: for when Christ, the shining light, was not recognized, John came forward, opened men's eyes and pointed out the shining light which was present; after that, on its own, without being pointed out by John, it was accepted, listened to, and recognized.

Now, I believe, we are at the end of the most difficult and most profound part of this Gospel, for what else is written is easy and smooth and deals with what the other evangelists also tell about John and Christ—although, as I have said before, this part, too, by itself is not difficult. It has intentionally been made difficult through natural and human interpretations. Any passage will become difficult, if a word is removed from its ordinary meaning and given an alien one. Who would not wish to know what a human being is and would not imagine all sorts of strange thoughts if he should hear that a human being is different from what the world thinks. This has happened here to the simple clear words of the evangelist.

Still, John has his own particular manner of presentation in this that he constantly directs John the Baptist's testimony toward the divinity of Christ because of Cerinthus, while the other evangelists do not do this; they direct their testimony solely toward Christ, without particular reference to his divinity. But here John says that John came to testify to the light and to announce Christ as the life, the light, and as God, as we shall hear.

Whatever has been said in the Advent season concerning John the Baptist is also to be understood here; just as he was the forerunner of Christ and directed the people to him, so the spoken word of the gospel should preach only Christ and point only to him. For only to that end was it ordained by God, just as John was sent by God (as we have heard), so that he should be the voice in the wilderness who with his office signifies the spoken preaching of the gospel. Just as the darkness was unable, on its own, to comprehend this light, even though it was present, John had to reveal and to bear witness of it. To this day natural reason on its own is unable to comprehend it, even though it is present in all the world. The spoken word of the gospel must reveal and proclaim it.

Now we see that through the gospel this same light is brought to us, not from afar, nor is it necessary to run after it a great distance; it is very near to us and also shines in our heart. Nothing more is necessary but that it be pointed out and preached. And whoever hears it preached, and believes, finds it in his heart; for faith can only be in the heart, and so this light cannot be anywhere except in faith. Therefore I say that it is close by and within us, but it is not comprehended by us on our own; it must be preached and believed. This is what St. Paul has in mind in Romans 10[:6–8] where he refers to Moses' statement in Deuteronomy 30[:12, 14]: "It is not necessary to travel across the ocean, nor to climb into heaven or into hell for it. It is near to you, in your heart and in your mouth." See, this is what was meant by the light shining in darkness and not being comprehended until John and the gospel came and revealed it. Then man is illumined by it and comprehends it, and yet it changes neither time, place, person, nor age, but only the heart.

Again, just as John did not come of his own initiative, but was sent by God, so neither the gospel nor any other preaching concerning this light can come from its own initiative or from human reason, but God must send it. For this reason the evangelist denigrates here all doctrines of men; for what men teach never reveals Christ, the light; indeed, it only hinders it. But whatever reveals Christ, is certainly sent by God and not invented by men. Therefore the evangelist mentions the name and says: "His name was John." John, however, in Hebrew signifies grace or favor, showing that such preaching and proclamation are sent forth, not because of any merit of ours, but because of the pure grace and favor of God; they bring nothing but God's grace and favor. St. Paul says the same in Romans 10[:15]: "How can they preach, if they have not been sent?" From all of this we see that the evangelist deals with Christ in such a manner that he is recognized as God. For if he is the light, which is present everywhere and shines in the darkness, and needs nothing more than that it be revealed through the word and perceived through faith in the heart, then surely it must be God. No creature can shine in this manner so close to all places and hearts. Yet the light is God in such a manner that it is nevertheless human and that it is preached among and by this same human being. To continue:

> "He came to be a witness, to bear witness to this light, so that everyone might believe through him" [John 1:7].

See, it is now clear from what is said here that the gospel only proclaims this light, the man Christ, and causes the darkness to comprehend it, but not through reason or experience, but through faith. For he says clearly that everyone should believe through him. Likewise, he came to be a witness and he should bear witness. It is the nature of bearing witness that it speaks of something which others do not see, know, or feel, but they must believe the witness who bears the testimony to it. Thus the gospel, too, does not demand rational decision and agreement, but a faith, that is above reason; otherwise this light may not be comprehended. It was stated above with sufficient emphasis, how the light of reason fights and rages against this light, to say nothing of the fact that it is being comprehended and agreed with. For the statement which says "the darkness does not comprehend this light" stands firm, and because of this, reason with its light must be captured and blinded, as is said in Isaiah 60[:19]: "I shall cover your sun (i.e., your reason) with a cloud," i.e., with the gospel or the word of God or the witness of John which demands faith and makes a fool of reason. Similarly, he states: "Your sun shall not shine for you anymore, and the light of your moon shall no longer be within you, but your God shall be to you an eternal light." This light is attested to by the word, so that reason should keep silent and follow the testimony; then it would comprehend the light in the same faith and its darkness would be illumined. If it could comprehend this light by its own power, or agree with it, there would be no need of

John and his testimony. Thus the gospel has only one aim: to be a witness to self-willed, blind, and stubborn reason, to strive against it, and to lead it away from its own light and arrogance into faith through which it might comprehend the living and eternal light.

"He was not the light, but came to bear witness to this light" [John 1:8].

My dearly beloved, why does he say this and why does he repeat once more the words that John was only a witness to this light? A necessary repetition it is! In the first place, it is necessary in order to show that this light is not simply a human being, but God himself; for, as I have said, the evangelist was anxious to proclaim in all his words the divinity of Christ. If John, the great saint, is not the light, but only a witness to it, then this light must be something more than all that is holy, whether it be an angel or a human being. If holiness could make such a light, they would have made one out of John; but this light is beyond holiness, and so it also must be beyond the angels who are not beyond holiness.

In the second place, this repetition is necessary in order to counter the impious preachers who witness not to Christ, the light, but to themselves. It is eminently true that all who preach human doctrine make a human being into a light, lead the people away from this light to themselves, and put themselves in the place of this true light, as the pope and his followers have done. For this reason he is also the "Anti-Christ"; he is against this true light. The gospel cannot tolerate any other teaching beside it; it wants only to be Christ's witness and to lead the people to this light, Christ. Therefore, O Lord God, these words: "He was not the light," would truly be worthy to be written with capital letters and they should be used industriously against those who put themselves forward and want to give to the people doctrines and law of their own fabrication, who pretend to illumine the people, but lead them, with themselves, into the abyss of hell. They do not teach faith and cannot teach it; no one except John, who is sent by God, teaches the holy gospel. Much could be said about this point.

In brief, reject whoever does not preach the gospel to you and do not listen to him. He preaches the gospel to you who teaches you to have faith in Christ and to put your trust in the eternal light and not to rely on your own works. Therefore beware of everything that is told you that does not agree with the gospel; do not put any trust in it, and do not, under any circumstances, consider it the light which could illumine and improve your soul. Consider it rather as an external matter, such as eating and drinking to take care of the needs of the body, which you may use at your pleasure or to please somebody else, but under no circumstances as something contributing to your eternal salvation. For nothing but this light should be useful or necessary to you for your salvation. How gruesome are the teachings of men, which are rampant now and have driven this light into exile! They all want to be this light themselves, and not witnesses to the light; they teach themselves and their things. They are completely silent about this light, or teach it in such a manner that they actually teach themselves in addition to the light; this is even worse than to be silent. This action produces Samaritans who half serve God and half serve idols, II Kings 25 [17–41].

"It was a true light which enlightens every man who comes into this world" [John 1:9].

Neither John nor any other saint is the light. Yet it is a true light to which John and all evangelical preachers bear witness. Enough has been said concerning the nature of the light, how it is recognized through faith and how it eternally preserves us in life and death so that no darkness ever can hurt us. It is however, remarkable, that he says: "it enlightens all people who come into this world." If this is said of the natural light, his words are contradicted that it is the true light; for he said above: "the darkness does not comprehend it," and all his words are aimed at the light of grace. Then follow the words: "He came into the world and the world did not recognize him and his own did not accept him." But he whom the true light illumines, is illumined with grace and recognizes the light. On the other hand, one is driven to believe that these words are not spoken about the light of grace because he says "it enlightens all people who come into this world"; this is without a doubt said of all human beings who are born. St. Augustine says one must interpret the passage to mean that no man is enlightened except by this light, in the same way that one customarily says of a teacher in a city, where there is no other teacher, that this teacher teaches everyone in the city, i.e., there is no teacher in this city except this one.[17] He alone has all the pupils. Saying this does not mean that he is teaching all the people in the city, but merely that there is only one teacher in the city and that nobody is taught by another person.

Thus here, too, the evangelist did not intend that John or any other human being or any creature should be the light, but that there is only one light which illumines all men and that not a single human being could come upon the earth who could be illumined by anybody else. I do not know how to disagree with this interpretation; for in the same manner also St. Paul writes in Romans 5[:18]: "As through one man's sin condemnation has come over all men, so through one man's righteousness justification has come over all men." Yet not all men are justified through Christ, nevertheless he is the man through whom all justification comes. It is the same here. Even if not all men are illumined, yet this is the light from which alone all illumination comes. The evangelist has freely used this manner of speaking; he did not avoid it even though some would stumble over the fact that he speaks of all men. He thought he would take care of such offense by explaining before and after and by saying that "the darkness has not comprehended it," and that the world has never recognized him and his own have never accepted him. Such passages should have been strong enough so that nobody could say he had intended to say that all men are enlightened, but that he alone is the light which enlightens everybody and that, without him, nobody is enlightened.

If the reference, however, is to the natural light of reason, then this would be an insignificant statement, inasmuch as it enlightens not only all men who come into the world, but also those who leave the world, and even the devil. The same rational light remains in the dead, the devils, and the damned; indeed, it only becomes brighter so that they are all the more tormented by it. Since he mentions only the men who come into this world, he shows that he is talking of this light of faith which shines and helps only in this life; for after death nobody is illumined by it. It must

---

[17] Augustine, *On the Gospel of John* (*In Ioannis evangelium*), Tractate 2, 7 (MPL 35, 1392).

happen here through faith in the man Christ, yet by his divine nature. After this life we shall see it no longer in its humanity and in faith, but we shall see the pure godhead itself openly. The evangelist carefully chooses his words so that he does not reject Christ, the human being, and yet, at the same time, declares his divinity. For this reason it was necessary that he say "all men," so that he might preach only one light above all others and so that he might warn us that we should not accept in this life human lights or other lights. No human being is to shine for another, but this light alone is to shine for all men. Preachers are to be only precursors and witnesses of this light to men, in order that all should believe in the light.

After saying: "it illumines all people," he saw that he had included too much and therefore he added: "who come into this world," so that he might make a light out of Christ in this world. For in that world the light will cease and will be changed into eternal brightness; St. Paul says in I Corinthians 15[:24]: "Then Christ will hand over the kingdom to the Father." But now he reigns through his humanity. Just as he will hand over the kingdom, so will he also hand over the light. Not that there are two kinds of light or that we shall see something different from what we see now. We shall see the same light, even the same God, whom we now see in faith, but in a different manner. Now we see him in faith, darkly; then we shall see him revealed. It is as if I see a golden statue through a painted glass or veil, and later see it bare and uncovered. Thus St. Paul says in I Corinthians 13[:12]: "Now we see in a mirror, darkly, but then we shall see him as he is." Behold, now you see of what sort of light the evangelist speaks, namely, that Christ is the light of men by means of his human nature—that is, in faith—through which his divine nature shines as through a mirror or a colored glass, or as the sun through thin clouds, so that the light is always attributed to the divine nature, not to the human nature. Yet there is no contempt for the human nature which is the cloud and the curtain of this light.

This language is clear enough, and he who has faith understands well what is the nature and character of this light. But he who does not believe does not understand it, and it does not matter either, for he is not supposed to understand it, and it would be

72

better for the unbeliever if he knew nothing of the Bible and did not study it; for he misleads himself and everybody else with his fallible light, which he thinks is the light of Scripture, but which for all that cannot be understood without the right faith. For this light shines in the dark places, but is not comprehended by them.

This passage may also mean that the evangelist wishes to say that the gospel and faith are preached in all the world and that this light has risen in the sight of all the people of this world, as the sun rises over all people, exactly as St. Paul says in Colossians 1[:23]: "The gospel is preached among all creatures under heaven," and as Christ himself says in Mark 16[:15]: "Go into all the world and preach the gospel to every creature." Psalm 19[:6] also says of him: "His going forth is from the rising of the sun until the setting, and there is nobody who could hide from his heat." How this is to be understood, has been explained above, in the Epistle for Christmas Eve.[18] Thus it is a clear and simple interpretation, that his light enlightens all people who come into this world, so that neither the Israelites nor anyone else dare set up their own light anywhere. This interpretation harmonizes well with the preceding passage. Even before John and the Gospel witness to this light, it shines in the darkness and is not comprehended. But after it is promulgated and testified to publicly, it shines over all people as far as the world extends, even if not all accept it, as is expressed in the following passage:

"It was in the world, and the world was made through it, and the world did not recognize it" [John 1:10].

All this is said of Christ, the human being, and especially of him after his baptism. When he began to shine after the testimony of John, he was, indeed, in the midst of the world. But which place in the world knew it? Who bothered about him? Is it not true that he was not accepted by them among whom he was present in person, as it is stated:

"He came to his own people and his own did not receive him" [John 1:11].

---

[18] Cf. Luther's treatment of Titus 2:11, WA 10[I], 1, 21 f.

These words, too, are spoken concerning the coming of his preaching, and not concerning his birth. For his "coming" is his preaching and illumining. As the Baptist says in Matthew 3[:11], Luke 3[:16], Mark 1 [:7], and John 1[:27]: "There is one who will come after me whose shoelaces I am not worthy to untie." It is on account of this "coming" that St. John is called his forerunner. As Gabriel says in Luke 1[:17] to Zechariah, John's father: "He will go before him and prepare his way." For, as said above, the gospels begin with Christ; after his baptism he began to be the light and to do the things for which he had come. Therefore he now says: "He came to his own people right in the midst of the world, and they did not accept him." If this were not said of his coming to give light through his preaching and shining, then he would not castigate them so for not having accepted him. Who could know that it was he, had he not been revealed? Therefore they are guilty for not accepting him because he came and was revealed by John and by himself. Therefore John also says in John 1[:3]: "For this reason I have come and am baptizing with water, so that he might be revealed in Israel." And he, himself, in John 5[:43] says: "I have come in my Father's name and you have not accepted me. Another one will come in his own name, and him you will accept." This, too, is clearly said concerning the arrival of the preaching and revelation.

He calls the Israelites his own people because they were chosen out of all the world to be his people and because a promise had been made to them through Abraham, Isaac, Jacob, and David. No promise was made to us Gentiles, strangers that we are and alienated from Christ. Therefore we are not called his own. But we have been received out of pure grace and we have become his people, even though, alas, we still permit him to come through his gospel every day and pay him no heed. For this reason, too, we have to suffer that another one, namely, the pope, comes in his place and that he is received by us. We are forced to serve the evil foe because we refuse to serve our God.

However, we must not forget in this connection that the evangelist twice refers to Christ's divine nature: the first time, when he says: "The world was made through him"; the second time, when he says: "He came to his own." For it belongs to the qualifications of a true god that he have his own people. The Israelites were always God's own people, as the Bible says many times. If then they are Christ's own people, he must certainly be the God to whom the Bible ascribes that people. The evangelist leaves to the thoughtful contemplation of each individual what a disgrace and shame it is for the world not to recognize its creator and for the Israelites not to receive their God. How could one reproach the world more strongly than by saying that it does not recognize its creator? How many evil vices and reports flow from this single fact? What good can be found there where there is nothing but ignorance, darkness, blindness? What evil should be absent there where knowledge of God is not present? Ah woe, what a horrible, frightening thing the world is! He who knows the world and reflects properly on this matter, should fall all the more deeply into perdition. He would not be happy in this life for which such evil things had been written.

"But as many as received him, to them he gave the power to become children of God, who believe in his name" [John 1:12].

Here we see what sort of light it is of which the evangelist was speaking previously. It is Christ, the comforting light of grace and not the natural light of reason. For John is an evangelist, not a Platonist. All who receive the natural light, or reason, receive him in accordance with that light. How else should they receive him? Exactly as they receive the natural life from the divine life. Nevertheless, that same light and life do not impart to them the power to become the children of God. Indeed, they remain enemies of this light, do not recognize it, and do not accept it. For this reason there cannot be any mention of the natural light in this Gospel, but everything relates only to Christ, with the intention that he be recognized as true God. Henceforth this Gospel will be well known. For it talks of believing in Christ's name, namely, that such believing creates children of God. These are choice words and they powerfully attack those who insist on works and the law. Good works never change a person. Therefore, although those who are works-righteous do their works and improve them—at least to their manner of thinking—yet they remain the same person as before and their works become only hypocrisy and covers for infamy! But faith changes a person and makes an enemy into a child. It does this secretly, so that external works, position, and manner of life remain, provided the works are not by nature bad. This has been explained frequently. Thus faith brings along the whole heritage and sum of righteousness and salvation, so that it is not necessary to obtain either of these by means of works, as the false work-teachers foolishly tell us. For if someone is God's child, he already possesses God's inheritance because of that filial relationship. If faith bestows such a filial relationship, it is indeed clear that good works are to come about freely and without payment, solely in order to glorify God; they are done by those who already possess salvation and God's inheritance through faith, as has been explained sufficiently above in connection with the other Epistle lesson.[19]

> "Those who are born, not of blood nor of the will of the flesh nor of the will of man, but of God" [John 1:13].

This he says to clarify for himself what faith brings about and how everything that is outside of faith is of no avail whatsoever. Truly, here he does not praise nature, light, reason and that which is not faith, but he mightily destroys them. The filial relationship is too high and noble to come out of nature or for it to be demanded of nature.

The evangelist enumerates four kinds of filial relationship, the first growing out of blood, the second from the will of the flesh, the third from the will of a man, the fourth from God. The first filial relationship, stemming from blood, is easily understood: it is the natural one. With it the evangelist takes a stand against the Israelites who glory in their descent from Abraham and the patriarchs and boastfully cite the Scripture passages where God promised to the seed of Abraham blessing and the inheritance of salvation. Because of it they claim that they alone are the true people and children of God. But he says here: There must be more here than blood, otherwise there is no filial relationship with God. For even Abraham and the patriarchs did not possess the inheritance because of blood, but because of faith, as St. Paul teaches in Hebrews 11[:8 ff].

---

[19] Luther is referring to the Epistle for the Early Christmas Service, Titus 3:4–7. Cf. WA 10[I, 1], 95–128, esp. 119–28.

If natural kinship were sufficient to establish this filial relationship, then truly, Judas, the traitor, Caiaphas, Annas, and all the evil Israelites who in times past were damned in the desert could lay claim to this inheritance, for all of them were of the blood of the patriarchs. Therefore the passage does not read: "Those who are born of the blood," but "those who are born of God."

The other two kinds of kinship, of the will of the flesh and of the will of a man, are not sufficiently clear to me as yet. But I clearly see that by means of them the evangelist wants to disavow everything that nature is and does, and wants to emphasize birth of God alone. Therefore there is no risk involved in how we discuss and divide these two items, as belonging to nature outside the realm of grace. It really makes no difference. Some understand the filial relation born of the will of the flesh to be one which comes not from the blood, but from the law of Moses. He ordered that the next of kin had to marry the wife of a deceased man to beget children to bear the name of the deceased and to be his heirs, in order that the bloodline of his kinsman should remain intact. Under this heading belongs also the "step-blood" relationship, which in every respect comes from the will of the flesh and not from the regular bloodline. Here, however, the evangelist calls "flesh" man as he lives in the flesh, as is the usage of Scripture. Thus the meaning might be: not as people outside of the blood relationship have children, for all this is still completely carnal and human and comes about from man's free will; but what is born from blood comes about without free will and naturally, man willing or not willing.

The third kind of "from the will of a man" they take to be the alien filial relationship called adoption, where a man chooses a strange child and accepts it as his own. Now even if you were Abraham's or David's genuine child or stepchild or adopted child, or friend, it would not help you one bit. You must be born of God. Even Christ's own relatives did not believe, as John 7[:5] states.

If you wish, you may define "kinship" so that "from the blood" is understood to include all those who belong to the blood, whether through physical relationship or "step"-relationship. "The will of the flesh," then, would be all relationships outside the blood relationship, as, e.g., adopted children, as has been mentioned. But "out of the will of man" may refer to spiritual children, as, e.g., pupils in their relationship to their teachers. Thus the intention of the evangelist would be to destroy everything in the power of blood, flesh, nature, reason, knowledge, teaching, law, and free will, so that nobody would have the audacity, by means of his teaching, work, knowledge, or free will to help or permit anybody on earth to be helped to the kingdom of God, but, casting all this away, one should strive only after the divine birth. I believe that in Scripture man is commonly referred to as one who carries out, who rules, leads, and teaches others. For these above all deserve to be cast out and to be so identified. For no clan makes more obstinate and wanton claim and relies more on its own strengths, with the result that it always resists and persecutes grace most vehemently.

In this matter everyone may hold to his own opinion, except that he must know that nothing is of any avail which is outside of being born of God. For if anything had been of any avail, the evangelist, with his thorough investigation, surely would have mentioned it alongside the "born of God," and he would not have solely praised the divine birth.

The divine birth, then, is nothing else but faith. How does this work? I have mentioned above how the light of grace fights and blinds the natural light of reason. The gospel comes and promulgates the light of grace, namely, that man must not act and live according to his arrogance; rather, his natural light must be discarded, killed, and removed. If man accepts and obeys this testimony, if he surrenders his light and selfconceit, if he willingly agrees to be a fool and to be led, taught and illumined, behold, a change takes place in his chief part, i.e., in his natural light. His old light goes out, and a new light, faith, enters. He holds to this faith through life and death. He clings only to the testimony of John or of the gospel, even if this should mean the loss of his possessions and prowess. Behold, then he is newly born of God through the gospel in which he abides, giving up his light and his arrogance. As St. Paul writes in I Corinthians 4[:15]: "I gave birth to you in Christ through the gospel." And in James 1[:18] we read: "Of his gracious will he gave birth to us through the word of truth, so that we would be a beginning of his creation." For this reason St. Peter calls us "new born children" of God, I Peter 2[:2]. For this reason also the gospel is called God's womb: in it he conceives us, carries us, gives birth to us, as a woman conceives and carries a child in her womb and gives birth to it. Isaiah 46[:3] states: "Hear me, you poor little remnant, you whom I carry in my womb," etc. But this birth truly reveals itself when tribulation and death approach; then we find out who has been born according to the new or the old birth. Then reason, the old light, struggles and writhes and is loathe to yield its thoughts and will; it does not like to turn to the gospel, to trust in it, and to let go its own light. Those, however, who are newly born or are being newly born at that point, surrender the old way and follow the new, giving up light, life, goods, reputation and whatever they have. They trust in the testimony of John and cling to it. For this reason, too, they attain the eternal inheritance, as the true children.

Behold, if the light, reason, the old conceit, is now dead, dark, changed into a new light, then man's entire life and powers must follow after the new light and be changed. For wherever reason goes, there the will follows. Wherever the will goes, there love and desire follow. The whole man must crawl into the gospel and become new. He must shed his old skin as does the snake. When the snake's skin becomes old, it looks for a narrow hole in the rock, crawls in it, sheds its skin, and lets it lie outside in front of the hole. In like manner must man enter into the gospel and the word of God, must boldly believe its promise that God does not lie; in doing so he sheds his old skin and leaves lying outside his light, his conceit, his will, his love, his desire, his words, his deeds. Then he becomes entirely different, a new being who looks at all things differently from the former way. He judges and considers differently, thinks, wills, speaks, loves differently, desires, performs and behaves differently. Thereafter he can recognize all classes and works of all men, whether they behave rightly or wrongly, as St. Paul says in I Corinthians 2[:15]: "The spiritual man judges all others, and he is judged by no one." Then he perceives with great clarity what great fools they all are who want to become pious through works, and he will not give one penny for all the tonsures of priests, monks, bishops, and popes nor for cowls, incensing, ringing of bells, burning of candles, singing, making noise on the organ, and reciting prayers with all their external performance. He sees how all this is nothing but idolatry and foolish sham, exactly as the Israelites worshipped Baal Ashtaroth and the calf in the desert, a precious matter under the influence of the old light of their self-willed and egotistical reason.

From this it is now clear that no blood relationship, no relatedness, no law, no teaching, no reason, no free will, no good works, no Carthusian order, no clerical status, even if it were an angelical one, is useful or helpful to this filiation with God. In fact, they are only obstructive. For if reason is not first renewed, but becomes associated with one of these things, then it clings to it, is hardened and blinded, so that it can never, or only with great difficulty, be helped to become free of it. It is then of the opinion that its nature and status are right and good, and it rants and rages against all who despise and reject its nature. In this situation reason must remain the old man, the enemy of God and his grace, of Christ and his light, must cut off the head of John, his witness, i.e., of the gospel, and instead set up its own human doctrine. This is how, in the establishment of the pope and the clergy, the game goes on now and is whooped up with full pomp and power. None of them knows anything of this divine birth, and they mumble and mutter with their teachings and laws about certain works through which they expect to attain grace. And yet they remain in their old skins! But assuredly what is said here will remain: this birth comes about not out of blood, not out of the will of the flesh or that of a man, but out of God. We must give up all reliance on our will, works, and life, for they are poisoned through the false, self-serving, self-oriented light of reason, and we must listen, above all, to the voice of the Baptist and to his testimony, and believe and follow him. If we give up that reliance, the light of Christ will illumine us, renew us, and give us power to become the children of God. To that end he came and became man. As the following passage puts it:

"*And the Word became flesh and dwelt among us, and we saw its glory, a glory as that of the only begotten Son of the Father, full of grace and truth*" [John 1:14].

"Flesh" here means total humanity, body and soul, according to the usage of Scripture which calls man "flesh." Such is the usage above, where the evangelist says: "Not out of the will of the flesh," and in the Creed where we say: "I believe in the resurrection of the flesh," i.e., of all people. Again Christ in Matthew 24[:22] says "If the days were not shortened, no flesh could be saved," i.e., not a single person. And Psalm 104 [78:39] states: "He remembered that they are flesh and as a wind which goes and does not return." Likewise John 17[:2] states: "You have given to your Son power over all flesh, so that he might give eternal life to all whom you have given him." I repeat this so assiduously because this passage suffered many attacks from heretics at the time of great learned bishops. Some, like Photinus and Apollinaris, taught that Christ was a man without a soul, and that the divinity was in him instead of a soul.[20] Manichaeus taught that Christ did not have natural and true flesh, but that he only appeared [to be human]; he had passed through Mary, his mother, in such a way that he had not laid hold of her blood and flesh, as the sun shines through a glass without taking on the nature of the glass.[21]

For this reason the evangelist used an understandable expression, saying he "became flesh," i.e., a human being, like any other human being that has flesh and blood and body and soul. Thus Scripture had to be tested and proved at that time, one piece after the other, until the time of the Antichrist who suppresses Scripture, not a piece at a time, but in its entirety. For it was prophesied that at the time of the Antichrist all heresies would be lumped together into one bilge-water pool and overcome the world. This could not take place more easily than at a time when the pope has deposed all of Scripture and has set up his own laws. Therefore at this time the bishops are no longer heretics, neither could they become heretics, for they have nothing of that book out of which heretics could develop, i.e., the gospels, and they have heaped all heresies upon themselves.

In previous times, the heretics, no matter how bad, still re-

---

[20] Apollinaris (ca. 310–ca. 390) taught that Christ as the Word of God had assumed human flesh and biological life but not a human mind or spirit. In Christ the human spirit was replaced by the divine Logos; cf. O.D.C.C., p. 70. Photinus was a fourth century theologian whose views, known only through his opponents, were apparently a variant of Arianism. Both Apollinarianism and Photinianism were formally condemned at councils in the late fourth century.

[21] Manichaeus (Mani), a third century heretic, had a syncretistic and strongly dualistic theology. He taught that Christ, being spiritual, would have been contaminated had he possessed a real human body.

mained within Scripture and left certain pieces untouched. But what is left now, since this birth of God as well as faith are no longer recognized or preached, and nothing but human laws and works are put forth? What does it matter whether Christ is or is not God, whether he is flesh or only appears to be, whether he has or does not have a soul, whether he came before or after his mother—and whatever other errors and heresy have existed—if we have no more of him than these heretics? Nor is there any need of him. It is as if he became man for nothing, and everything written about him was in vain, if we have discovered how we, through our works, can attain the grace of God.

Therefore there is no difference between our bishops and all the heretics who have ever lived, except that we use the name of Christ with our mouth and our pen as a cover and pretense, but under such pretense get rid of him and so little turn him to use and benefit as if he were the one whom all heretics have foolishly said he was; such was prophesied by St. Peter in II Peter 2[:1]: "False teachers will appear among you, who deny the God who has purchased them and who curse the way of truth." What does it avail that Christ is not as the heretics have pictured him in their preaching if, for all that, he means (or does) nothing more to us than to them? What does it avail that we condemn such heresy with our mouths and know Christ correctly if, nevertheless, our hearts do not consider him differently than they do? I do not see to what they might point as the reason for the need of Christ, if I am able to attain God's grace through my own works. It is not necessary for him to be God and become man; in short, nothing written concerning him is necessary. It would be sufficient to preach God as a person, as the Israelites believe, and then I would attain his grace with my works. What more could I wish for? What more would I need? Thus there is no need of Christ and of Scripture, if the teachings of the pope and the universities are valid. For this reason I have said that the pope, the bishops, and the institutions of higher learning are not good enough to be heretical. No, they surpass all heretics and they are the bilge-water pool of all heresies, errors, and idolatries which have existed from the beginning of the world. With them they push Christ and the word of God completely to the side, and they only keep their names as a cover-up. This sort of thing no idolater, no heretic, no Israelite has ever perpetrated, and the Turks, too, do not act in the same fashion. If it is true that before the birth of Christ the pagans were without Christ and Scripture, nevertheless, they did not act against Scripture and Christ as do these. For this reason the pagans assuredly are better than the papists.

Therefore in this worst era of the Antichrist let us be wise and cling to the message which does not teach that our reason is a light, that men are capable of teaching us, but which presents Christ to us as the one without whom we cannot get along, and which says: The Word through which all things are created is life and this life is the light of men. Believe confidently the truth that he is the light of men; without him there would be nothing but darkness in man, so that he could not know what he should do and how he should do it, not to mention how he should attain God's grace with his works (as the mad institutions of higher learning teach under the guidance of their idol, the pope, and thereby seduce all the world). In order that he should become the light of men, i.e., in order that he should become known, he came, bodily and personally, showed himself among them, and became man. Here the light was placed into the lantern. It was not the lost penny which through its work and light ran after the lantern and looked for it, but the lantern looked for the penny and with its light found it and moreover with the right kind of broom swept the whole house, i.e., the world. It looks and searches in all corners, sweeps and continues to find down to the Last Day.

It is, however, an important article that only the Word has become flesh, and not the Father, even though both of them are one, full, unique, and true God. Faith comprehends it all, and it is fitting that reason does not comprehend. For this took place and was written, in order that reason should not comprehend but should become totally blind, dark, foolish, and step forth into a new light out of its old, false light. This article does not oppose the light of reason which says: one must serve God, have faith, and lead a godly life. All this is not changed by this article. But when reason is to be precise and state who this God is, then it jumps back and says: this is not God, and it wants to call God whatever comes to its mind. Therefore when reason hears that this Word is God, and that the Father also is the same God, it shakes its head and does not want to consider it. It believes that this is not right and not true and continues to hold to its self-conceit, claiming that it knows better than anybody what and who God is.

Behold, it is thus that the Israelites stay with their self-conceit. They do not doubt that one should believe in God and honor him, but they reserve for themselves the explanation of who this same God is. In this matter they want to be the master. For them God himself must be wrong and a liar. Behold, reason always behaves this way in connection with every work and word of God. It keeps on shouting that one must honor God's work and word, and yet it wants to use its preference and judgment to determine what are God's work and word. It wants to judge God in all his works and words and be exempt from his judgment. Supposedly it is up to reason's caprice what God is or is not. Look whether God in Scripture does not justifiably take a stand against such formidable sacrilege and whether he does not prefer, and justifiably so, male and female public sinners to such "saints"? What is more vexatious than such heinous arrogance? I say this so that we correctly discern the tender fruit—who it is to whom so much is given and attributed by the pope and the universities so that, without Christ and by itself, it should be capable of attaining God's grace with its deeds, even though it is God's worst enemy and wants, above all, to annihilate him so that it alone may be God and attain God's grace. In my opinion, these are indications of real darkness!

Thus reason is forced to create idols; it cannot do otherwise. For it knows well how to speak of God's honor, but constantly goes ahead and renders such honor to whatever it imagines to be God; this "whatever" then assuredly is not God, but its own self-conceit and error, lamented in the prophets in many places. It does no good, either, for somebody to say, as do the Israelites: Yes, I mean the God who has created heaven and earth, then I can never make a mistake and I am bound to hit it right. God himself answers through Isaiah 48[:1]: "You swear by the name of God and appeal to the God of Israel, but not in truth or in righteousness," and in Jeremiah 5[:2]: "Even if they say 'by the living God,' yet they swear falsely." How does this happen? It happens in this way: whoever does not accept God in one aspect, especially in the one which he causes to be emphasized, cannot be helped when he wants to accept him in those aspects which he himself chooses. What would it have availed Abraham if he had wanted to say when he was ordered to sacrifice his son Isaac, that it was not God or God's work, and if he had gone along with his reason and said he did not wish to sacrifice his son but in other respects he would serve God, the maker of heaven and earth? He would have lied; for, he would have rejected the God who made heaven and earth; he would have fashioned a different god under the name of the God who created heaven and earth. He would have treated with contempt the true God who had given him the order.

In like manner all those are lying who say that they have in mind the true God who has made heaven and earth and who yet do not accept his work and word, but rank their self-conceit above God and his word. Now if they truly believed in the God who made heaven and earth, they would know that the same God also is a creator with respect to their self-conceit and that he should be able to make it, break it, and direct it as he wills. Since they will not let him be a sovereign creator over them and their self-conceit in one small way, it cannot be true that they believe in him as the creator of the universe.

You say: All right, what if I am misled and this is not God? Answer: Be silent, dear fellow; God does not permit a heart which does not insist on its arrogance, to be misled. For it is impossible that he should not come into such a heart and dwell therein, as the mother of God says: "He fills the hungry" [Luke 1:53], and Psalm 104 [107:9] states: "He fills the empty souls." If somebody is misled, it is certain that he did insist on his self-conceit secretly or openly. Therefore an empty heart always lives in fear of the things concerning which there is uncertainty, even though they are from God, but the self-conceited suddenly make up their minds and consider it sufficient that it glistens and seems good to them. On the other hand, whatever is assuredly from God, is quickly accepted by the "empty ones," but the self-conceited persecute it.

There is no surer sign that something is of God, than the fact that it is against self-conceit. The self-conceited, of course, are of the opinion that there is nothing more certain (and thus not from God) than what is against their self-conceit; for they are godmakers and teachers of God. Whatever suits their self-conceit must be God and God's. Thus all must be misled who insist on their own judgment. All who come to their self-conceit and give it up celebrate the true sabbath. Where this self-conceit arrives at the point that it uses the word of God to justify its presumption and attacks Scripture with its light, there is no more counsel nor help; for then this self-conceit thinks it has God's word on its side and its duty is to defend it. This is the last fall and Lucifer's misfortune, concerning which Solomon says: "The just man falls seven times and rises again, but the unbelievers fall into nothing but misfortune" [Prov. 24:16].

But enough of this. Let us return to the pericope. The evangelist says: "the Word which became flesh dwelt among us," i.e., he walked among men on earth just like any other man; even though he is God, still he became a citizen of Nazareth and Capernaum; and he deported himself like any other man, as St. Paul also says in Philippians 2[:7–8]: "He laid aside his divine nature and became like other people and in all his bearing he was found to be like a man; he humbled himself and became obedient even unto death." For this reason this "becoming like" other men on the part of Christ and his dwelling on earth must not be understood with reference to his human nature. For with reference to his human nature he became like men through being born of Mary, and it was here that he came into human nature and became like men with reference to nature. Rather his "becoming like" other men must be understood with reference to his external essence and behavior, that he was involved with eating, drinking, sleeping, walking, work, rest, house and town, walking and standing, clothes and garment, indeed every human behavior and deportment, so that nobody would have been able to recognize him as God, had not John and the gospel so proclaimed him.

He continues: "And we have seen his glory," i.e., his divinity, in his miraculous signs and his teachings. The little word "glory" we have also heard above in the Epistle where he says of Christ: "He is a reflection of his glory," and thus refers to Christ's divinity.[22] However, if I wanted to express this in real German, I would say that this glory, called *cabod* in Hebrew, *doxa* in Greek, and *gloria* in Latin, is, in German, the same as *herlickeyt*. For we say of

---

[22] Luther is referring to his comments on Heb. 1:3; cf. WA 10$^{\mathrm{I, 1}}$, p. 154.

86

a lord or a prominent man: he has done it *herlich*, and we say something was done with great *herlickeytt* if it was done at great cost, with lavishness and stateliness. Thus *herlickeytt* signifies not only mighty clamor or widespread honor, but also those things on the basis of which such fame is carried abroad, as, e.g., expensive houses, vessels, clothes, food, servants, and the like. As Christ says of Solomon in Matthew 6[:28–29]: "See how the lilies grow! I tell you that Solomon in all his glory, i.e., in all his magnificence, was not clothed like one of these." Here he certainly calls *gloria herlickeytt*. Esther 1[:4] also states that King Ahasuerus prepared a great banquet "to demonstrate the riches of the *herlickeytt* of his kingdom." Therefore we chose to translate the above passage in the Epistle into German thus: "He is a reflection of his *herlickeytt*." Similarly we say in German: that is a magnificent [*herlich*] thing, a magnificent [*herlich*] matter, *gloriosa res*, a magnificent [*herliche*] deed. Here the evangelist writes to express that, too: "We have seen his *herlickeytt*," his magnificent, majestic essence and deed, which was not an ordinary, common garden variety of *herlickeyt*, but:

"A *herlickeyt* as of the only begotten Son of the Father." Here the evangelist explains who the Word is concerning which he and Moses have spoken so far, namely, the only Son of God, who has all the glory that his Father has. Therefore he calls him the only Son and the only-begotten, in order to separate and elevate him above all the children of God, who are not natural children, as this one is. In this manner his true divinity is indicated once more, for were he not God, he could not be called the only-begotten Son in preference to the others. This says as much as: he and no other one is the Son of God, and this cannot be said of the holy angels and men. None of them is solely the Son of God, but they are all brothers and creatures who were created one as the other, children chosen out of grace and not born from nature. But one must not refer the "seeing" of his glory solely to the bodily sight, for the Israelites, too, saw his glory, and yet they did not consider it the glory of the only begotten Son of God; rather such seeing refers to the believers seeing and believing it with their hearts. The unbelievers, whose eyes look at secular glory, did not pay attention to this divine glory. These two do not get along either; he who wants to be glorious in the sight of the world must be base in the sight of God. And he who is base in the sight of the world for the sake of God is glorious in the sight of God.

"Full of grace and truth." These two words Scripture normally places next to each other. "Grace" means that everything he is and does is pleasing in the sight of God. "Truth" means that everything he is and does is good from the start and right in him; there is nothing in him that is not pleasing and upright. The opposite is the case with men: there is nothing but lack of grace and falseness so that everything they do is displeasing to God. It is also false from the beginning and nothing but glitter, as Psalm 116[:11]: "All men are liars," and Psalm 51 [39:6]: "All men are vain," state. I say this against the arrogant papists and Pelagians who find something additional which, they say, is good and true outside of Christ in whom alone there is grace and truth. As has been said above, to be sure, some things are true and pleasing, as the natural light which says: three plus two equal five, God must be honored, etc. But this light never comes to its task, for as soon as reason is supposed to strike and to bring this light into use and practice, it turns that which is farthest behind into something farthest in front; it calls that good which is evil, and that evil which is good, names the honor of God that which is dishonor, and vice versa. Therefore man is nothing but a liar and puffed up, so that he cannot even make use of this natural light, except in opposition to God. We have said a good deal about this above.

There is no need to look for the most solid portion of this Gospel. It is all solid and important, laying a foundation for the article of faith that Christ is true God and man and that, without grace, nature, free will, and works are nothing but lies, sin, error, and heresy—contrary to the views of the papists and the Pelagians.[23]

---

[23] The Pelagians were followers of Pelagius, a fifth century British monk who taught that man's salvation was due to the faithful exercise of his free will. This teaching was condemned at councils in Ephesus (A.D. 431) and Orange (A.D. 529).

THE GOSPEL FOR ST.
STEPHEN'S DAY,
MATTHEW 23[:34-39]

This is a harsh Gospel directed against those who persecute the believers. But the harsher it is against these persons, the more comforting it is for the persecuted believers. This Gospel teaches us what obstinate things the natural light, self-conceit, and reason are. Where reason gets mixed up with works and with the commandments, it refuses to hear anybody, as was stated in the last Gospel.[1] Only reason's operation and self-conceit, are right. It does no good to preach to reason: no matter how much one preaches to it, no matter how many prophets God sends to it, everything that is against reason must be persecuted and killed. St. John portrays her as the scarlet murderess in Revelation 17[:3-5]: "Her name is the great whore, Babylon; she is arrayed in a scarlet and purple robe, sits on a beast which is also scarlet and has in her hand a golden drinking vessel filled with the filth and abomination of her whoredom," i.e., teachings of men wherewith she leads the pure and believing souls away from the faith and ruins them. She strangles all who resist her.

The present Gospel also describes such obstinate, murderous wilfulness in the first place in this way, that God tries various things with Jerusalem. He sends her various preachers whom he enumerates under the three names of prophets, wise men, and scribes. Prophets preach solely by inspiration of the Holy Spirit, and they have not derived their preaching from books or through men; Moses and Amos were such prophets. These are the highest and the best; they are wise and can make others wise; they can set forth sacred writings and interpret them. In this category belong almost all the fathers prior to and contemporary with Moses; after

---

[1] Cf. above, pp. 58 f.

him there were many others, especially the apostles, who were laymen and completely uneducated people, as Luke says in Acts 5[4:13]. Wise men derive their message not only from God, but also from books and human beings. They are the disciples and followers of the prophets, yet they preach and teach with their own mouths and speak their own words. Such a one was Aaron: he spoke everything Moses commanded him to say, as God says to Moses, Exodus 4[:15–16]: "Put my word into his mouth and make him preach to the people for you, and you shall be a god to him." Priests are supposed to be like this, as Zechariah 11[:11] states. The scribes or those learned in the law teach by means of writings and books when they are unable to teach by talking because they are at another place. The apostles belong in this category, too, as do the evangelists and their followers, e.g., the holy fathers. However, they do not write and set forth their self-conceit, but the word of God which they have learned from the wise men and from Holy Scripture. Here, then, are the three ways in which truth may be revealed: in writing, in words, in thoughts, writing by means of books, words by means of the mouth, thoughts by means of the heart. By no other means can one receive the teaching than through heart, mouth, and writing.

Now all of this is of no avail in dealing with self-willed reason. It does not listen to words, nor to what is written nor to illumination. God may try this with it or that: it suppresses and burns writing and books as did King Jehoiakim with the writings of Jeremiah, Jeremiah 36[:21–24]; it prohibits, silences and condemns spoken words; it chases away and kills illumination together with the prophets. Oddly, no prophet was killed, chased away, or persecuted because he was chastising coarse sins, with the one exception of John the Baptist whom Herodias put to death because he had castigated her adultery [Matt. 14:3–12]. Such an eminent man had to have nothing but the most ignominious cause for his death, although the Israelites, too, were not his enemies for this reason, but because he refused to concede that they were right, and so they said that he had a devil. Thus the controversy has always been over the true and false kind of divine worship.

Abel was murdered by Cain for the purpose of invalidating his divine worship [Gen. 4:3–8]. All prophets, wise, and learned men have castigated as idolatry that divine service which consisted of reason and works, without faith; natural self-conceit acted up and said that it was doing it in honor of God and that it was acting rightly. For this reason the prophets had to die, presumably as those who banned and castigated divine service, honor, and good works. As Christ says in John 16[:2]: "The hour will come when those who kill you will think that thereby they are doing God a service." So all the idolatry in the Old Testament was done by them; not that they worshipped wood and stone, but that they wanted to serve the true God in this way. Since God had forbidden this and it happened out of their own self-conceit and without faith, it clearly follows that it came from the devil and not from God. Therefore the prophets said that these people were not serving God, but the false gods: that kind of statement these people would not tolerate nor listen to. On the other hand, the prophets, acting on God's command, could not be silent; therefore they had to die, be chased away, and be persecuted because of their testimony.

For this reason the entire controversy centers around the fact that the pseudo-saints are quarreling with true saints about the service of God and good works. The former say: this is serving God. The latter say: no, this is idolatry and an erroneous faith. Such controversy has existed from the beginning and will continue to the end. Thus also the papists have invented for themselves good works and a way to serve God with their external works and statutes; yet all this is devoid of faith, is solely based on works, lacks God's sanction, and is nothing but worthless human striving. We say to them: this is not service of God, it is service of yourselves and the devil, as is all idolatry. We also say, that it leads people astray from the Christian faith and common brotherly love. But they do not want to tolerate our view and so they cause the misery which obtains at the present time. Both sides are unanimous that one must serve God and perform good works. But in the interpretation of what constitutes service to God and good works, the two sides will never come to an agreement. The one side says it is faith that counts; nature and reason with their works are out. The other side says, faith amounts to nothing, and nature with its works is good and right. Likewise, there is unanimity in this: gross sins,

91

murder, adultery, robbery are wrong. But with respect to the main works relating to the service of God they differ like winter and summer. The one side clings to God and his mercy and fears him. The other side runs to wood and stone, food and clothing, days and seasons, and wants to win God by building churches, by setting up endowments, by fasting, by reeling off prayers, and by shaving the head. They fear nothing and are insolent, full of arrogance. What a holy, learned, wise crowd, for whom even God with all his prophets, wise men, and scribes, is neither holy, nor learned nor wise enough.

The Gospel raises several questions. Let us look at them. First, why does Christ say that all righteous blood, beginning with Abel, is to come upon the Israelites, even if they have not shed it all? Answer: the words of Christ are directed to the whole multitude and the progeny of those who, from the beginning, have persecuted the prophets. This is so, since he addresses not only the contemporary people, living at that time, but the whole of Jerusalem: "O Jerusalem, Jerusalem, you who kill the prophets and who stone those who are sent to you! How often have I wanted to gather your children," etc. [Matt. 23:37]. This refers, surely, not only to the contemporary, but also to the former inhabitants of Jerusalem. Likewise, when he says: "You killed Zechariah between the sanctuary and the altar" [Matt. 23:35], for this same Zechariah was killed by King Joash (II Chronicles 26 [24:21]) more than eight hundred years before the birth of Christ. Yet he says: You killed him. In like manner, too, they killed Abel and will also kill the prophets and the wise men. It is as if he should say: It is one people, one sort, one race; like fathers, like children. The arrogance which rebels against God and his prophets in the fathers is the same arrogance that is rampant in exactly the same manner in their children: there is no difference between the mouse and the mouse's mother. The Lord's purpose in saying that all the righteous blood shall come upon them is to indicate that the people must shed righteous blood; that is its nature; it does not act otherwise. The blood that is shed, they shed; therefore all of it will come upon them.

But why does he mention only Abel and Zechariah, especially since Zechariah was not the last one whose blood was shed, but after him there were Isaiah, Jeremiah, Ezekiel, Uriah, Micah and virtually all who are prominent in Holy Writ? To be sure, Zechariah is the first of the prophets named in Scripture as one whose blood was shed. But Christ speaks here of the blood not only of the prophets, but of all the righteous of whom a great many were killed in the reign of King Saul. Likewise many prophets, whose names are not recorded, were killed in the reign of King Ahab.

For this I have no other answer than that Christ goes along with scriptural usage and furnishes us an example that we should not say, maintain, or mention anything which is not clearly founded on Scripture. Although Isaiah and other prophets were killed, yet not a single one has been described in the Old Testament by name, as to the manner of his death, after Zechariah. Therefore, even though he is not the last whose blood was shed, he is the last whose name is given in the account of how he in his time preached and was killed, so that, accordingly, Christ indicates the first and the last righteous one mentioned in Scripture. And in this manner he includes all the other righteous blood which is not mentioned and yet was shed before and after. It is true, it is written of the prophet Uriah in Jeremiah 26[:23], that he was killed by King Jehoiakim long after Zechariah. But this is merely narrated by others as something that happened long ago; Scripture writes nothing about him at the time he was living, nor does it even mention his existence when it describes King Jehoiakim's times and deeds in the accounts in II Chronicles [36:4 ff.] and II Kings [23:34 ff.]. Therefore the Lord does not include him here.

The question is also asked why Christ calls him the son of Barachias whereas Scripture calls him the son of Jehoiada. The text in II Chronicles 26 [24:20–22] reads as follows: "The spirit of God strengthened Zechariah, the son of Jehoiada, the priest, and he stood up in front of all the people and said to them, 'God the Lord has this to say to you, "Why do you transgress the commandments of God, so that you will not fare well, and why do you forsake God so that he in turn should forsake you?"' Then they all gathered against him, and by command of the king they stoned him in the churchyard; as he was dying, he said: 'May God see and avenge,'" etc. This also happened because he had preached against the kind of worship they had instituted. St. Jerome is of the opinion that he is called the son of Barachias for a spiritual reason, namely, because Barachias in Latin means *benedictus*, the blessed one.[2] But others have clearer comments: his father Jehoiada had the surname Barachias, perhaps because he had bestowed many good things on that king and on the people, for which reason they called him the blessed one; after his death, to express their gratitude, they killed his son. This is exactly how things usually go in the world, as the proverb says: If you help a person to escape from the gallows, he in turn gives you a hand onto the gallows. So it happened with the Son of God; God bestowed everything that is good on all the world, and the world crucified his dearly beloved son—as is prefigured by this.

Finally the question is asked: since nobody can resist the will of God, why then does he say: "How often have I wanted to gather your children together, and you did not want it to happen?" Commentators have interpreted the passage in various ways. Some have based their interpretation on free will and its power, although it seems that it is not free will that is castigated here, but self-will. It is bad freedom which acts only against God and therefore it is condemned and punished so harshly. St. Augustine forces the words into the following interpretation, as if the Lord intended to convey this much: as many of your children as I have gathered together, I have gathered despite your opposition.[3] But this is doing real violence to this simple text; it would be much easier to say that Christ was talking here as a human being who has borne all human concerns. In keeping with his human nature he has done many things which do not go with the divine nature; he had to eat, drink, sleep, walk, cry, suffer, and die. So one could say here, too, that, in keeping with human nature and motivation, he had said: I wanted to, and you did not want to. For, as I have often said, we must pay close attention to Christ's words, some of which refer to his divine nature, some to his human nature. Here, however, he introduces himself as God when he says: "I am sending to you"; the sending of prophets is God's sole privilege. According to Luke 11[:49] he spoke as follows: "Therefore the wisdom of God says: 'Behold, I will send prophets to them,'" etc. In addition, his words

---

2 Luther's source for this statement may have been Nicholas of Lyra's comments; cf. *WA* 10$^{\text{I, 1}}$, 277, n. 2.

3 Augustine, *Enchiridion*, chap. 97 (*MPL* 40, 277).

sound as if he wanted to gather the children of Jerusalem not only during his lifetime, but also before it, and often, so that the passage must be understood to refer to the divine will. Therefore we want to answer as follows:

The words are to be interpreted most simply without sophistication and as having to do with the divine will, in accordance with the usage of Scripture which speaks of God, for the sake of the simplest people, as if he were a human being. As is written in Genesis 6[:6]: "He repented that he had made man," and yet there is no repentance in God. Again, it is written that he is filled with wrath, and yet there is no wrath in him. Again, it is written in Genesis 11[:5]: "He came down from heaven and saw the building" that was going on in Babylon, and yet he remains seated always. In the Psalter the prophet often says: Wake up, why do you sleep so long? Again: Arise, come to me, and similar expressions, and yet he does not sleep, does not lie down, is not far away. Again in Psalm 1[:6] it is written that God knows nothing of the way of the unrighteous, and yet he knows all things. These passages are all written in accordance with our understanding and ability and not in accordance with the essential propensity of the divine nature. Therefore these words are not to be transformed into lofty speculation or recondite descriptions of the divine nature; rather, they are to be left for the simple people, to be spoken and interpreted in keeping with our understanding; for according to our understanding God acts as the words sound. This is a beautiful and comforting manner of speaking of God who is neither terrifying nor far removed. So here, too, the phrase "How often have I wanted," is to be understood to mean that he acted in such a manner that everybody could only think and feel that he was anxious to gather them together, that he acted as a man anxious to have it that way. Therefore we must give up these rarified speculations and stick to the milk and the simple meaning of Scripture.

But, in order that we derive our teaching from the gospel, the Lord sets up such a lovely picture and parable about faith and the believer, that I know of nothing lovelier in all of Scripture. Out of wrath and disgust over the Israelites he uttered many harsh words in this chapter and shouted horrible lamentations over their unbelief. Therefore he also acts as irate men are wont to act toward the ungrateful: they magnify with greatest emphasis their kindness and good will and say: I would gladly have shared with him the heart in my body, etc. In the same way the Lord, in the most affectionate manner possible, demonstrates here to the Israelites his good will and kindness, saying he would have liked to be their mother-hen, if they had wanted to be the chicks. O man, mark well the words and parable, how out of sheer and utter seriousness and out of his whole heart he poured this! In this picture you will see how you should act toward Christ, how he is beneficial to you, and how you should make use of and benefit from him. When you look at the mother-hen and her chicks you see a picture of Christ and yourself better than any painter can paint.

In the first place, our souls certainly are the chicks, and the devils and evil spirits are the hawks in the air, only we are not so clever as the chicks who take refuge under the mother-hen. Also, the devils are more cunning in their attempt to rob our souls than are the hawks in their attempts with the chicks. I mentioned above in an Epistle that it was not enough for us to be pious, do good works, and live in grace; not even our righteousness, much less our unrighteousness, may stand up before the eyes of God and his judgment.[4] Therefore I have said: faith, if it is true faith, is such that it does not rely on itself, on its believing, but it holds on to Christ and shelters itself under his righteousness; it lets this righteousness be its shelter and shield, even as the chick does not rely on its life and speed, but seeks shelter under the mother-hen's body and wings. To survive before God's judgment seat, it is not enough for one to say: I believe and have received grace; for everything within him is unable to protect him sufficiently. Rather he holds up to this judgment Christ's own righteousness; he lets it deal with God's judgment and it stands up for him forever with all honors, as Psalms 111[:3] and 112[:3, 9] say: "His righteousness endures forever." Under this righteousness he creeps, snuggles, and crouches; he trusts and believes and does not doubt that it will keep him protected. Then it also comes to pass that way, and he is preserved through this same faith, not for the sake of faith, but for the sake of Christ and his righteousness, under whose protection he is liv-

---

[4] Cf. Luther's comments on the Epistle for the Early Christmas Service, esp. Titus 3:6, WA 10[I, 1], 121–22.

ing. It also follows that faith which does not act in this manner is not the true faith.

See, this is what Scripture has in mind when it says in Psalm 91[:1–7]: "He who remains under the shelter of the Most High and dwells under the shadow of the Lord, can say to God: 'You are my confidence and refuge and my God, my hope is in you.' For he will free you from the snare of the hunters and from the pestilence of adversity. With his shoulders he will cover you, and under his wings will be your confidence. His truth is a shield and breastplate; therefore you will not be afraid of the terror of the night, nor of the arrow that flies during the day, nor of the pestilence that stalks in the darkness, nor of the plague which destroys at noon. Even if a thousand fall on your left side and ten thousand on your right side, nevertheless none of these shall happen to you," etc.

Behold, this is all said concerning faith in Christ. This faith alone lasts; it is protected from all peril and destruction of false teachings, from the assaults of the devils on both sides, physical and spiritual, so that all other faiths must fall and suffer ruin. This happens because he shelters himself under Christ's wings and shoulders, where he places his refuge and confidence. This, too, is what Malachi 4[:2] says: "The sun of righteousness shall rise for you who fear my name, and salvation is under its wings." Therefore, St. Paul in Romans 3[:25] calls him *propiciatorium*, "the throne of grace," and teaches everywhere that we must be preserved in the faith through and under him.

If the believers and saints truly are in need of such great protection, where will those abide who move about outside of Christ with their free will and works? Oh, we must remain in Christ, on Christ, and under Christ and must not leave the mother-hen. Otherwise everything is lost. St. Peter says: "The righteous man is scarcely saved" [I Pet. 4:18]; it is so difficult to remain under this mother-hen. For many temptations, physical and spiritual, try to tear us from the mother-hen, as the Psalm above indicates.

Let us observe how a natural mother-hen acts. There is hardly an animal that takes care of its offspring so meticulously. It changes its natural voice turning it into a lamenting, mourning one; it searches, scratches for food and lures the chick to eat. When the mother-hen finds something, she does not eat it, but leaves it for the chicks; she fights seriously and calls her chicks away from the hawk; she spreads out her wings willingly and lets the chicks climb under her and all over her, for she is truly fond of them—it is, indeed, an excellent, lovely symbol.[5] Similarly, Christ has taken unto himself a pitiful voice, has lamented for us and has preached repentance, has indicated from his heart to everyone his sin and misery. He scratches in the Scripture, lures us into it, and permits us to eat; he spreads his wings with his righteousness, merit, and grace over us and takes us under himself in a friendly manner, warms us with his natural heat, i.e., with his Holy Ghost who comes solely through him, and in the air fights for us against the devil. Where and how does he do that? Surely not in a bodily manner, but spiritually; his two wings are the two testaments of Holy Scripture which spread over us his righteousness and take us under him. Scripture teaches this and nothing else, namely, how Christ is such a mother-hen, that we, in faith, are kept under him and through this righteousness. Therefore the above mentioned Psalm interprets the wings and the shoulders, saying: "His truth (that is Scripture, comprehended in faith) is breastplate and shield against all fear and danger" [Ps. 91:4]. We must seize Christ in word and sermon and must cling to him with a firm faith that he is what Scripture says he is. If we do this, we are certainly in this faith under his wings and truth, and will be well preserved.

Accordingly, this Gospel, and all other gospel lessons, are his wing or truth, for they all teach Christ in this manner, although more clearly in one place than in another. In an earlier Gospel he is called a light and life, as well as Lord and helper.[6] Here he is called a mother-hen, with the emphasis always on faith. His body is he himself or the Christian church, his warmth is his grace and the Holy Spirit. Behold, this is the loveliest mother-hen which all the time wants to gather us under herself, spreads her wings and lures us, that is, she causes the two testaments to be preached, she sends forth prophets, wise men, and scribes to Jerusalem and into all the world, but what happens? We refuse to be chicks, especially

---

[5] Luther's immediate experiences on the Wartburg provide the setting for this illustration.

[6] Cf. above, pp. (52 ff.; 56 ff.).

those arrogant "holy ones" who inordinately fight against him with good works, who refuse to acknowledge faith, so entirely necessary and blessed, who do not want to know about their peril and who insist that their way is right. Indeed, they carry on so that they themselves become hawks and boars; they devour and pursue the chicks with the mother-hen, tear apart wings and body, kill the prophets and stone those to death who are sent to them. But what will be their reward? Listen, terrible things will befall them:

"Behold, your house shall be left desolate for you" [Matt. 23:38]. Oh, this is a gruesome punishment. We see it in the case of the Israelites. They have killed the prophets so that God has stopped sending prophets to them. He has let them go for fifteen hundred years, without sermon and without prophets. He has taken his word from them and drawn his wings close to himself. Thus their house is desolate; nobody tills their souls, nor does God dwell among them any longer. It has happened to them as they wanted it to happen, as Psalm 109[:17] says, "They wanted no part in the blessing; therefore it shall come away from them. They wanted cursing, and it shall surely come on them." Here all the blood that is shed on earth comes upon them, and this Gospel is fulfilled over them. Likewise Isaiah 5[:5-6] said about them: "I will let you see what I will do to my vineyard. I will remove its fence and permit it to be torn up. I will break up its walls and permit it to be trampled, and it shall remain desolate. It shall not be pruned or hoed, and within there shall grow only hedges and thorns. I will command my clouds that they rain no rain on it." Oh, these are terrifying words! What does it mean that no rain may come over them, other than that they shall not hear of the gospel and the faith? They are not to be pruned or hoed; what does that mean other than that nobody will remonstrate with them about their errors and that nobody will speak openly about their failings? Therefore the vineyard is left to those who teach human doctrines, who tear it up and trample on it, so that it must remain desolate and bear nothing but hedges and thorns, i.e., works-righteous ones who are devoid of faith, bear no fruits of the spirit, but only grow up and are prepared for the eternal fire, as the hedges and thorns.

All of this, however, we Gentiles might also take to heart. We are, indeed, just as bad, if not a lot worse; we, too, have persecuted the mother-hen and did not abide in the faith. Therefore it has happened to us, too, that he has caused our house to lie desolate and the vineyard forsaken. There is no more rain in all the world; the gospel and the faith have become silent; there is no pruning and no hoeing; nobody preaches against the false works and teachings of men and would cut off such unprofitable things. Rather God allows us to be torn asunder and trampled to pieces by the pope, the bishops, priests, and monks, of whom all the world is utterly and completely full. Yet they do nothing but trample to pieces and tear asunder this vineyard, the one teaching this, the other that. This one tramples this place to pieces, that one another; everyone wants to set up his sect, his order, his estate, his teaching, his theses, his works. So we are trampled to pieces, so that there is no more knowledge of the faith, no Christian life, no love, no fruit of the Spirit, and nothing but firewood, hedges, and thorns, i.e., dissemblers, hypocrites, who presume to be Christians with their vigils, masses, foundations, bells, churches, recitations of the Psalter or of the rosary, cult of the saints, celebration of holy days, cowls, tonsures, robes, fasting, pilgrimages, and all the other foolishness without number. O Lord God, completely torn asunder, completely trampled to pieces, O Lord Christ, completely desolate and forsaken are we miserable men in these last days of wrath? Our shepherds are wolves; our watchmen are traitors; our protectors are enemies; our fathers are murderers; our teachers are seducers. Alas, alas and alas! When? When? When will your harsh wrath cease?

Yet, in the end, consolation is offered to the Israelites in the passage when he says: "Truly I tell you, you will not see me again, until you say: 'Blessed is he who comes in the name of the Lord.'" These words Christ spoke on the Tuesday after Palm Sunday, and they are the conclusion and the last words of his preaching on earth. It follows that they are not yet fulfilled and that they must be fulfilled. It is true, they welcomed him one time in this manner on Palm Sunday, but this does not constitute fulfillment. His words "You will not see me again," are not to be understood to mean that, after this, they no longer saw him in the flesh, for they crucified him after that. But he means they shall see him no more as preacher and Christ, in the mission and office for which he had been sent; in this his official capacity he was no longer seen by them after this event. In this sermon he took his leave of them and concluded his mission for which he had been sent. Thus it is certain that the Israelites will yet say to Christ: "Blessed is he who comes in the name of the Lord." Moses prophesied this in Deuteronomy 4[:30–31]: "In the last days you will return to God, your Lord, and obey his voice, for God, your Lord, is a merciful God; he will not forsake you altogether, nor blot you out totally, nor will he forget the covenant which he swore to your fathers." Likewise Hosea 3[:4–5]: "The children of Israel shall dwell a long time without king, without princes, without priests, without altar, without priestly garment and robe. Afterward the children of Israel shall return and seek God their Lord and David their king (that is Christ), and they will honor God and his goodness in the last days." And Azariah in II Chronicles 15[:2–4]: "If you forsake God, he will forsake you, too. Many days will pass in Israel without the true God, without priests, without teachers, and without the law; and when in their distress they return and call on the God of Israel, their Lord, then they will find him."

These passages should not be understood to pertain to any Jews in our own day. It is true, in the past they have not been without princes, prophets, priests, teachers, and the law. St. Paul, in Romans 11[:25–26], agrees and says: "Blindness has come upon one part of the people of Israel, until the full number of the Gentiles enter in, and so all Israel will be saved." God grant that the time is near—as we hope! Amen.

THE GOSPEL FOR THE
SUNDAY AFTER CHRISTMAS,
LUKE 2[:33-40]

It is quite clear that the preceding Epistle (Gal. 4[:1–7]) was appointed to be read for this Sunday from sheer misunderstanding and that he who appointed it assumed, because mention is made of a young heir who is the master of all goods, that the reference was to the young Christ-child. Many more of the Epistles and Gospels, as is known, were ordained to be read for days that do not fit, and the reason was the same sort of misunderstanding. However, the order is not important; it makes no difference which one is preached at which time, if only the right understanding of the order is retained.

Thus this Gospel took place on the day of our Lady's Candlemas, when she brought the child to the temple, and yet it is read on this Sunday.[1] I mention this, so that the sequence of events should not confuse anybody or impede the interpretation and sequence of the Gospel. I propose to divide it into two parts; one part will concern Simeon, the other Hanna. It is an extraordinarily rich lesson and nicely arranged: first the man, Simeon, then the woman, Hanna, both old people and saints.

The First Part Concerning Simeon

"His father and his mother were amazed at the things which were said about him" [Luke 2:33].

What were the amazing things and by whom were they said about him? These are patently the things which St. Simeon mentioned immediately before, as he took the infant Jesus in his arms

---

[1] Candlemas is the festival celebrated on February 2 in commemoration of the presentation of Christ in the temple and the purification of the Virgin Mary. This festival was also the occasion for the consecration and sale of candles which were to be used throughout the year; hence the name Candlemas.

in the temple and said: "Lord God, now dismiss your servant in peace; for my eyes have seen your Savior whom you have prepared in the presence of all people, the light to illumine the Gentiles, and for glory to your people Israel" [Luke 2:29–33]. Luke says that they were amazed at these things: that this aged holy man stood in front of them in the temple, took the infant into his arms and joyously talked about him in such glorious terms, namely, that he should be a light for all the world, a Savior of all people, a glory to all Israel, and that he himself had such a high opinion of him that he would gladly die, having seen the child. It is certainly something to be amazed at, to have such things said there publicly by the eminent man in that public, sacred place; for it was, after all, a poor, insignificant baby—the child's mother was poor and humble, and the father Joseph was not rich. How could this infant be regarded as if it were the Savior of all people, the light of all Gentiles, and the honor and glory of all Israel? After the child's true nature became known, all this no longer seems to be so amazing. But when nothing of the sort was known, it did look very strange indeed, and the poor little infant was so greatly unlike the mighty, grand being, as Simeon described him. But Joseph and Mary believed it, which is at once the reason for their amazement. Had they not believed it, Simeon's statements would have been a matter of contempt rather than amazement for them, and they would have appeared false and of no use. Therefore such amazement glorifies the noble and great faith of both Joseph and Mary.

But somebody might say: how is it they are amazed at this only? After all, they had heard before from the angels, too, that he was the Christ and the Savior. The shepherds also reported gloriously concerning him. It was most certainly astonishing that the kings, or magi, coming from faraway countries, adored him with their offerings. Mary knew very well how she had conceived him of the Holy Ghost and given birth to him miraculously, and how the angel Gabriel had told her that he should be called Great and the Son of God. In short, all the events had been marvelous up to this time; but now no miracle takes place, and mention is merely made of things which have not happened and are not yet visible in him. I do not think it is necessary to look far and wide for an explanation. The evangelist does not deny that Mary and Joseph had marveled before this occasion. The simple explanation is that the evangelist wishes to describe how they reacted when St. Simeon spoke so gloriously of the child, as if he wanted to say: when Simeon was telling such marvelous things concerning the child, his parents did not despise them, but believed them firmly. For this reason they stood, listened, and marveled at his speech—how else could they react to it? Saying this does not deny that previously they had marveled just as much, if not more.

We shall investigate the spiritual meaning of this amazement later; right now we are concerned with the literal meaning. It serves as an example of our faith: we, too, should learn how marvelous God's works are concerning us and that the beginning and end are quite dissimilar. The beginning is nothing; the end is everything. Just as here the infant Christ does not appear very significant and yet, in the end, he became the Savior and light of all the people. If Joseph and Mary had judged in accordance with what they saw, they would not have regarded Christ as more than a poor little child. But they disregard the external evidence and cling to Simeon's words with a firm faith; therefore, they marvel at his speech. In like manner we, too, must disregard the external evidence when contemplating God's works and cling only to his words, lest our eyes or senses offend us.

Another reason why it is written that they marveled at these words of Simeon is to teach us that God's word never goes forth and is never preached in vain, as he says in Isaiah 55[:11]: "My word which proceeds out of my mouth (i.e., out of the mouth of God's messengers) is not to return to me empty, but it is to do all I desire and it is to be prompt in all for which I send it." Thus the evangelist wants to say that Simeon delivered a heartwarming, beautiful sermon, preaching nothing but the gospel and God's word. What else is the gospel but a sermon about Christ, declaring that he is a Savior, light, and glory of all the world; such a sermon fills the heart with joy, and it marvels joyfully at such grace and consolation, provided it is received in faith. But no matter how beautiful and wondrously comforting this sermon was, there were very few who believed it; indeed, many despised it, considering it foolishness. They walked about and stood in the temple—one prayed, another did something else, and they paid no attention to these

104

words of Simeon. Yet, because the word of God must bring forth fruit, there were there some who received it with joyful wonder, namely, Joseph and Mary. Here the evangelist also covertly rebukes the unbelief of the Israelites: there were many of them present (for all this took place publicly in the temple), and yet no one wanted to believe—they took offense at Christ's infancy. So we learn here that we should gladly hear the word of God; for it does produce good fruit.

This takes us to the spiritual significance of this amazement on the part of Joseph and Mary. The temple is the habitation of God; hence it signifies all places where God is present. Thus it also signifies Holy Scripture wherein one finds God as in his proper place. To bring Christ into the temple means nothing else than to follow the example of the people in Acts 17[:11]. When they had accepted the gospel with complete desire they went into Holy Scripture, examining daily whether things were so. Now we find Simeon in the same temple; Luke says of Simeon that he is a personification of all prophets filled with the Holy Ghost. They spoke and wrote as they were inspired by the Holy Ghost, and they waited for the coming of Christ as did Simeon, and they never ceased to do this until Christ had come, as St. Peter says in Acts 4 [3:24] that all prophets have spoken of the time of Christ. And Christ himself says in Matthew 11[:13] that all the prophets and the law have prophesied until John, i.e., until Christ's baptism when he began to appear as the savior and the light of the world. This is signified in Simeon, who was not to die until he had seen Christ. For this reason, too, his name is Simeon, i.e., one who hears, for the prophets had only heard of Christ as of one who was unborn who should come after them; they had him on their backs, so to speak, and heard him. If we come into the temple in this manner with Christ and the gospel and look at Holy Scripture that way, then the statements of the prophets take their places warmly next to him, take him up in their arms, and say with great joy: This is the man, of whom we have spoken. Now our words have come to their end with peace and joy. And right there they begin to give the most beautiful testimonies: how this Christ is the Savior, the light, the consolation and glory of Israel—and everything else that Simeon is saying and preaching.

Concerning this St. Paul says in Romans 1[:2] that God promised the gospel through the prophets in Holy Scripture. He explains the meaning of Simeon and the temple. In Romans 3[:21] we read that the law and the prophets bear witness to the faith. And Christ says in John 5[:39]: "Search the Scriptures, for they give testimony of me"; and he also says: "If you believed Moses, you would also believe me, for he wrote of me" [John 5:46]. This should be demonstrated with examples, but there is no time to do so here. We have noted examples of this in our sermon for Christmas Day, in the Epistle and Gospel lessons for the main service, showing how the apostles adduce testimony nicely and aptly from Holy Scripture.[2] In the Gospel lesson for Christmas Eve, too, we talked about this in connection with the infant's diapers.[3] For the present, the statement of Moses in Deuteronomy 18[:15], which the apostles refer to in Acts 8[7:37] and Acts 13[3:22] as well as in other places, must suffice. There Moses says: "God will raise up a prophet from the midst of your brothers, to him you shall listen as you listen to me." With these words Moses ends the anticipation of the people and his own public teaching which pointed toward this prophet Christ to whom they should henceforth listen. These words are a testimony that Christ should be a light and Savior after Moses and, without a doubt, better than Moses; otherwise Moses would not have stated that his teaching and guiding would come to end, but that it would continue in addition to Christ. Again, Isaiah 28[16] says: "Take heed, I shall lay in Zion a precious, choice foundation and cornerstone, and he who believes in him shall not be disgraced." Look, how beautifully and smoothly these and similar statements agree with the gospel, for what they assert concerning Christ is exactly what the apostles preached concerning him—and what all of Holy Scripture proclaims continuously.

Therefore Simeon had to be an old man, in order that he would be a perfect and exact image of the prophets of old. He does not take the child into his hands or onto his lap, but into his arms. Although there is hidden here a deeper meaning, it is enough to say for the present that the prophecies and statements of Scripture present Christ in a straightforward manner and offer him to every-

---

[2] Cf. WA 10I, 1, 145 and above, pp. 41 ff.
[3] Cf. above, pp. 41 ff.

body, and do not keep him for themselves, just as we do with what we carry in our arms. St. Paul speaks of this in Romans 4[:23] and 15[:4] when he writes that everything is written not for their sake, but for ours. And I Peter 1[:12] reads: The prophets did not present these things for themselves, but for us, to whom Christ has been announced.

Luke did not say that Joseph and Mary marveled at what Simeon said; rather he says that they marveled at those things which were spoken of the child. He does not mention Simeon's name; he wanted to divert our attention away from Simeon to this spiritual meaning so that thereby we should understand the statements of Scripture. Only his father and mother marvel at these sayings. The evangelist has established here a distinguishing mark: he does not mention Joseph and Mary by name; he calls them father and mother, in order to point out the spiritual meaning. Who, then, are Christ's spiritual father and mother? He himself names his spiritual mother in Mark 3[:34–35] and Luke 8[:21]: "He who does the will of my father, that one is my brother, my sister, and my mother." St. Paul calls himself a father in I Corinthians 4[:15]: "Even if you have ten thousand schoolmasters in Christ, yet you have not many fathers; for I gave birth to you in Christ through the gospel." Thus the Christian church, i.e., all believing persons, is Christ's spiritual mother, and all apostles and teachers of the people, who preach the gospel, are his spiritual father. As often as a man becomes a believer, Christ is born of them. These are the people who marvel over the statements of the prophets, that they apply so nicely and accurately to Christ, speak of him so gloriously, and bear witness to the whole gospel so masterfully. There is no greater joy in this life than to see and experience this in Scripture. But the great mass of unbelievers despise this Simeon, mock him, and twist his words as if he were a fool; they engage in monkeyshines and mischief in the temple, even placing idols and altars from Damascus there, as was done by King Ahab [I Kings 16:32]. Those are the people who play mischief with Scripture, bring it into discredit, interpret it according to human understanding, and introduce into it that anointed idol, namely, reason, thereby changing it into a religion of works, doctrine, and man-made laws. Indeed, they even profane and demol-

107

ish the scriptural temple and in it they carry on their sin and shameful deeds, as the pope does and has done with his decretals and the universities with their Aristotle. At the same time, they are "pious"; they consecrate many churches built of stone and wood, chapels and altars; they grant dispensations; they are angry at the Turks who desecrate and destroy these churches; and they hold that God should reward them for desecrating and destroying, ten thousand times worse, his most precious temple which is immeasurably better and eternal. It is a blind, mad, clumsy mob; let them go, one blind man following the other, into eternal destruction!

A simple soul might be disturbed that Luke calls Joseph the father of Christ and shows no respect for the virginity of Mary. But Luke said this according to common usage—that is how they were regarded among the people and how they were called. According to the legal custom, stepfathers were called fathers, as is the usage everywhere. Moreover he is rightly called his father, because he was his mother's sole betrothed and bridegroom. Luke did not hesitate to express himself in this way; the reason for it is that previously he had written so clearly about her virginity, that he could well think that nobody could take Joseph to be Christ's natural father. On account of his precautions he could write without any hesitation. The preceding text convinces us abundantly that Mary is his natural mother and Joseph his father according to the common usage of that word. Therefore, it is true that he has a father and he has a mother. There follows:

"And Simeon blessed them" [Luke 2:34].

This blessing is nothing else but Simeon wishing them good joy and blessedness, honor and every good thing. He did not bless only the child, but, according to Luke, all of them—child, father, and mother. This blessing seems to be a simple, slight matter; for people generally bless and wish each other well in a similar manner. But to bless Christ and his parents is an exalted and exceptional deed. Why? Because Christ and nature are completely opposed to each other. He condemns everything the world chooses, gives us a cross and misfortune, and takes away all worldly gaiety, possession, and honor. He teaches that everything with which people are concerned is foolishness and sin. But nobody wants to, nobody can, tolerate this from him. This is where malediction and blasphemy and persecution of Christ and his followers begin. There are only a few Simeons who bless him, but the world is full of those who curse him and wish him evil, disgrace, and misfortune. For whoever is not disposed willingly to despise all things and to be prepared to suffer, will not bless and praise God for long, but will take offense at him quickly. To be sure some praise and bless him, as long as he does what they desire and as long as he allows them to be what they want. But then he is not Christ, neither does he do Christ's work with them, but he is what they are and desire. As soon as he sets out to be Christ to them, demanding that they forsake their ways and allow him and him alone to be in them, there is nothing but desertion, blasphemy, and cursing. Similarly, some believe that if they could see the infant Christ with his mother in the flesh, just as did Simeon, they would be willing, too, to bless him joyfully. But they lie; his infancy and poverty, like his humble appearance, would surely have caused them to turn away. They prove this by disregarding such poverty and humble appearance in the members of Christ, among whom they still might discover every day Christ the head. Therefore, just as they now flee from the cross and hate its humble appearance, so they would also react even if he were before their very eyes. Why do they not honor the poor? Why do they not honor the truth? Simeon was not minded that way; he took no offense at his appearance; indeed, he confessed that he was to be a sign of opposition and he took pleasure in the fact that Christ rejects all pretensions and carries forth the cross; in addition, he blesses not only Christ, but also his members, mother and father.

In this blessing, Simeon, as a preacher and friend of the cross and an enemy of the world, gives a great and remarkable example of how to praise and honor Christ, who was despised, cursed, and rejected in his own person, and who today suffers the same in his members who for his sake bear poverty, indignities, death, and all sorts of ignominy. Yet nobody relieves them, or takes them in, or blesses them; rather, people want to be pious and Christian through praying and fasting, through bequests and the performance of good works.

Here the spiritual meaning also comes to the fore. The spiri-

109

tual Christ, his spiritual father and mother, i.e., the Christian church, with its apostles and their followers, are subject to all kinds of ignominy and, as St. Paul says [I Cor. 4:13], they are the sweepings, chaff, and filth of this world. Hence they surely need to obtain their blessing and consolation elsewhere. They obtain it from Simeon in the temple, i.e., from the prophets in Holy Scripture, as Paul says in Romans 15[:4]: "Everything that is written is written for our instruction, so that we through patience and the consolation of Scripture endure in hope." A Christian therefore must not plan or scheme to arrange his affairs so that he may be praised and blessed by the people of this world. No, it has already been settled that he must expect disgrace and ignominy and must submit himself willingly to them and be prepared for them. He must not expect a blessing, except from Simeon in the temple. Scripture is our consolation, and it praises and blesses all who, for the sake of Christ, are reproached by the world. This is the sum of the teaching of Psalm 36, also Psalm 9, and many others; they all tell how God delivers those who are suffering in this world. And Moses, in Genesis 4[:9], writes that God was so concerned about pious Abel after his death that, even without a request, he was moved to avenge him solely by his blood, doing much more for him after his death than he had during his lifetime. Thereby he indicated how he cannot disregard even the dead; indeed, he will remember those who believe in him more when they are dead than while they are alive. On the other hand, when Cain was slain, he remained silent and paid no attention to him. These and similar statements of Scripture are our consolation and blessing, if we are Christians; we must cling to them and be satisfied with them. There we see how blessed are they who suffer reproach, and how accursed are our persecutors. The former God cannot forget or forsake, the latter he does not wish to remember or know. Could we wish for more precious and greater consolation and blessing? What is the blessing and consolation of this world compared with this consolation and blessing of Simeon in the temple?

> *"And he said to Mary, his mother: 'Behold this one is set for the fall and rising of many in Israel and for a sign that is spoken against. And a sword will pierce through your own soul, that thoughts out of many hearts may be revealed there'"* [Luke 2:34–35].

110

Why does he not say this to his father as well, and why does he, in addition, call his mother by her name? He observes nature here, calls his natural mother by name, and not his father. Since Jesus was her natural child, his mother experienced quite naturally the pain that came over him. There is also the possibility that Simeon addressed Mary because Joseph would not be alive at the time of Christ's passion which would engulf only his mother. She had to suffer like a poor lonely widow, and Christ suffered like a poor orphan. This was so extraordinarily pitiful; according to Scripture God himself watches out diligently over widows and orphans, calling himself an advocate of the widows and a father of the orphans. Mary was a member of all three estates, the estate of virginity, that of matrimony, and that of widowhood, the last being the most pitiable, having neither protection nor assistance. A virgin has her parents, a wife has her husband, but a widow is forsaken. In this pitiable condition she will suffer much—this Simeon prophesies to her. And so he indicates and interprets for her his blessing as a blessing of God, and not of the world. For in the sight of the world it would be reversed: not only would she be unblessed, but her child, too, should become a target and an aim of everyone's curses, just as the arrows and bows are aimed at the bull's eye. This is, in my opinion, the meaning of the blessing in the temple. There was, indeed, a great need for her to be strengthened and comforted through a spiritual and divine blessing against the barrage of future maledictions, because she was to endure and suffer alone in her soul that great tempest of her son's curse.

First of all, Simeon states that Christ is set up for the fall and rising of many in Israel. This is the first consolation his mother was to experience and secure from him, that many would take offense at him, even in Israel, which was, after all, the chosen people. In the eyes of men, it is indeed a poor comfort that she is the mother of a son who should be for so many, even in Israel, the cause of offense and falling. Some have interpreted this passage to mean that many have been offended by Christ, and their pride has fallen, in order that they should rise again in humility, even as St. Paul fell and rose again, as also all who consider themselves righteous because of their works, fall and must despair of their trust in themselves and rise again in Christ, if they are to be saved. This is a good interpretation, but not good enough here. Simeon speaks of Christ in such a manner that many Israelites would take offense at him and stumble, thereby falling into unbelief, as it has happened in the past and still happens. This was indeed a sad picture and sight, as well as a terrible announcement which the ears of this holy mother had to hear. However, the cause of this falling is not Christ, but the arrogance of the Israelites, and for this reason: Christ has come to be the light and the Savior of the world, as Simeon says, so that, through faith in him, everyone should be justified and saved. Therefore, the attainment of righteousness by our own means, through works, at the exclusion of Christ, had to be repudiated. The Israelites would not permit this, as St. Paul says in Romans 10[:3]: "Not recognizing the righteousness which God gives (through faith), they set out to find how to establish their own righteousness; and so they do not submit to divine righteousness." So they take offense at faith, fall ever deeper into unbelief, and become hardened in their righteousness, so that they persecuted mightily all those who believed. All practitioners of works-righteousness too, must do the same. They rely on their works, take offense at faith, and stumble at Christ, burning, condemning, persecuting all who reject their works or insist that they are useless. This we observe today with the pope, the bishops, doctors, and all papists. They do this, thinking that they perform a service for God, in order to protect the faith and to preserve Christendom, exactly as the Israelites pretended that they were defending God's true service and the law of Moses when they persecuted and killed the apostles and the Christians.

Therefore, as Simeon here prophesies to Christ's mother that not everyone in Israel would accept him as light and Savior, and that not only a few, but many, would take offense at him and fall, so Christ's spiritual mother, the assembly of the Christians, must not marvel when many false Christians, especially members of the clergy, do not believe. For such are the people who rely on works and seek their own righteousness; they must take offense at Christ and faith in him and stumble, even as they persecute and kill everybody who opposes them. That, too, was prophesied a long time ago by the spiritual Simeon, namely, the prophets who almost without exception, testify concerning this fall. Isaiah 8[:11–15] reads as follows: "God speaks to me with strength and teaches me, I must not walk in the path of this people, and he commands me to say to them: you shall not call this rebellion or revolt; for everything this people says is only concerning rebellion. But be not afraid and frightened by it, sanctify God the Lord, let him be your fear and terror; he will be your sanctification, a stone of stumbling and a rock of offense for the two houses of Israel, and a rope and a snare for the citizens of Jerusalem; many of them will take offense, stumble, fall, be snared and trapped," etc. There are many more statements, from which it can be shown that Christ must be a rock against which the best and highest will stumble, as is stated in Psalm 78[:31]: "He has slain the fat ones of Israel and smitten her elite." For Christ has been ordained a Savior and he cannot step aside nor change; but these arrogant people are also tough and stiff-necked, and, furthermore, will not give up their vanity. So they run against Christ with their heads, and thus, naturally, one part must break and fall, but Christ must remain and cannot fall, and so they must fall.

Again, just as he firmly stands against the "works-righteous" ones, without yielding an inch, so he also stands up for all who put their trust in him, as Isaiah 28[:16] says: "I shall lay a cornerstone for a foundation, and all who believe in him, shall not come to shame." And Christ himself says in Matthew 16[:18]: "On that rock will I build my church and the hellish portals shall not overpower it." The falling and breaking mentioned here is nothing else than unbelief and clinging to works, even as rising and being built on this rock is nothing else than faith and disregarding works. This takes place for the believers, for whom Christ alone is set for a rising. Even as at the time of Christ many in Israel rose in him, so it will continue until the end of the world; nobody can rise through works or through the teachings of men, but solely through Christ. This comes to pass through faith, as has often been stated, without any works and merit; works must of necessity come after we have risen.

You see how the entire Bible speaks only of faith and rejects works as useless, indeed as offensive and as an obstacle to righteousness and our own rising. Christ alone wants to be set up for the rising of many; otherwise he becomes the reason for their fall. He does not permit anything to be set next to him to bring about our rising. Is the life of the papists and the clergy not horrible? They run against this rock so vehemently and directly, and their walk is so utterly opposed to the Christian life, that it may well be called the Antichrist's nature and rule. Of this rising does the spiritual Simeon speak to Christ's spiritual mother. For all the prophets teach Christendom that only in Christ can all men rise, as St. Paul says in Romans 1[:17], and Hebrews 10[:38] quotes Habakkuk 2[:4]: "The righteous man lives by his faith."

Thus we see how this falling and rising by Christ is entirely spiritual and that the falling pertains to other people than does the rising. The falling pertains only to those who are thoroughly important, highly educated, mighty and "holy," who trust all-too-firmly in themselves. The gospel tells us, that Christ had no quarrel or conflict whatsoever with sinners, but dealt with them in a most friendly fashion. But with the privileged, the scribes, the high priests, he cannot get along at all, nor does he find favor with them. Hence, even as the falling is only for those who already stand, so the rising is only for those who lie prostrate and have fallen. Those are the souls who thirst for grace, who realize that they themselves are nothing and that Christ is everything.

It is significant that Simeon added the little word "Israel"; for Christ is promised by all the prophets only to the people of Israel. It was also announced that many of the same people would fall, solely on account of their self-righteousness. This is certainly terrifying for us Gentiles, to whom nothing has been promised. We have been added out of sheer grace—we did not think about it or hope for it—and have risen with Christ as St. Paul teaches in Romans 15[:9] and as was declared above in the Epistle lesson for the Second Sunday in Advent.[4] The fall of the people in Israel should surely touch our heart, as the apostle admonishes, in Romans [11:20], that we should not fall likewise; indeed, we have fallen and are seduced through the Antichrist worse than the Jews and the Turks, so that we bear the name of Christ only to the dishonor of God and to our harm.

In the second place, Simeon says that Christ has been set for a sign that will be spoken against. But is it not a calamity that the

---

[4] Cf. WA 7, 482 ff., 486 ff.

Savior and the light of the world should be spoken against, condemned, and damned, when people ought to run after him and seek him from one end of the world to the other? From this we learn what the world is and how human nature uses free will. The world is clearly the devil's realm and God's enemy and not only acts contrary to God's commandments, but with mad rage persecutes and kills the Savior who would help to keep God's commandments. One thing, however, leads to the other. Those who take offense at him must also speak against him and cannot do otherwise. On the other hand, those who rise through him must confess, defend, and preach him, and cannot do otherwise either; it is their souls that the sword will pierce through, as we shall see. Now pay attention to the text: Simeon does not say that Christ will be spoken against, but that he has been set for a sign so that he will continually be spoken against, just as a bull's eye or a target is set up for the marksmen, so that all crossbows and muskets, arrows and stones are aimed at that. It is set up that the shots are aimed not at some other place, but toward the mark. And so Christ is the mark everybody is after; all the speaking against is aimed at him, so that even if those who do the speaking against are at variance with each other, they nevertheless are united when they speak against Christ. This is illustrated by Pilate and Herod; they were deadly enemies and yet became united against Christ [Luke 23:12]. The Pharisees, too, and the Sadducees were at odds with each other beyond measure, but they all were united against Christ, so that David wonders about it in Psalm 2[:12]: "Why do the people rage? And why does the mob seek such vain things? Why do the kings of the earth gang up in this manner, and the rulers become united against God and against his anointed?"

Likewise all the heretics, no matter how greatly they differ with each other and oppose each other, are of one mind against the one Christian church. Even today, this is true, when no bishop gets along with another and no cathedral chapter, religious order, or convent honors the other. And although there are almost as many sects and divisions as there are heads, yet all of them are of one mind against the gospel, just as the prophet Asaph writes in Psalm 83[:6-8] that the people were gathered together against the people of Israel, namely, "Edom and the Ishmaelites, Moab and the Hagrites, Gebal and Ammon and Amalek, Philistia with the inhabitants of Tyre and Assyria"; yet none of them was of one accord with the other. Wickedness and deceit are, to be sure, at odds one with the other, but unfailingly they are united against truth and justice, all conflict and disagreement violently being directed against this target. They believe that for this they have ample justification, for every faction fights only against its own adversary, Pilate against Herod, Pharisees against Sadducees, Arius against Sabellius, monks against priests. In addition every faction has more allies and friends, and their feuds and their concords are only partial.

But Christ is entirely discourteous and unreasonable: he rebukes them all. To him Pilate is as much as Herod, the Pharisee as much as the Sadducee, and he does not side with any of them. Thus, as he is against all of them, so likewise, they are all against him. Thus truth is against all lies and falsehood. Therefore all lies join together against truth and make it into a sign of contradiction. This must take place in this manner, for Christ and truth do not find a single person to be godly and acceptable to God; as the Psalter expresses it [116:11]: "All men are liars." Therefore Christ must rebuke them all, without distinction, and reject their doings, in order that they all feel the need of his grace and thirst for it. But not all accept or want it; only a few will believe and accept it.

So we have two Simeons: the natural Simeon announces to the natural mother how Christ in his own person is set as a target for those who speak against him; thereby he indicates what the spiritual Simeon, i.e., the prophets, would teach Christendom concerning the Christian faith, namely, that this faith and gospel, the living word of truth, are a rock at which many stumble and rise, and that this gospel is a target that is spoken against. Of this Isaiah 53[:1] speaks with astonishment: "Who, tell me, believes our preaching?" as if he were to say that only a few believed it. Again Isaiah 8[:15] and 28[:13] say that many will stumble over this word, so that scarcely the dregs of the people will be saved. The writing of the prophets abundantly describes such stumbling, rising, and speaking against.

Simeon said before that Christ is the light and the Savior of all the world—something also declared by the prophets. These words

116

announce what Christ is and his attitude toward the world. But here, where Simeon speaks of falling, rising, and speaking against, he announces what Christ will achieve, what the world is, and what attitude it takes toward Christ. Thus it turns out that Christ is indeed willing to be the light and the Savior of all the world and to prove this richly and abundantly to the people. But the world not only does not receive him, but also becomes worse in its behavior; in addition it speaks against him and persecutes him most vehemently.

From this we recognize that the world is the realm of the devil, not only full of wickedness and blindness, but also loving these, as Christ says in John 3[:19]: "The light has come into the world, and the world loved darkness rather than light." Here we see how our pilgrimage on earth is one among devils and the enemies of God, so that, indeed, this life should be horrible for us.

From this we learn and know that, when men take offense at our word and faith and speak against them, especially the great scholars and clergymen, then we can comfort ourselves and rejoice. This is a sign that our word and faith are right, for they are treated as Simeon and all the prophets anticipated. God's word must experience rebuffs, falling, rising, and contradictions; that is the way it must be. He who wants it to be otherwise, must look for another Christ. This Christ is set up for a stumbling block and a rising of many in Israel, and as a sign which is spoken against; and so, assuredly, every member of his body, i.e., every Christian, must be like him for the sake of his faith and message. Our text has the word *antilegomenos*, "spoken against." His words must be condemned, banished, cursed as the worst heresy, error, and foolishness; wherever this happens, he has received his due. Where it does not happen, there is neither Christ, nor his mother, nor Simeon, nor the prophets, nor faith, nor the gospel, nor any Christians. What other meaning should there be to "speaking against" than not only to deny, but also to blaspheme, curse, condemn, banish, forbid, and persecute with all shame and disgrace as the worst heresy?

But there is one other consolation in the text. Simeon says Christ is a sign which is spoken against, but which will not be overthrown or uprooted. The whole world may condemn my faith and word, call them heretical, and turn and twist them in a most shameful manner. But it must let them remain and cannot take them from me. It gets nowhere with its ranting and rage; it merely speaks against me, and I must be the mark and target. And yet it will fall, and I stand. Let them speak against as much as they wish—God also resists them and battles with his deeds against their words. Let us see who will be the victor in this battle. Here are the deeds of God which establish this sign firmly and strongly upon a good foundation. It is a target set up by God—who will upset it? On the other side, however, are nothing but fleeting words and a powerless breath that come out of the mouth. The flies flutter mightily with their wings and sharpen their bills; however they only dirty the wall and must let it stand.

From this it follows that the doctrine and faith of the pope, the bishops, the charitable institutions, the convents, and the universities are nothing but worldly and devilish things; for no one takes offense at them or speaks against them, nor do they permit it. There is nothing but glory, power, wealth, peace, and pleasure; they are our Lord's fattened pigs in his sty. Occasionally a few may be found who are tormented by the devil with spiritual temptations concerning faith and hope. For wherever Christ is and his faith, there must be opposition or it is not Christ. If men do not oppose openly, then devils do it secretly. Those are severe tribulations in unbelief, despair, and blasphemy. These may be preserved and saved, but the great multitude live without Christ, without Mary, without Simeon, without any truth—and yet they celebrate many masses, sing high and low, display their tonsures and clerical robes and are apes of Solomon and cats of India. Indeed, since they will tolerate being spoken against and are not worthy of it, and since they also have nothing and do nothing that would call forth opposition, they themselves become those who speak against. What else should they do? It is their peculiar doing to condemn, forbid, curse, and persecute the truth. I say this because I wish to have performed my duty and to have pointed out to every Christian the danger in which he lives, so that he should know how to protect himself against the pope, the universities, the clergy, where God's word does not prevail. These are as the devil's own kingdom and essence, and he should govern himself in accordance with the gospel and should watch for opposition and praise. If there is no opposition, Christ is not there either. This opposition is not from the Turk, but from our closest neighbors. Christ has not been set up as a sign to bring about the fall of many residing in Babylonia or Assyria, but of many in Israel, i.e., among the people where he is living and who boast to be his own.

In the third place Simeon says to Mary: "A sword will pierce through your soul." This is not said of an actual sword, but should be understood as it is written about Joseph in Psalm 105[:18]: "Iron has pierced through his soul," and Psalm 107[:10]: "He has delivered those who were sitting in darkness and shadow of death, in suppression and in iron." Again Deuteronomy 4[:20]: "I have delivered you out of the iron furnaces of Egypt." It means that she would carry great sorrow and grief in her heart, even though she would not actually be tormented in her body. Everybody knows exactly how this took place. We must understand this expression after the Hebrew manner, speaking of great sorrow and pain of the heart, exactly as we speak of "heartbreak," or say "my heart is going to break" or "my heart is going to burst."

We shall speak in greater detail of this during the Passion season. For the present it is sufficient for us to notice how Simeon interprets his blessing with a bitter footnote, lest it be understood as a worldly blessing. But what is the significance of Simeon saying such things only to Mary, the mother, mentioning her by name, and not also to Joseph? It patently signifies that the Christian church, the spiritual Virgin Mary, continues to exist on earth and will not be destroyed, although the preachers and their faith and the gospel, the spiritual Christ, are persecuted. Joseph died before her and before Christ suffered, so that Mary became a widow and was deprived of her child, yet she lived on and this misery overwhelmed her soul. Thus the Christian church remains forever a widow, and the fact that Joseph, representing the holy fathers, dies and that the gospel is tortured goes through her heart; she must suffer the pain of the sword and yet she must live on until Judgment Day. What can be more bitter for a Christian than to see and experience how the tyrants and the unbelievers mercilessly persecute and destroy the gospel of Christ? This is happening at present under the pope more than in the past. This is in accord with her name; for Mary means a "sea of bitterness," which indicates that there is in her not merely a drop, nor a stream, but a whole sea of bitterness; a deluge of suffering inundates her, so that she is well named "Mary," a "bitter sea."

Finally, Simeon says all this will happen in order that the thoughts of many hearts may be revealed. Oh, what a blessed and necessary outcome of this falling and speaking against! But in order to understand this, we must note that there are two kinds of offense and temptation among men. The one kind is gross and finds expressions in gross sins, e.g., to be disobedient to parents, to kill, to be unchaste, to steal, to lie, to slander, etc.; these are sins against the second table of the law. The people who do these need not take offense at a sign to be spoken against; their thoughts are clearly visible through their evil behavior. Of this offense Scripture speaks little. The other one is prefigured by Cozbi, the beautiful daughter of Prince Zur of Midian; on her account twenty-four thousand Israelites were slain, as Moses writes in Numbers 25[:15]. Here you have the real offense and seduction: in the "holy" and "beautiful" sins of good works and the service of God this lady plunges the whole world into misery; nobody is able to guard sufficiently against her. These are sins against the first table of the law, against faith, God's honor, and his works. For there is no bigger, more dangerous, more poisonous stumbling block than the external good life lived in good works and blameless conduct. The people living such lives are such upright, sensible, honorable, pious people, that not a single soul could be saved or remain unseduced, if God had not set up his sign and target, over which they stumbled and revealed the thoughts of their hearts. Through their beautiful words and good works we see into their hearts and discover that these eminent saints and wise men are heathen and fools; for they persecute the faith for the sake of their works and they want to be unpunished in their conduct. Thus their thoughts are discovered and become visible, showing how they trust in their works and in themselves and how they not only sin unnecessarily against the first commandments, but also, full of hatred, strive to blot out and to destroy everything pertaining to faith and to God. They always behave as if they were doing so for the sake of God and in order to preserve the truth. The pope, the bishops, and almost all the clergy are of this disposition; they have filled the world with their snares and offenses by turning the spiritual life into external glitter. And yet there is no faith, but only works; the gospel does not rule here, but only human laws.

All of Scripture speaks of this offense and God fights against it with all his prophets and saints. This is the true gate to hell and the broad highway leading to damnation. Thus, this harlot is aptly named Cozbi, *mendacium meum*, "my lie."[5] Everything that glitters is falsehood and deception, but her beautiful adornment and jewels deceive even the rulers of Israel. She is named not only *mendacium*, but *meum mendacium*, "my lie," because her deception entices and tempts everybody. In order to protect us from this, God has set up his Christ to be a sign, and they are to stumble at it, to fall and to oppose, lest we, misled by their works and words, take their life to be good, and follow it. We should recognize how, before God, no good life is valid without faith. Whenever there is no faith, there is only Cozbi, nothing but lies and deception. This is revealed as soon as one preaches against them and treats their conduct with contempt in comparison with faith. When you do this then you and your faith are called heretical. They lash out and reveal themselves unknowingly and unwillingly so that we see what shocking abomination of unbelief lies under that "nice" life, what a wolf is under the sheep's clothing, what a harlot is under the virginal wreath who immediately and shamelessly insists that such shame and vice of hers be adjudged honor and virtue or she will kill you. God does well to say to her through Jeremiah [3:3]: "You have acquired a harlot's forehead and you refuse to be ashamed," and Isaiah 3[:9]: "They have not covered their sin, but declare it publicly as Sodom and Gomorrah." Would she not be considered a mad, shameless harlot who had her adultery extolled even in the presence of her husband? This is done by the preachers of works and the faithless teachers who unashamedly preach works and who, in addition, condemn faith, matrimonial chastity, and say that their whoredom is chastity and call true chastity whoredom. All of this would remain hidden, and nature and reason would

---

[5] This is a reference to Num. 25:6–15. Cozbi, a Midianite woman, and Zimri, an Israelite man, were slain by the priest Phinehas because they had transgressed the command that the Israelites and Midianites keep separate from each other. A listing of Hebrew names published in Basel in 1514 gave the meaning of Cozbi as "sin or lie"; cf. WA 10[I, 1], p. 408, n. 1.

never discover such vice: their actions are too nice and their manners too cultured. Indeed, human nature thinks up all of this and delights in it, believing that it is right and well done and sticking to it and becoming hardened in it.

For this reason God sets up a sign so that our nature should stumble and everybody should learn how much higher Christian life is than nature and reason. All their virtues are sin, all their light is darkness, all their paths are error. We need a new heart, and nature; the old heart reveals itself as God's enemy. A long time ago this was indicated by the Philistines [I Sam. 5:6] whom God plagued with tumors when they had God's ark in their country. The tumors are the thoughts of an unbelieving heart which break out as soon as the ark of God comes to them, i.e., when the gospel and Christ are preached, which they do not want to endure. And so the heart of these saints, whom nobody can recognize in themselves, is also revealed if we hold Christ up against them; St. Paul says in I Corinthians 2[:15]: "A spiritual man judges all men, and he is judged by nobody." He knows of what mind they are and what the attitude of their hearts is when he hears that they do not accept God's word and faith. The text continues as follows:

[The Second Part Concerning Anna]

"And there was a prophetess named Anna, a daughter of Phanuel, of the tribe of Asher; she was very old and had lived with her husband seven years from her virginity and as a widow till she was eighty-four. She never went away from the temple and served God with fasting and praying day and night" [Luke 2:36–37].

Somebody could say here: You see in the story of Anna that good works are praised, as for example fasting and praying and going to church. Therefore they certainly are not to be rejected. Answer: Who has ever rejected good works? We reject only false good works, those that seem to be good and are not. Fasting, praying, going to church are good works, if they are done in the right spirit. But the trouble is that the blind heads rush into Scripture, clump about in boots and spurs, paying attention only to the works and examples of the saints; immediately they want to learn from them and to do likewise. They become only monkeys and hypocrites, for they do not contemplate how Scripture speaks more about the person than about works. Scripture praises Abel's sacrifice and work, but, before that, even more his person. They let the person lie and only observe the example; thereby they only grasp the works and miss the faith. They eat the bran and throw away the flour, as we read in the prophet Hosea [3:1]: "They look to another god and love the dregs of the grapes." If you want to fast and pray with Anna, that is all right. But first of all, emulate her character and then her works. First be like Anna. But let us see how Luke treats her works and her character, in order that we correctly understand her example.

In the first place Luke says that she was a prophetess, without a doubt a saintly, pious prophetess. Assuredly the Holy Spirit was in her, and so she was good and justified without any work; her subsequent works were also good and justified. You see that St. Luke does not wish to say that she became pious and a prophetess through works, but that she was, first of all, a pious prophetess and that good works came into being through her. Why do you want to destroy her example and the gospel and turn them upside down, reading first and solely about works, when Luke writes first of the character and not of works.

In the second place Luke praises her as a widow who performed works suitable to her widowhood and stayed with her station in life. But thereby Luke does not cite these works as if they alone were the right kind of good works and divine service, rejecting all others. St. Paul, I Timothy 5[:3–6], describes a widow's life as follows: "Those widows you shall honor who are widows indeed. For if there is a widow who has children or grandchildren, she shall first learn to manage her household in a Christian manner and to do good in turn to her parents; that is pleasing to God and good. The one, however, who is a widow indeed and alone, she places her hope in God and continues in prayer day and night. The one, however, who lives in pleasure, is dead while she is still living."

From this you see that Anna must have been a lone widow, without children and parents to take care of—otherwise she would not have served God, but the devil, by never leaving the church and neglecting to manage her household in a God-pleasing manner. Luke indicates this when he writes she had been a widow until her eighty-fourth year. Everyone can easily calculate that her parents must have been dead and her children provided for, so that she, being an old mother, was taken care of by them and that there was henceforth nothing more for her to do except to pray, and to fast, and to forego all carnal desires. Luke does not say that she had lived all of her eighty-four years in this manner, but that she began to live thus at the time when Christ was born and brought into the temple, when, children and parents having been taken care of, she became very lonesome.

And so it is a rather dangerous thing, if one looks only at the works and not at the person or station or calling. It is most unpleasing to God for somebody to give up the duties of his calling or station and to want to take up the works of the saints. Hence if a married woman should want to follow Anna and forsake husband and children, house and parents, in order to go on a pilgrimage, to pray, to fast, and to go to church, she would only tempt God. To confound the matrimonial estate and that of widowhood, to leave one's own calling and to attach oneself to alien undertakings, surely amounts to walking on one's ears, to veiling one's feet, to putting a shoe on one's head, and to turning everything upside down. Good works must be performed, and one should pray and fast to the extent that the work of one's calling and station are not neglected or impeded. Serving God is not tied to one or two works, nor is it confined to one or two callings, but it is distributed over all works and all callings. Anna's work and that of lonely widows is nothing but fasting and praying, and St. Luke agrees with St. Paul. The work of a married woman is not continuous praying and fasting, but the godly administration of children and the household, and the taking care of parents, as St. Paul says [I Tim. 5:4]. The evangelist, when wanting to write concerning the works of Anna, was moved to emphasize with many words, so diligently, her estate and age, in order to rebuff all those who wished to make a big to-do of her works and suck poison out of roses. He reminds them, first of all, of her calling.

In the third place, for the same reason Luke also writes that she lived seven years with her husband from her virginity. By this expression he praises her married state and the duties of this estate, so that nobody should get the idea that he considers only praying and fasting good works. For she did not do this while she was

124

living with her husband, nor before she was married, but after she had become a lonely old widow. And yet her virginity and married estates, with their works, are also praised and set up as examples, as being proper good works. Why did you then want to disregard them and cleave only to the works of a widow? Nor did the evangelist first praise her matrimonial state and then her widowhood for nothing: he did so in order to pull the rug from under the blind legalists. There was a godly maiden, a godly woman, a godly widow, and in all three estates she took care of the respective works. You, likewise, must pay attention to your estate; you will find enough good works to do, if you wish to be pious. Every estate has enough works, without needing to look for strange ones. It is true service of God, just as St. Luke says that Anna served God with fasting and prayer day and night. But those work-fanatics do not serve God, but themselves and, indeed, the devil, because they do not perform their proper works and because they stray from their own calling. It is clear that anything good with respect to works depends on the persons and their callings, something which is also mentioned above in the Gospel for the Day of St. John the Evangelist.[6] Let this suffice for now. Now let us see what Anna signifies, if we look at her allegorically.

Simeon, as mentioned above, signifies the holy prophets who speak of Christ in Holy Scripture; thus Anna must signify those who stand by and hear and confess the message and apply it to themselves, as Anna did, standing there as Simeon spoke of Christ. Accordingly, Anna is nothing else but the holy synagogue, the people of Israel, whose life and history are written in the Bible. For Anna is found in the temple, that is, in Holy Scripture. Just as Mary signifies Christendom, the people of God after the birth of Christ, so Anna signifies the people of God before the birth of Christ. Anna is old and over a hundred years of age, close to her death, while Mary is young and in the prime of life; the synagogue at the time of Christ was at its end and the church at its beginning.

Thus the saints living before the birth of Christ understood the prophets and believed them and were all preserved in Christ and his faith, as indicated by Christ himself in John 8[:56] where

---

[6] Cf. *WA* 10$^{\mathrm{I, 1}}$, 306 ff., 315 ff. The Gospel for the Day of St. John the Evangelist is John 21:19–24.

he says of Abraham: "Abraham, your father, desired to see my day. He saw it, too, and rejoiced"; and again Luke 10[:24]: "Many prophets and kings desired to see what you see and to hear what you hear"; again St. Paul writes in Hebrews 13[:8]: "Christ is the same today and yesterday and forever"; and a lot clearer yet in I Corinthians 10[:1–4]: "You must know, dear brethren, that our fathers were under the cloud and that all went through the Red Sea; and all were baptized under Moses in the cloud and the sea, and ate this spiritual food and drank this spiritual drink; for they drank from the rock which followed them: and this rock is Christ." This and similar passages show how before the birth of Christ all the saints received their salvation in Christ, exactly as we do. Thus we read in Hebrews 11 many examples of faith: of Abel, Enoch, Noah, Abraham, Moses, and others, who lived their lives in Christ and pointed toward him whom they heard and understood through the prophets, in whom they believed, and for whose coming they waited.

For this reason, too, all the narratives of the Old Testament point so nicely and beautifully to Christ and confess him; all of them, indeed, stand around him, just as Anna physically stood in his presence. It affords great pleasure to read and hear how they all look and point toward Christ. Let us note just one example: Isaac was sacrificed by his father and yet remained alive, being replaced by a ram, which Abraham saw behind him entangled in the thicket by his horns. This signifies Christ, the Son of God. He is in all respects like a mortal human being who died on the cross; yet the divine nature remained alive, and the human nature was sacrificed in place of it; like the ram with his horns (that is, the preaching of the gospel which rebukes and castigates the perversity and obstinacy of the scribes and priests) which was caught in this same thicket behind Abraham, so Christ's human nature came after him in time. Many additional great lessons are hidden in this story.

Another example: Joseph was sold into Egypt and became a ruler over the country after his imprisonment. This happened and was written that he might prefigure Christ, who became through his passion Lord of all the world. Who has time enough to explain all these stories and to see how Samson, David, Solomon, Aaron, and others literally and accurately signify Christ? St. Luke used the

126

word *epistasa*, here, that is, Anna "stood over," or "next to," or "at," such happenings as took place with Christ in the temple. In the Latin version we read *superveniens*, meaning that she happened to come along, although that would be true, too. But the Greek term is better. She "stood over" what happened; this means the same as that she placed herself at the spot; with great effort she pressed herself to the spot, in order to see him, exactly as we say: Look, how the people press toward this or that. In this manner all narratives of Holy Scripture act with reference to Christ, indicating that they are prefigurations of him.

But in this the saints would not have been saved, and probably they themselves did not know at the time that their actions prefigured Christ's. Prefigurations and interpretations are not enough on which to lay the foundation of the faith; the foundation must be laid by means of clear Scripture, understood according to the sound and meaning of the words. Then, after such words and foundation of faith, such interpretations of the narratives must be built upon the faith, which is nourished and strengthened in this manner. Therefore, as I have said before, they were types of Christ only externally in their works, through which nobody would have become holy, but they heartily believed in the Christ who was to come because of clear statements from God's word, understood without recourse to allegory.

Thus Adam and Eve were promised after their fall, as God said to the serpent, Genesis 3[:15]: "I will place an enmity between you and the woman, between your seed and her seed. He is to crush your head and you will crush the soles of his feet." In this promise Adam and Eve are saved; they believed in the seed of the woman who was to crush the head of the serpent. So it was until Noah who received another promise, Genesis 6[:18]: "I intend to make my covenant with you." And so, when Eve gave birth to her first son, Cain, she rejoiced and believed that this was the seed of which God had spoken, and she said happily: "I have gotten a man of God," as if she should say: this will undoubtedly be that man, the seed, who is to fight against the serpent. She would have liked to see Christ, but the time had not as yet come. Afterwards she realized that Cain was not he, and her faith had to look forward to another woman.

Then came the clear promise made to Abraham, Genesis 12[:3] and 22[:18], when God said: "In your seed shall be blessed all the nations of the earth," of which we spoke in connection with the Epistle.[7] The faith of all the saints before the birth of Christ until the time of his coming was based upon this passage so that undoubtedly this same statement can be understood to be implied in "Abraham's bosom" of which Christ speaks in Luke 16[:22]. This statement was later also extended to David, but by virtue of the promise made to Abraham. Mary's child is now the seed of the woman. It fights against the serpent, in order to destroy sin and death. For this reason the text says that the seed is to bruise the serpent's head; without a doubt he meant the serpent which seduced Eve; that was the devil within the serpent. Adam and Eve assuredly understood it that way, too. Who could put forward another son or seed who is to bruise the head? If it were said of a mere human being, then Adam would have had the same chance as any one of his children. But it was not to be done by Adam, nor by a son of Adam, but by the son of a woman, the son of a virgin. It is beautifully noted that this seed bruises the devil's head, the seat of all life. The devil, in turn, does not bruise the head of this seed, but his heels or the soles of his feet. This means that the devil violates, destroys, and kills, the external, corporeal life of Christ and his activity and work. But the head, the godhead, keeps on living and raises also the soles of his feet, the human nature, that was crushed by the devil. Likewise in all Christians he crushes their soles, thus violating and killing their lives and works; their faith, the head, he must leave alone, and through the head their work and life are brought back. But, the devil's feet remain; his strength and fury continue to rage. But his head, that is, the sins and the inner being, are bruised, and therefore, in the end, his feet, too, must be bruised, and he, together with sin and death, must die forever. Behold, in this manner God has redeemed the fathers of old through his word and their faith, preserving them from sin and the power of the devil, as they looked toward the Christ to come; they are represented by saintly Anna.

For this reason Anna does not take the child into her arms, as did Simeon, neither does she say anything concerning him, as did

---

[7] Cf. WA 10[I, 1], 342, 355 f., 357 f.

Simeon, but she stands close by and speaks about him to others. For the dear fathers of old and the saints did not prophesy concerning Christ as did the prophets, nor did they say anything concerning him. But they watched and stood by with strong faith, when the prophets made their announcements, and they carried the message to other people and to their children's children, as Luke says here of Anna. All her characteristic traits agree with Luke's account. In the first place, she is a prophetess, that is, she has the understanding of the prophets. Thus all the saints of old understood Christ to be in the passages of Scripture, and consequently they were all prophets. In the second place, her name is Anna, which in Latin is *gratia*, meaning "favor" or "grace." The two names, Anna and John, are almost one and the same name in Hebrew. Anna means gracious or she who is favorably and graciously inclined. This signifies that the fathers and saints of old did not have such faith and promise of God by their own merit, but by the favor and grace of God, in whose sight they were "gracious" because of his mercy. In the same fashion all men are acceptable and lovely, not on account of their worthiness, but only by God's mercy. This is in accordance with nature which often throws her favor upon an unlovable thing; this agrees with the proverb that favor and love fall as often on the frog as on the purple. And another proverb says: What pleases me, nobody can make unpleasant for me. In the same way God loves us who are sinners and unworthy, and we must all be his beloved little Johns and Annas. In the third place, she is a daughter of Phanuel. In Genesis 32[:30] after Jacob had wrestled and fought with the angel, he called that place "Peniel" or "Phanuel" and said: "I have seen God face to face, and because of it my soul has been saved."

Now the meaning of "Peniel" is "face of God." But "face of God" is nothing else but the knowledge of God. Nobody knows God except through faith in his word. The word and promises of God declare nothing but consolation and grace in Christ; therefore, whoever believes them sees God's mercy and goodness. This amounts to knowing God properly and this makes the heart joyful and blessed, as David says in Psalm 4[:6-7]: "Raise up the light of your countenance over us, thereby you bestow joy upon my heart." And Psalm 80[:3] says: "O God, show us your face, then we shall be blessed." Many things are written in the Bible about the turning away and the turning toward of the face of God. Behold, in this manner all the fathers and saints of old were children of Phanuel, of the divine knowledge and wisdom which made them joyful. Their faith in the divine promises guided them and made them prophets. But they obtained faith and the promise only because they were dear little Annas, i.e., out of God's favor and compassion.

The fourth point is that she belonged to the tribe of Asher. "Asher" means "bliss" [cf. Gen. 30:13]. Faith makes us children of divine wisdom and blessedness. For faith destroys sin and redeems from death, as Christ says in Mark 16[:16]: "Whosoever believes will be saved." Salvation is nothing but redemption from sin and from death. Thus Anna is a daughter of Phanuel and of Asher, full of wisdom and of a good conscience in the face of all sins and the terrors of death. All this is bestowed by faith in the divine promise of his mercy, so that one follows after the other: Anna, the prophetess, a daughter of Phanuel, from the tribe of ·Asher. By God's grace we receive his promise and believe in it; thereby we learn to know God and his kindness; thereby the heart becomes joyful, confident and saved, completely freeing us from sin and death.

We come to the fifth point, penetrating still deeper into the spiritual meaning. She was married for seven years, living with her husband, and afterward she was eighty-four years a widow without a husband. The whole Bible might well be understood by these numbers, should we have the time and the skill for it. In order, however, that we may see that we Christians in no wise have need of Aristotle or of human teachings, but could find enough to study in the Bible to fill an eternity, should we care to do so, let us examine these numbers in relation to the wondrous matters of the Bible which we have already mentioned. The number seven, according to common interpretation, refers to our temporal life, the life of the body, for the reason that all time is measured by the seven days of the week (Genesis 1). This is the first and foremost measurement of time found in the Bible. For in Genesis 1, Moses says that God in the beginning created the days and that he then measured them, first of all, into seven; afterward the weeks were measured in months, the months in years, the years in lives, etc.

130

Thus, these seven years signify the whole life of the saints of old, their external, corporeal existence. But who was the husband? St. Paul in Romans 7[:2] interprets that a married man signifies the law; for as a woman is bound to her husband as long as he lives, so all, who live under the law, are bound to it. Now the law was given to no people on earth, except to this Anna, the Israelites, as Paul says, Romans 3[:2], that God's oracles are entrusted to them before all the heathen. And Psalm 147[:19–20] notes that God promulgates his word to Jacob, and his judgments and laws to Israel. To no other people did he do this, nor did he reveal to them his judgments. Again Psalm 103[:7] says: "He has revealed his ways to Moses, and his will to the children of Israel." But the gospel he revealed not only to this people, but to all the world, as we read in Psalm 19[:14]: "Their voice has gone into all the world and their words to all the ends of the world." This means the words of the apostles. And so Anna, for seven years married to her husband, signifies this people under the law, according to the external life and corporeal existence.

Now we have heard in the Epistle for today that they who live under the law, do not live well, for they do only the works of the law, unwillingly and without desire, and they are servants, not children.[8] For the law considers nobody just, unless he keeps it of his free will. Such will, however, is bestowed only by faith in Christ, as has been stated often. But where faith is, there will be righteous works and fulfillment of the law. It is immaterial to the believer whether he is under the law or not, as Christ, too, was under the law. St. Luke or, rather, the Holy Spirit, wants to show that this holy Anna, the holy people of old, was not only under the law and a servant. He goes on to indicate how she, in addition to her life under the law, also walked in faith and the spirit and how she fulfilled the law not with works alone, as do the servants, but with her faith. That is the meaning of the eighty-four years of her widowhood, which signified the spiritual life in faith of the saints of old; for widowhood which means living without a husband, signifies that they were free of the law. Thus both kinds of life came together simultaneously. According to the soul, they are not under the law, and the works of the law are justified only through

---

[8] Cf. WA 10I, 1, 364 ff., 369.

faith; in this they were real widows. But according to the body, they were under the law and its works, and yet not in the sense that they were justified thereby. Rather having been justified in advance through faith, they kept the law quite freely in honor of God. Whoever lives thus may also keep the law, and its works will not harm him or make him into a servant, for this is how Christ and the apostles kept them. They are those who at one and the same time live seven years with a husband and eighty-four years without a husband, who are simultaneously under the law and not under the law, as St. Paul says of himself in I Corinthians 12 [9:20]: "To those who were under the law, I became as one under the law, even though I was not under the law." How is he, simultaneously, under the law and not under the law? In this manner: he performed works externally and gladly, to render service to others; but inwardly he clung to faith, and through faith he justified himself without any works of the law. For he performed the works of the law and yet he did not claim to be justified through them, for this would be impossible. In this way the whole Anna, that is, the holy people, kept the law. For the person who believes and is justified through faith, can perform the law and the works of all the world, not only God's law, and yet they do not impede him; for he does them freely, not thinking he might thereby become righteous.

But those who are simply the married Anna for seven years and not also the widow Anna for eighty-four years, are the ones who live solely under the law, without spirit and without faith. They are unwilling servants who believe that they become righteous if they keep the works of the law. As a result they never become righteous or justified, as has been explained sufficiently in the Epistle.[9] And yet there is a nice order in setting first the seven years of matrimony and then the eighty-four years of widowhood, for St. Paul, too, says in I Corinthians 15[:46]: "The bestial, sensual man is before the spiritual one." If man is to become spiritual and obtain faith, it is necessary that first he be under the law. For without the law no one recognizes himself and what he is lacking; and he who does not know himself, does not seek grace. However when the law comes, it demands so much that man senses and

---

[9] Cf. WA 10I, 1, 364 ff.

must confess that he cannot meet the law's demands. He must despair of himself and, with all humility sigh for the grace of God. See, that is why the seven years come first, and the law precedes grace, exactly as John the Baptist preceded Christ. The law kills and condemns the bestial, sensual man, so that grace might raise up the spiritual, inner man. Nothing is said about the years of Anna's virginity, which signify the barren life before the law and before grace, for this is nothing in God's sight. Thus virginity was wholly despised and rejected in the Old Testament as a barren estate.

But how is it that the number eighty-four signifies faith or the spiritual life of the inner person who is a widow without a man and not under the law? At this point let us follow St. Augustine's custom and take a little spiritual walk and play a little spiritual game. Everybody knows that the numbers seven and twelve are the most glorious ones in the Bible; many times the numbers seven and twelve are found in it, undoubtedly on account of the twelve apostles who began and founded the Christian faith in all the world. Their teaching and essence is nothing but faith. Just as Moses, being one, received the law from the angels, by means of which he created the married Anna and exacted works in the external man, so the apostles, of whom there were twelve times more than Moses, received the gospel not from angels, but from the Lord himself, and through it they justified without any works all who were true widows, that is free believing persons.

Now the Old Testament saints had this same apostolic faith in addition to the law, as has been pointed out. So they attained not only the number seven, but also the number twelve, and not only the one Moses, but they owned the apostles who were twelve times more, and they lived, as we have heard, in both kinds of teaching and character. The number seven, then, nicely signified Moses, and the number twelve the apostles, of whom there were twelve times as many as Moses. We conclude, therefore, that the number twelve signifies the apostles, the apostolic teaching, the apostolic faith and the true state of being a widow which is spiritual and free of the law estate; just as the number seven signifies Moses, Moses' teaching, the works and character of the law, the real matrimonial, obligated estate. The twelve apostles are signified by the twelve patriarchs, by the twelve precious stones on the sacerdotal robe of Aaron, by the twelve princes of the people of Israel, by the twelve stones in the Jordan, the twelve pillars and gates of Jerusalem, and many similar things. For all of Scripture emphasizes the faith and the gospel which is started and founded by the apostles. Therefore, this same faith is also signified by these eighty-four years, wherein the number twelve is miraculously contained.

To begin with, eighty-four is exactly twelve times seven. This signifies that there is only one teacher of the law, Moses. He is equal to only one times seven, i.e., his law and the life of the law. But the number of the apostles is twelve and twelve times as great as that of Moses. Inasmuch, then as eighty-four to seven is as much as twelve to one, and the law is given through one, whereas the gospel through twelve, it is most fitting that seven signifies Moses and eighty-four the apostles and that, consequently, Moses' people should be the married Anna and the apostles' people the widow Anna, the one external in body and works, the other inward in spirit and faith. In this way we also demonstrate that faith surpasses works as twelve surpasses one and eighty-four surpasses seven. Faith includes the sum total and the inheritance, as the apostle calls it in I Thessalonians 5[:23]; he says it is *holocleros*, "the whole inheritance," just as the number twelve includes the whole people of Israel divided into twelve tribes. For he who believes, has it all; he is heir, child, and saved. Therefore look at the divine order: since Anna could not be a widow in her twelfth year nor married when she was only one, God nevertheless arranged it so that by the use of seven and eighty-four years the numbers one and twelve should be brought together and correspond. In addition, he gave an added significance to the number seven and to the married and widowed estates, as we have seen.

In the second place, the mathematicians teach the division of numbers which they call *aliquotten*; i.e., they observe how many times a number can be divided in such a manner that all parts are equal. Twelve, for example, can be divided five times, always into equal parts; for twelve is, in the first place, twelve times one (and the parts are all equal); in the second place, it is six times two; in the third place, four times three; in the fourth place, three times four; in the fifth place, two times six. Aside from these divisions there is no additional one which would result in equal parts; seven plus five are also twelve, as are three plus nine and one plus eleven; but the pieces are unequal and this is not a division into equal parts.

Now they take the number of the same equal parts and add them up to see the sum total; take, for example, the number twelve which is divided five times; if I add up one, two, three, four, and five the total comes to fifteen, three more than the original sum. For this reason they call such a number a rich, redundant number, because dividing it into equal parts amounts to more than the number itself. On the other hand, the division of some numbers amounts to less than the amount of the original number. So, for example, eight is equally divisible three times: eight times one, four times two, two times four. Now one, two, and four add up to only seven, one less than eight. This they call a deficient number. Between these two, mathematicians place a third kind of number where the total of the parts amounts to the same as the original sum; thus six is six times one, three times two, and two times three. Now one, two, three add up to six also. So here, too Moses and the number seven cannot be divided in this way; the same is true of all other odd numbers, for this division into equal parts can only be done with even numbers. But the apostles and the number eighty-four are a rich, redundant number, equally divisible eleven times; for Judas the traitor refuses to participate in the rich division, even if he is part of the number. He leaves a gap in the division, so that the outcome is not twelve, and yet he brings the number of the apostles up to a full twelve. He figures along in the number and the name, but not in deed. First, this number eighty-four is eighty-four times one; second, forty-two times two; third, twenty-eight times three; fourth, twenty-one times four; fifth, fourteen times six; sixth, twelve times seven; seventh, seven times twelve; eighth, six times fourteen; ninth, four times twenty-one; tenth, three times twenty-eight; eleventh, two times forty-two. Now add up the num- bers of the division: 1, 2, 3, 4, 6, 7, 12, 14, 21, 28, 42. The total is one hundred forty, a good sixty-six [fifty-six] above the original number.

What does all this mean, except that the undivided Moses, the law, just like the number seven, which stayed within itself, has not progressed farther than into the Hebrew people, and has included neither less nor more people? But the apostles, the grace-endowed spiritual life, and the gospel have broken out of the banks and overflowed richly into all the world. And just as one compared with twelve is so poor and little that it could not be less or poorer, so seven compared with eighty-four is a solitary poor thing. For the law with its works gives absolutely nothing to all its servants, except temporal goods and the honor of this life—a poor, miserable boon which does not increase, but only consumes itself. On the other hand, twelve compared to one is a rich thing and, what is more, it increases and does not simply consume itself; for faith is blessed and overflows eternally with goods and honor. Let this be enough of our rambling for this time. It has shown us how not a single tittle in Scripture is written for nothing, and how the dear fathers of old with their faith have provided us with examples, and how they, with their works, always pointed out what we are to believe, namely, Christ and his gospel. Hence nothing concerning them is read in vain: rather everything concerning them strengthens and improves our faith. Now let us go on with Anna.

Luke says, she never left the temple. Oh, this is a beneficial and necessary admonition! We have heard that this temple signifies the Holy Scripture. There was a peculiar plague among the Israelites, namely, that they greatly liked to listen to false prophets and to human teachings. They demonstrated this by erecting many altars and places of worship outside the temple, on mountains and in valleys. Moses had strictly forbidden them to do this in Deuteronomy 4[:2] and 12[:32] where he said: "Whatsoever I command you to do, those commandments keep and do not add to them or take from them." It was as if he wanted to say: I want you to be like Anna who never leaves the temple. But they were not at all like Anna, and so they left the temple for their altars, that is, they departed from God's commandment and in addition to it, they also followed their own devices and false prophets. But this was as nothing compared with our present situation: not only have we been led away from the temple by the pope's and human teaching; we have also demolished and profaned the temple with all kinds of desecration and abomination, and live our lives in an utterly self-willed manner, more than we can express. It should rather be as St.

Anthony diligently taught his disciples, namely, that nobody would propose to do anything which God did not command or advise in Scripture, so that we would surely remain in the temple.[10] Of this Psalm 1[:2] says: "Blessed is the man who does not walk according to the counsel of the godless and does not stand in the path of sinners and does not sit on the seat of the seducers, but his pleasure is in the law of God and on this law he meditates day and night." St. Peter says: "The righteous man," who is in the temple, "will scarcely be saved" [I Pet. 4:18], that is, the evil spirit snatches even at those who build solely and exclusively on the foundation of God's word; even they can scarcely remain firmly grounded. Where, then, will the secure and reckless spirits remain who move to and fro on human teachings?

Oh, a godly life is unable to tolerate human teachings; they are offensive and dangerous to it—like a snare that has been placed in one's path. A godly life must remain in the temple and never leave it. This is what the saints of old did of whom St. Paul says in Romans 10 [11:4] that God spoke to Elijah: "I have kept for myself seven thousand men who have not worshipped Baal." David complains about such hunters and seducers in Psalm 140 [:4–5]: "Protect me, O Lord God, from the hands of the godless and preserve me from violent people who plot to push my feet from the path. For the arrogant conceal their snare from me, and they stretch out their ropes as a net along the way and try to trap me in many ways." All this is directed against human teachings which tear us away from the temple. For the word of God and the teachings of men cannot tolerate one another in one and the same heart. Yet these raving killers of souls, the papists with their Antichrist, the pope, state that we must believe and observe more things than are stated in the Bible. Thus they lead all the world into hell with their ecclesiastical estates and orders.

Finally St. Luke says that Anna served God day and night with fasting and prayer. At this point the works of faith follow: first, she must be Anna, a prophetess, the daughter of Phanuel of the tribe of Asher, married for seven years, a widow for eighty-four years never departing from the temple; only then are fasting and

---

[10] Luther may have been drawing on his knowledge of *The Lives of the Fathers* (*De vitis patrum*) for this comment; cf. WA 10 I, 1, p. 431, n. 3.

praying right; only then is Abel's sacrifice acceptable; only then is God served wih fasting and prayer day and night.

He who starts with works, turns everything around and gains nothing. In the same way St. Paul after he had taught faith to the Romans, undertakes to teach them many good works saying that they should offer their body as a holy, living, agreeable sacrifice in the service of God. This takes place when one chastises the body with fasting, staying awake, getting dressed, and working. This is what Anna does. All the saints of old did the same. "Fasting" refers to all chastisement and discipline of the body which, although the soul is justified and holy through faith, is still not entirely free of sin and evil inclinations. Thus it is necessary that the body become subdued and chastised and subservient to the soul, as St. Paul says of himself: "I chastise my body and bring it under control, so that I, who am teaching others, am not myself disqualified" [I Cor. 9:27]. St. Peter, too, teaches the same thing in I Peter 2[:5]: "You are to offer spiritual sacrifices," not sheep and calves, as in the law of Moses, but your own body and yourselves through putting sin to death in the flesh and through the chastisement of the body. Nobody does this unless faith is there previously.

For this reason I have said frequently that the works that come after faith should have the sole purpose and intention of chastising the body and serving one's neighbor; they are not intended for earning a lot of merit or for making someone pious, for that must be present prior to the works. This is the real service of God in the works, if these works come about quite freely, to honor God. Otherwise what use does he have for your fasting, unless you quell thereby the sin and the flesh which he wants quelled? Those who fast for certain saints and on special days and times, without regard to the chastisement of the body do not do this; they only turn their fasting into a sterile work. But Anna does not have certain special days. She does not fast on Saturdays and Fridays, nor on the eves of the days of the apostles or on the quarter-year-days. Nor does she make a distinction between foods, but day and night, as St. Luke says, she fasts and thereby serves God. This means that without ceasing she chastises her body, not as if she were thereby performing a work, but in order to serve God and to blot out sin. St. Paul also teaches about fasting of this sort in II

Corinthians 6[:5], stating among other things that in many fastings we should show ourselves as servants of God. But our foolish fasting, thought up by men, thinks it is doing something worthwhile if it does not eat meat or eggs, or butter, or milk for several days. It is not at all directed toward the chastisement of the body and of sin, that is, toward serving God; rather with this fasting we serve the pope and the papists—and the fishermen.

Anna prayed day and night, and this surely indicates, too, that she was awake. But this must not be understood to mean that she prayed and fasted day and night, without interruption; naturally, she also had to eat, drink, sleep, and rest. The meaning is rather that such works made up her life; these were the things she did, day and night. What a man does during the day and night must not therefore be understood to refer to the whole day and the whole night. This is the second part of serving God, wherein the soul is offered up to God, just as the body is offered up through fasting. "Prayer", too, is understood to be not only oral prayer, but everything the soul does in god's word—hearing, speaking, composing, meditating, etc. Quite a few psalms are recited as prayers and yet in them scarcely three verses offer petitions; the other verses say and teach something; they punish sin, they invite us to talk with God, with ourselves, and with people. Such works were the service rendered to God by all the dear fathers and the saints of old. With them they sought nothing but that the honor of God and the salvation of mankind might be achieved. Thus we read in the Bible many sighs and yearnings of the ancient fathers for Christ and the salvation of the world; these are especially plain to see in the Psalter. But our prayer today occurs solely in the mumbling of the appointed hours, the counting of the beads of the rosary, and the babbling of words of that kind. Nobody thinks seriously to ask or to receive something from God; rather prayer is undertaken as an obligation and one leaves it at that. Like a thrasher who thrashes with his flail, that is the way they thrash with their tongues, and so they earn only bread for the belly. They give no thought at all to the fact that they should serve God with prayer, that is, that they should pray for the common needs of Christendom; even the "best" of them think they do well if they are pious and pray for themselves. For this reason, too, they merit

139

(like hypocrites) nothing but hell with their praying; for they serve neither God nor the people, but only their bellies and their advantage. If they were to serve God and their neighbor with their praying, as they should, then they would be obliged to give up and forget about the counting of words. They would not think of the number of psalms or individual words they had prayed; rather they would think about how seriously they were seeking in these things God's honor and their neighbor's salvation, which is the true service of God. They would often spend a whole day praying about the one thing that was troubling them most. That would be true prayer and divine service like that of Anna. Luke had a purpose in stating that she served God with her prayer. He did so in order to reject all the swarming and mumbled throng of our foolish prayers, whereby we merely multiply and increase sin, simply because we do not serve and seek God in them. Now let us return to the text once more:

> "She was present at that very hour and gave thanks to God and spoke of him to all who were waiting for the redemption in Jerusalem" [Luke 2:38].

Our Latin texts read: "for the redemption of Israel." But the Greek text says: "those who were waiting for the redemption in Jerusalem." Thus Anna would be speaking to those who in Jerusalem were waiting for the redemption. Since she never left the temple, she was unable to tell anybody of this unless they were in Jerusalem, regardless of whether they were townsmen or were visiting in the city. However, whether she was standing "above" or "close by," enough has been said about this in the allegorical interpretation. For when we come with Christ into the temple of Scripture to offer him to God and to give thanks, then this saintly Anna appears at the same time, with all the saints of the whole synagogue, and they all look at him and interpret him with their faith and their whole lives. But, in addition and in a tangible way, this saintly woman was also shown that she was worthy of great honor in that she received the grace to recognize in this poor child the true Savior. Undoubtedly, there were priests present who received similar offerings from Mary and Joseph and yet did not recognize the child and who, perhaps, considered the words of Simeon and

140

Anna as old wives' tales. There must have been a special illumination of the Spirit in her, and she must have been regarded as a great saint in the eyes of God, that he gave her the light in preference to all other people. Notice that there are five persons meeting together: the Christ-child, his mother Mary, Joseph, Simeon, and Anna; yet in that small number various stations of life are represented: man and woman, young and old, virgin and widow, married and unmarried. Thus at a very early age Christ begins to gather to himself all stations which are blessed; he does not care to be alone. Therefore whoever is not found in one of these states, is not in the state of blessedness.

"She gave thanks to God." The Hebrew language employs the word "confess" in a very broad sense; we can scarcely cover the meaning with three words: as "confess" our sins, "confess" [our faith] and "give thanks." Hence when the Hebrew language wants to give thanks, it says: "confess." This usage is, in fact, not bad or inappropriate. For to render thanks is nothing else than to "confess" the receipt of a benefaction, the benefactor's goodness, and the unworthiness of the one in need. Whoever recognizes and confesses this, renders thanks rightly. Beyond this "confess" also means to take a stand concerning a thing; as Christ says in Matthew 10[:32–33]: "Whoever confesses me before men, him will I confess before my father in heaven. But whoever denies me before men, him will I also deny before my father in heaven." Even as it was said above concerning the blessing of Simeon, that it is an extraordinary virtue to bless Christ whom all the world curses, so it is a remarkable work to give thanks to God for this same Christ. Those who recognize him do this, but their number is small. The others blaspheme God, condemn, persecute, and oppose Christ and his teaching. What they do to his teaching, they also do to him and to God, his father, as he says in Matthew 10 [Luke 10:16]: "He who despises you, despises me, and he who despises me, despises him who has sent me." It is terrifying that the world should be so full of blasphemers and people given to cursing and that we should live among them. Thus Paul prophesied in II Timothy 3[:1–4] that in these last times there would be many blasphemers, a prophecy which the pope now fulfills, along with the universities, religious foundations, and monasteries, for they do nothing but condemn, persecute, and curse Christ's gospel. Therefore do not consider it an insignificant grace, when you can confess Christ and thank God for him, that you do not consider him a condemned, accursed heretic and seducer, and that you do not slander, despise, and forsake God in his teaching, as the great multitude do. For Christ is not interested in having his person and name greatly honored, as are all his enemies; rather he wants his teaching to be honored. This is the greatest art. As he says in Luke 6[:46]: "Why do you call to me 'Lord, Lord,' and not do what I say?" And in Mark 8[:38] he says: "Whoever confesses me and my words among this evil, sinful people, him I will also confess," etc. Here you hear that it is his teaching which is the important issue to him. The pope and his followers also call him Lord; in his name and in his honor and service they condemn his teaching, strangle Anna, and persecute her in all the world. It is terrifying and unbearable to see this countless mass, blaspheming God and Christ and going to hell with frantic speed. He is a sign that is spoken against, and more stumble against it and fall than has happened up to now. "Thanks be to God" [*Deo gratias*] is a common saying, but scarcely one in a thousand says it sincerely. In Elijah's time only seven thousand men were left among so many Israelites (of whom there were, without a doubt, ten times one hundred thousand)—and that was still a time of grace; what would it be now, in the last age without grace which Daniel 11 [8:19] calls a time of wrath? We could well say to God with the words of Psalm 89[:47–48]: "Almighty God, where is your mercy now which in times past was so great; have you created all mankind for nothing?"

Furthermore, Anna did not only thank God, but she also spoke of him to all who were awaiting the redemption. Luke does not idly add that Anna spoke of Christ only to those who were waiting for the redemption. Undoubtedly there were not many, and none among the superlearned priests. What could such high, holy, educated people learn from listening to an old, foolish woman? We are the real teachers of the people! That is undoubtedly the way her words were regarded by these great lords. For the word of God concerning Christ must necessarily be contemptible, foolish, heretical, culpable, and arrogant in the high, learned, ecclesiastical ears. Therefore it is received only by the hungry and longing souls who

142

are awaiting redemption, as Luke says here; those who feel their sins, yearn for light and consolation, and who know nothing of any wisdom and righteousness of their own. Faith and knowledge of Christ cannot remain silent. Faith breaks forth and testifies in order to help others and to share its light, as Psalm 116[:10] says: "I have believed, and so I also speak." Faith is much too kind and good to keep such treasure for itself alone. However, if it opens its mouth, it encounters all sorts of misfortune from these faithless "saints." But faith is not bothered by this; it just marches ahead. Who knows how Anna fared? If they had not taken into account her age and her sex and had not looked down upon her as a stupid fool, her life would hardly have been spared for spreading such errors and heresy and talking so much about Christ. What she said was new and unheard of and contrary to all the teaching and arts of the learned priests and teachers of the law, who are filled with wisdom and righteousness, who need no redemption, but who look only for the crown and reward of their works and merits. For if we want to speak of Christ's redemption, we must claim that we are prisoners of sin and blindness; but it is an insult to such great ones that they should be blind sinners. Therefore it is unbearable for them to hear about Christ and his redemption or to permit somebody to talk about it; they insist we should condemn it as a pernicious error and satanic heresy.

From this we may easily understand how the spiritual Anna gives thanks to God and talks about Christ to all who were waiting for the redemption in Jerusalem; for the dear saints in the Old Testament truly recognized Christ. For this reason with their whole life they praise and thank God, proclaim what is in the Bible, and also talk of nothing else but of the redemption, of how Christ is given only to the needy and hungry; all the Bible narratives demonstrate this. For God has never yet helped those who were self-secure and unforsaken in their own estimation. On the other hand, he has never forsaken those who were needy and desirous of this help. Many, in fact, all the examples in the Bible, could be cited in support of this, as is clear enough and obvious to anybody who reads them. The reason that such speaking, hearing, and waiting are located in Jerusalem, is that "Jerusalem" means "vision of peace"; it signifies the hearts which only look for peace and are not quarrelsome. St. Paul writes in Romans 2[:8] that those who are quarrelsome cannot grasp the truth. Divine truth wants to have quiet hearts which listen and desire to learn; but those who storm and are noisy, who are obstinate or first want to know signs and reasons, before they catch the truth, they are in the confusion of Babylon and not in Jerusalem, with its vision of peace. Therefore they neither await Anna's message and the redemption nor do they listen to them. Whoever wants to read "Israel" for "Jerusalem" may do so. There is no great danger in the exchange of these two words.

> *"And when they had fulfilled everything according to the law of God, they returned home to Galilee, to their own city, Nazareth"* [Luke 2:39].

What the things are which they fulfilled according to the law of God, the Gospel for Our Lady's Candlemas will furnish.[11] The significance of Galilee and Nazareth is to be told in connection with the Gospel for the Annunciation.[12] We must note here the words of St. Matthew that after the magi had found Christ at Bethlehem and brought offerings of gold, frankincense, and myrrh, etc., they returned home; the angel having appeared to Joseph in his sleep and ordered him to flee to Egypt with the child and the mother, Joseph had acted accordingly. How does this agree with what Luke says, namely, that they returned home again to Nazareth after six weeks and after fulfilling all things according to the law of God. Here we have a choice of two possibilities: either that soon after the six weeks, they moved, first to Egypt and then later, at the appropriate time, they left Egypt and returned home to Nazareth or—as I think, and I will stick with this explanation—that they first went home directly after the six weeks, as Luke says here. I assume that the appearance of the angel who commanded them to flee to Egypt, of which Matthew speaks, took place in Nazareth and not in Bethlehem; no doubt it took place after the magi had left, as Matthew states, but not immediately afterward. Matthew states that it happened afterward for the sake of the

---

11 For Luther's treatment of the Gospel for Candlemas, Luke 2:22–32, see *WA* 12, 421–26.

12 For Luther's treatment of the Gospel for the Annunciation, Luke 1:26–28, see *WA* 12, 457–62.

arrangement of his account. For after the account of the magi, he immediately records the flight to Egypt; he omits what Luke writes here about the offering in the temple. Thus it becomes clear that the two evangelists are not contradicting each other.

In addition, the cross we are to bear is all the better depicted thereby. After the poor mother had been away from home seven or eight weeks because of the impending birth of the child, and after they had hardly arrived back home and settled down again to rest, and had started household affairs again, they had to get up quickly and leave again. They had to let everything lie and travel farther than before. Our Lord Christ starts out on his pilgrimage with his birth and forever remains a pilgrim on this earth, with neither fixed city nor place. How differently from other children is this child treated and brought up! Such treatment would certainly appear unfair and hard to us! But the poor mother must flee with her child to Egypt to escape the wrath of Herod, of which we will hear more in the Gospel lesson at the proper time.

"And the child grew and became strong in the spirit and was filled with wisdom; and the grace of God was in him" [Luke 2:40].

There have been some persons who were impertinently inquisitive, not satisfied with the statements of Scripture. They wanted to know what Christ had done in his infancy. Their curiosity was satisfied by a fool or a knave who came forward and fabricated a book about the infancy of Christ; he was utterly without fear and shame in proclaiming his lies. He dreams up stories about how Christ went to school and many more foolish and disgraceful swindles.[13] Thus with his lies he pokes fun at the Lord, whom all angels adore and fear and before whom all creatures tremble. The knave deserved to have a millstone hung around his neck and to be drowned in the deep sea for not esteeming his Lord and the Lord of all more than to poke fun at him. Yet we find people who print and read and believe such books—which was, in truth, what this knave wanted. Therefore I say that if the pope, the bishops, and universities were Christians, they should burn such books. But in-

---

[13] Luther is referring to a book that was published in Augusburg in 1503 and entitled *On the Childhood of Our Lord Jesus Christ* (*Von der kinthait unnsers herren iesu cristi*); cf. WA 10I, 1, 444, n. 1.

stead they produce much worse ones, and remain blind leaders of the blind. Christ did not go to school, for schools did not exist at that time. Neither did he ever receive the simplest education; for the gospel says that the Israelites marvelled and said: "How does he know Scripture, since he never studied it?" [John 7:15]. Similarly they wondered also about his learning and said: "Is not this Joseph's son and Mary's? Do we not know his relatives? Where, then did he acquire such wisdom and all this?" [Matt. 13: 54–56]. It seemed strange to them that a lay person and a carpenter's son should be so learned without ever having gone to school. For this reason, too, they took offense at him, as the gospel states [Matt. 13:57]; they thought he must be possessed by an evil spirit.

Let us stay with the gospel; it tells enough of his childhood. As Luke writes here: "He grew and became strong in the spirit and was filled with wisdom," etc. And again later, Luke states that he was obedient to his parents [Luke 2:51]. What more should the evangelist write? It was not yet time for him to perform miracles. He developed and was brought up like any other child, except that some children are more capable than others, and so Christ was a more capable child than others. There was nothing more to write about him than what was written by Luke. If he had recorded what he ate and drank and wore each day, how he walked, stood, slept, and acted while he was awake—what kind of narrative would that have been? Therefore it is not necessary to believe— indeed, I think it is not true—that his knitted coat, which those who crucified him did not want to divide, grew with him from his youth. Perhaps his mother did not make that coat, but it was an ordinary garment of the kind worn by the poor people. We should have a pure faith that believes nothing without a foundation in Scripture. Everything which we are to believe is abundantly contained in Scripture, especially since Christ's miracles and works first started after his baptism, as is written in John 2[:1 ff.] and Acts 2 [1:22].

Next, the cunning people also labor over Luke's words, about how Christ, if he was always God, could have grown in spirit and wisdom. They do concede that he did grow; that is something to marvel at, inasmuch as they quickly invent miracles where there are none, despising those which actually were. Such labor and

146

inquiry they create for themselves, for they have invented an article of faith, namely, that from the first moment of his conception, Christ was full of wisdom and spirit, so that nothing more could be added, as if the soul were a wineskin which one fills until nothing more will go in. As St. Paul writes in I Timothy 1[:7] they do not know "what they are saying or the things about which they are speaking." If I could not understand what Luke means when he writes that Christ grew in spirit and wisdom, I would want to honor his word, as the word of God, and believe it to be true, even if I never could find out how it could be true. I would let go of my own imaginary article of faith as being human foolishness which is far too small as a measuring stick and standard for divine truth. Surely we must all admit that Christ was not always equally joyous, even though he who is full of the spirit, is also full of joy, inasmuch as joy is a fruit of the spirit; Galatians 5[:22]. Again, Christ also was not always equally sweet and mild. He was filled with wrath and disgust when he drove the Israelites from the temple, John 2[:15–17]. He became sad and angry over their blindness, Mark 3[:5]. Therefore we must understand Luke's words in the simplest manner as referring to Christ's humanity which was a tool and a dwelling of the godhead; and even though he was always filled with the spirit and with wisdom, the spirit did not always move him in the same way but aroused him now to this, and now to that, as necessity required. Thus, although it is true that the spirit was in him from the moment of his conception, as his body grew and his reasoning powers increased in a natural manner as in other human beings, in the same way the spirit descended ever more into him and moved him more and more as he became older. So it is not mere delusion when Luke says: "He grew strong in the spirit"; rather, as the words clearly say, in the most simple manner he truly became bigger as he grew older, and more intelligent as he grew bigger, and stronger in spirit and filled with wisdom, as he grew more intelligent before God and within himself and before the people. You need no gloss to understand this passage! This interpretation can be accepted without any danger; it is Christian. It does not matter that it is against their imaginary articles of faith.

St. Paul agrees with this when he says in Philippians 2[:6–8] that Christ emptied himself of his divine form and took the form of a servant; he became like other men and he was found in human form. Paul does not say these words about the likeness of Christ's nature compared to our own; for he says: Christ, the man, after he had taken on human nature, became like other men and took on their form. Now, however, all men naturally increase in body, reason, spirit, and wisdom, and no one develops differently. Thus Luke agrees with Paul that Christ, too, grew in all respects and that he was an exceptional child, that grew more markedly than did others; for his physical stature was nobler, and God's gifts and mercies were richer in him than in others. Therefore these words of Luke have an easy, clear, and simple meaning, if only the smart sophists would leave their subtleties outside. So much about this Gospel.

THE GOSPEL FOR NEW YEAR'S DAY, LUKE 2[:21]

On this day it is customary to distribute new year's gifts from the pulpit, as if one did not have enough useful and beneficial matters to preach about, and it were necessary to hand out such useless tales instead of the word of God and to turn this serious office into a game and a joke. The Gospel demands that our sermon be about the circumcision and the name Jesus, and we are going to observe this.

Let us, first, ask that smart woman, Madam Jezebel, natural reason: Is it not foolish, ridiculous, futile that God demands circumcision? Could he find no other part of the body except this one? If Abraham had followed reason in this matter, he would not have believed that it was God who demanded such a thing from him; to our mind it is always a most foolish thing—there could hardly be a more foolish one. In addition, the Israelites suffered a great deal of humiliation and shame because of it. They were despised by all the world because of it and were almost considered to be an abomination. Moreover, there is absolutely no good in it; what purpose is served by injuring the body? It does not make a person any better, since everything depends upon the soul. But all of God's commands and works are exactly that way and such they are intended to be; in our eyes they appear as most foolish, humiliating, and useless, in order that proud reason, which considers itself clever and wise, may be disgraced and blinded, give up its arrogance and subject itself to God, render honor to him, and believe that everything he presents is most useful, honorable, and wise, even if reason does not see it and has entirely different thoughts about it. If God had given a sign that, in the estimation of reason, had been appropriate and useful, wise and honorable in its foolish conceit, reason would have remained completely unchanged; it

149

would not have come down from its high horse, but would have persisted in its custom of looking for and loving only honor, profit, and prudence in this world, and thus it would have become ever more deeply rooted in worldly, temporal things. By presenting foolish, useless, disgraceful things to reason, however, God pulls it away from the pursuit of profit, honor, and wisdom, teaching it to look only to the invisible divine wisdom, honor, and profit and gladly to suffer for them lack of temporal honor, profit, and wisdom and to be foolish, poor, insufficient, and disgraced for God's sake. Therefore, God was not concerned about circumcision, but about the humbling of proud nature and reason.

So, too, in the New Testament we have baptism, in which we must be immersed in water and believe that there we become cleansed of our sins and saved. Again, we believe that Christ's body is in the bread of the altar; again, we adore the crucified man as Lord and God. All of this is immeasurably above and contrary to reason. Thus all works and words of God are contrary to reason, and reason, in turn, is contrary to God, and they collide over the sign which is spoken against. It was certainly foolish speech in the sight of men, when Noah built the ark and said the world would be flooded [Gen. 6:14 ff.]. Again, Lot must have been a fool, when he said, Sodom and Gomorrah would perish [Gen. 19:14]. Moses and Aaron were fools before King Pharaoh [Exod. 5 ff.]. In short, God's word and his preachers must be fools, as St. Paul says in I Corinthians 1[:18–23]. In all this God is looking only for humility, that man take captive his reason and be obedient to divine truth. Thus, this foolish rite of circumcision was given Abraham and his seed so that in this way they would give glory to God and permit him alone to be wise. Circumcision was an external sign, whereby God's people were recognized as different from other peoples, just as we see that every prince gives to his people and army his banner and password, whereby they recognize one another, and foreigners know to which lord they belong. God has never yet left his people without such signs or passwords, by which one should know externally in the world where his people are. The Israelites are recognized by circumcision; that was their divine password. Our passwords are baptism and the body of Christ. For this reason the ancient fathers called such signs *caracteres, symbola, tesserae,* i.e., passwords or insignia; we now call them sacraments, that is, sacred signs. For where there is baptism, there are certainly Christians, wherever they are in the world. It does not matter if they are not under the pope, as he asserts. He would be only too happy to make himself into a sacrament and Christian password.

Let this be enough concerning the external reason for circumcision. We will look for its spiritual meaning and significance. First of all, why did he not command the circumcision of the fingers, hands, feet, ears, eyes, or some other member of the body? Why does he select that one member which has no useful purpose or service in human conduct and was created by God solely for procreation and natural increase? If the purpose was to cut off evil, then in fairness, the hand or the tongue should have been circumcised in preference to all other members, inasmuch as through the tongue and the hand all evil is perpetrated among men. It is said that this was done because evil lust shows itself most in this part of the body. For this reason Adam and Eve also sensed the disobedience of their flesh there and sought a cover for their shame.

All this is true, but something else—which we always stress—is portrayed here too, namely, that God does not condemn or redeem a person for the sake of the works, but the works for the sake of the person. Therefore our deficiency does not lie in our works but in our nature. Our person, nature, and entire existence are corrupted through Adam's fall. Therefore not a single work can be good in us, until our nature and personal being are changed and renewed. The tree is not good; therefore the fruits are evil. Thus, by circumcision, God very early taught everyone that no one could become righteous through works or through the law and that all works and efforts to become righteous or to be saved are in vain, as long as the nature and person are not renewed. If he had commanded that the hand or the tongue be circumcised, that would have been a sign that the deficiency to be corrected had to do with the words and the works; it would have been a sign that he was disposed toward the nature and the person and that he had hatred only for his words and works. Now, however, in choosing that member which does not perform anything except that the nature and personal existence originate through it, he lets it be clearly understood that there is deficiency in the whole natural being, that its

151

birth and everything connected with its origin are corrupted and sinful.

That is to say hereditary sin or natural sin or personal sin is the truly chief sin. If this sin did not exist, there would also be no actual sin. This sin is not committed, as are all other sins; rather it *is*. It lives and commits all sins and is the real essential sin which does not sin for an hour or for a while; rather no matter where or how long a person lives, this sin is there too. This natural sin is the only one to which God pays attention. It cannot be driven out by any law or any punishment, even if there were a thousand hells. Only the grace of God, which makes nature pure and new, can sweep it out. The law only points out this sin and teaches one to recognize it; but the law does not help against sin. It only impedes the hand and the members, but it cannot impede the person and nature from being sinful, for, since birth nature has anticipated the law and has become sin before the law had a chance to issue its prohibitions. As little as it is in anyone's power to be born and to receive his natural existence so little is it in his power to be without sin or to get rid of it. He who creates us, also must do away with it. For this reason he first of all gives the law, whereby man finds out about this sin and thirsts for grace; thereafter he gives the gospel and saves him.

Second, why does he command the male only to be circumcised when woman, too, is involved by her nature and birth? The prophet, in Psalm 51[:5], laments more over the mother than the father, when he says: "Behold, I was brought forth in sin, and in sin did my mother conceive me." It was done, obviously, for the sake of Christ and his mother, for the reason that he was to come as a natural man and person, could be born of a woman, without sin and without intercourse. But in all conception from a man, there is sin in both, man and woman, and conception cannot take place without sin on both parts. For this reason Christ did not want to be conceived by a man, lest his mother, too, be obliged to sin and conceive him in sin. So he made use of her womanly flesh and body for natural birth, but not for a natural conception, and he was a true man, conceived and born without sin. Because there may come a pure, innocent birth, nature, and person from a woman, and, because on the other hand, nothing but a sinful birth, nature, and person may come from a man, therefore circumcision is laid only on the male, to show how every birth is sinful and condemned when coming from a man, and that it must be circumcised and changed. On the other hand, that which comes from a woman alone, without a man, is innocent and not condemned and is not in need of circumcision or change. And to this might be applied what John 1[:12–13] writes: "He gave them power to become the children of God, to them who believe in his name, who were born, not of blood, nor of the will of the flesh, nor of the will of a man, but of God," provided we understand the "will of a man" as meaning "the birth from man." If more women could give birth without a man, these births would, all of them, be pure and holy; but this was reserved for this one mother alone.

In the third place, why did the circumcision have to take place on the eighth day? Here natural sin is once more demonstrated. The poor infant surely had no sin of its own; yet he has to be circumcised and must receive the sign of the cleansing from sin. If God had commanded to circumcise after eight years, one might say that this took place because of the sins that had been committed and in order to avoid future sins. Now he declares invalid both the notion that circumcision takes place for the sake of past sins or for the sake of the future sins by commanding circumcision on the eighth day. There is no doubt that a greater sin than any actual sin is born and has become a part of the human nature.

However, here somebody might object that Abraham together with his servants and household were circumcised when they were old (Genesis 17[:23])! Thus, circumcision might signify actual sin. The answer is: Scripture anticipates and resolves the notion that Abraham was justified by circumcision and that he was already justified of his sins when he received circumcision; for in Genesis 15[:6] we read how he was justified through his faith before his circumcision, when he was eighty years of age or a bit older, and he received circumcision when he was ninety-nine years old; circumcision obviously came some twenty years after his justification, just as St. Paul, too, in Romans 4[:11], concludes against the Israelites, that it is not circumcision that justifies, but faith without circumcision, as Abraham's example compellingly shows.

And so circumcision is not a taking away of sin, but a sign of such taking away, which takes place solely through faith, as happened with Abraham. Circumcision demands, as in Abraham, so also in all men, faith, in order that it remove the nature of sin and make the person righteous and acceptable. If now Abraham's faith had not been mentioned before his circumcision, it would have been a sure sign of original sin in him, as it is in children whose faith is not mentioned before; Scripture has so arranged it that Abraham first believed and was circumcised later, and that the others were first circumcised and believed afterward, in order that both truths would be established, first, that circumcision is only a sign of justification and that nobody is made righteous through it; second, that faith alone, without collaboration of circumcision, justifies and that, consequently, faith and its sign must be clearly differentiated and that any justification is opposed that is presumed to be resting on works.

In addition, the eighth day is perhaps appointed for physical reasons, that the infant should first become a little stronger so that it should not appear that it had died from circumcision if it were circumcised soon after birth and should die from weakness. Yet the spiritual meaning is of greater import. Seven days signify the time of this world up to the Last Day, because these times are measured by weeks or seven days (described in Genesis 1). The eighth day is the Last Day after this time, when weeks, months, and years shall cease and when there will be one eternal day. On that same day this circumcision will be fulfilled, when not only the soul, but also the body, shall be freed from sin, death, and all impurity, and will shine like the sun. In the meantime the soul is circumcised through faith from sin and a bad conscience. Thus we see, how Scripture everywhere insists on faith, but only on faith in Christ. For this reason, too, circumcision was given through the law of Moses not to the fathers before Abraham, but to Abraham, to whom Christ, his seed, was promised as a blessing, so that bodily circumcision everywhere might agree with the spiritual circumcision.

Why, then, has circumcision come to an end, even though the same faith in Christ, which it signifies, goes on and remains? The answer is that God has always maintained *one* faith from the beginning of the world until the end, the faith of Christ, but he has not assigned *one* sign of it. If all signs remain which have to do with faith, who might keep them? But now, since faith is inward and invisible, God has represented it to man with many external signs, in order that he thereby be incited to believe as by many examples. God has permitted each sign to continue for its appointed time. How many signs did Moses do alone in Egypt and in the wilderness? And yet all of them have passed away; they lasted for their appointed time, and all of them were signs of faith. So when God promised to Abraham the blessing in his seed and gave him as a sign of it circumcision, it could certainly not exist, by virtue of that very promise, longer than up to the fulfillment of that promise. But when Christ, the blessed seed, came, the promise was fulfilled; one did no longer have to wait for it. So, of necessity, the sign, too, must be finished and must cease; whereupon should it continue, when the promise on which it depended, was finished? The meaning of faith continues forever, no matter whether the promise goes or stays with its sign.

Yet circumcision is not abolished so that it would be sin to be circumcised, as St. Jerome and many others maintain.[1] It has become free; whoever wishes, may have himself circumcised or remain uncircumcised, provided he does not think that it is necessary or commanded, or that God's promise to Abraham remains unfulfilled, or that he may attain righteousness thereby. Of these opinions not a single one is compatible with faith; so it is not the work that counts, but the thought and the opinion connected with the work. He who is circumcised in the same fashion he trims his hair, beard, or skin, to please somebody or to serve him, would not commit a sin, for he would do it unbound by the law and without the need of justification, nor against the fulfilled promise of God, but out of free volition and his own choice, because the promise is fulfilled and the sign attached to it has come to an end. In addition, God never has had the custom that he raise up a sign again after it has come to its termination, but he has always instituted new and different signs. Thus, after the fulfillment of his promise, he raised, after the coming of Christ, for Abraham's seed a different, new sign, namely baptism. This, to be sure, is the last instituted sign prior to Judgment Day, because he instituted it through himself. Nevertheless there remains

---

[1] Jerome, *Commentary on the Epistle to the Galatians* (*Commentaria in epistolam ad Galatas*), II, 5 (*MPL* 26, 394).

the same faith in Christ which was in Abraham; for that faith knows neither day nor night, nor of any external alteration. This baptism signifies exactly what circumcision signified; of this we shall say something in due time.

Finally, it was customary to give the child a name in connection with circumcision, as we see here and in the case of John the Baptist, to whom, too, his name was given when he was circumcised. However, just as Christ was not obliged to be circumcised, and this sign was empty in his case, so, too, his name was given him beforehand through the angel, so that he did not obtain it through circumcision. This happened and was written that he should be free in every respect from the law and sin before all men and that he was solely serving us by submitting to the law and becoming like us, in order to save us from it, as Paul says in the Epistle lesson: "He was put under the law so that he might redeem them who were under the law" [Gal. 4:4–5]. For when death overcame him and slew him, without however having any claim or cause against him, and he willingly and innocently permitted himself to be slain, death became indebted to him, having done him wrong and having sinned against him and having handled all things inattentively, so that Christ has an honest claim against it. The wrong which death perpetrated against him, is so great that death is unable to pay or to atone for it. And so death must be under Christ and in his power forever. Thus death is overcome in Christ and strangled. But since Christ did this not for himself, but for us, and since he has made us a present of this overcoming of death in baptism, consequently all believers in Christ must be masters over death; death must be their subject, indeed, their criminal, whom they must judge and execute, exactly as they do when they die and on the Last Day. Through the gift of Christ death has become guilty against all to whom Christ has presented this gift. Behold, this is what we mean when we talk about being beautifully and happily redeemed from death through Christ; these are the spiritual wars of Joshua against the heathen of Canaan, notably the five kings, upon whose necks the princes of Israel trod by his command [Josh. 10:22 ff.]. So, too, circumcision did Christ wrong. He was not obliged to it, and so it is rightfully subject to him, and he has become its master, has vanquished it and given it to us as a present, so that it must come to an end and no longer have any say over those who believe in Christ. He has freed us from circumcision, only in this way he innocently submitted to it and donated to us his claim against it. Behold, this means once more putting Christ under the law, in order that he might redeem those who were under it [Gal. 4:5].

To continue, he has put himself under all other laws also, though not obligated to a single one, being Lord and God over all. So they are all in bondage to him, have sinned against him, and must now rightly also be subject to him. This he has also given to us. If we believe in Christ and the law would want to punish us as sinners, and death would insist on its dues and our miserable conscience would want to drive us to hell, if you should hold up against them their sin and injustice, perpetrated by them against Christ your Lord: do you not think that they will be ashamed and be more frightened of you than you of them? Death will sense its guilt and flee in disgrace; the law will be obliged to give up its terror and smile in friendly manner upon Christ. So one must expel sin with sin; the sins which they have committed against Christ and now also against you because of your faith, are greater than those you have committed against them. God, the just judge, will not permit that a big thief hang the little one, but decree that if the big one should go free, the little one all the more must go free. Of this St. Paul says in I Corinthians 15[:55–57]: "Death, where is your sting? The sting of death is sin. But God be thanked who has given us this victory through Jesus Christ, our Lord; for death is swallowed up in victory." Behold, is this not a precious redemption from the law through him who has placed himself innocently under the law?

God be praised, what an abundant, rich, and mighty thing is faith! It makes of man in every respect a god to whom nothing is impossible, as Christ says in Mark 9[:23]: "Can you have faith? All things are possible to him who has faith." And so also Psalm 82 [:6] says: "You are gods and all of your children of the most High." Fittingly his name this day is called Jesus, that is, Savior; we call a savior someone who helps, redeems, saves, and who is wholly salutary for everybody; such a one the Hebrew language calls *Jesus*. Thus spoke the angel Gabriel to Joseph in his sleep, Matthew

1[:21]: "She will bear a son, and you shall call him Jesus, for he will save his people, freeing them from their sins." Here the angel himself explains why his name should be Savior, Jesus, namely, he is salvation and redemption for his people. We have heard how this comes to pass through faith, to which he conveys all his rights and goods which he has over sin, death, and the law. He makes the believer justified, free, and blessed. Now just as circumcision signifies our faith, as we have heard, so the naming of the children signifies that we, through faith, become known before God through our distinctive names. For all those who do not believe, God does not know, as Psalm 1[:6] says: "God knows the ways of the just, but the way of the unjust will vanish," and Matthew 25[:12]: "Truly, I say to you, I know you not." What then is our name? Without a doubt, as Christ bestows upon us all that is his, so he also bestows upon us his name. We all are called Christians after him, children of God after him, Jesus after him, Savior after him; as he is called, so we are called, too, as St. Paul writes in Romans 8[:24]: "You have been saved in hope"; for you are like Jesus or a savior. There is therefore no limit to the status and honor of the Christian estate. These are the abundant riches of his goods which he pours out over us, in order that our hearts become free, cheerful, peaceful, and undaunted, and so willingly and joyously keep the law. Amen.

THE GOSPEL FOR THE
FESTIVAL OF THE EPIPHANY,
MATTHEW 2[:1–12]

Like the Epistle, this Gospel speaks of the physical coming of the Gentiles to Christ.[1] This signifies, and is the beginning of, that spiritual coming to which the Epistle refers. It is a truly terrifying and yet comforting Gospel: terrifying to the great, the learned, the holy, the mighty, because they despise Christ; comforting to the lowly and the rejected, to whom alone Christ is revealed.

First, the evangelist refers to Herod the King to remind us of the prophecy of Jacob, the patriarch, in Genesis 49[:10]: "The scepter shall not depart from Judah, nor the ruler's staff from between his feet, until he comes to whom it belongs." This prophecy clearly shows that Christ had to be at hand when the kingdom or realm was taken away from the Jews and no king or ruler of the tribe of Judah occupied the throne. This took place when Herod, who was neither of the tribe of Judah nor of the race of the Jews, but a foreigner of Edom, was set over the Jews, to their great disgust, as king by the Romans. As a result, for almost thirty years he wore himself out in the struggle against them, shed much blood, and killed the noblest of the Israelites, until he stifled their resistance and subjugated them. When this first foreigner had ruled for thirty years, subdued the realm, and maintained his position by force, so that the Israelites submitted and could no longer hope to be rid of him, the prophecy of Jacob was fulfilled. The time was fulfilled, Christ came, and was born in the reign of this first foreigner. He appeared in accordance with this prophecy, as if to say: The scepter of Judah has departed, a foreigner is on the throne of my people. It is time that I come and be king; the kingdom is now my very own.

---

[1] The Epistle for the Epiphany is Isaiah 60:1–6. Luther's treatment of this lesson is in WA 10I, 1, 519–55.

159

The soothsayers are generally referred to as the Three Kings, perhaps because their gifts were three in number. We will leave this matter to simple folk; it is of no great consequence. We do not know whether there were two or three, or how many there were. Their gifts of gold, frankincense, and myrrh [Matt, 2:11], indicate that they certainly came from rich Arabia or Sheba, for, all three of these are precious in that country. It is inconceivable that they bought them elsewhere, for it is the custom in those eastern countries to offer gifts and show veneration with the finest products of the land and the best of one's possessions, just as Jacob, too, Genesis 43[:11], commanded his sons to take the best products of the land of Egypt as a present to Joseph, etc. If their gifts had not been the fruits of their own country, why would they have brought frankincense, myrrh, and gold, which are found in their country, rather than silver and precious stones, or the products of some other country? Therefore these gifts were not offered to Christ as the painters depict it, the one offering gold, the other incense, the third myrrh;[2] but all of them, as for one person, offered all three things together. No doubt they were a company, with several leaders among them, even as today a prince or a town might send some important men from their midst as ambassadors with a gift to the emperor; so it happened in this case.

Those whom the evangelist here calls magi, in German we call fortune tellers. They do not prophesy as the prophets do, but use black magic, as the Tartars or gypsies are accustomed to do. Therefore they are called wise men and wise women. They can tell people all kinds of things, have secret knowledge, and engage in strange practices. Their knowledge is known as magic and is practised with the aid of the devil. However, they do not always make use of it, as do witches and sorceresses. The magus imitates the prophet and prophesies like the true prophets, but not by the Spirit of God. Therefore at times they are correct in what they foretell, for their work is not purely the devil's as it is in the case of witches; it is rather a mixture of natural reason and the devil's aid. Similarly their miracles are not purely the devil's art, as is the case with witches, but are a mixture of natural works and the devil's works. Thus a magus always imitates true natural science; for

2 The reference is probably to the work of Albrecht Dürer.

160

there are many mysterious processes in nature, and he who knows how to harness them, like the alchemists who make gold out of copper, seems to be performing miracles in the eyes of those who are ignorant.

Solomon, by the Spirit of God, had a considerable awareness of this secret knowledge of nature and made fine use of it, too, when he gave his judgment to the two women in the case of the living and the dead child. He discovered who was the rightful mother by appealing to the deepest depths of nature (I Kings 3[:16–27]). Similarly, Jacob made use of the same knowledge when, with the aid of the streaked rods, he brought it to pass that all the sheep that were born were striped, speckled, and spotted (Genesis 30[:37–39]). This knowledge is a good and most natural one. It is the source of everything that physicians, and those like them, know and describe about the powers and uses of herbs, fruits, iron, minerals, and so on. It is often referred to in Scripture when in similes it mentions animals, minerals, trees and herbs, etc. This knowledge was highly developed in Persia and Arabia, and these countries of the East studied it and looked upon it as honest knowledge which produced wise people. But then, as happens with knowledge and learning, swine and numskulls invaded the field, deviated far from the right course, and adulterated that noble knowledge with their trickery and sorcery. They wanted to pursue that same knowledge and imitate it, but lacking the ability, they gave up genuine knowledge and became tricksters and sorcerers who practise soothsaying and fake miracles with the devil's aid, sometimes, however, with the aid of nature. The devil has retained much of this knowledge and at times uses it through the magi, so that magus is now an ignominious name and refers to those who prophesy and work miracles with the aid of the evil spirit. It is true, at times they hit the mark and supply help, but only because the evil spirit is able to mingle the works of nature (which cannot lie) with his own works.

So these magi or soothsayers were not kings but men learned and experienced in such knowledge of nature. Yet undoubtedly not all they did was above board; they also indulged in much trickery. Even nowadays these same easterners practise great and manifold sorcery, and it was from here that sorcery spread into the whole

161

world after that knowledge had become worthless and had fallen
into decay. Prior to this they concentrated on stars and their courses
in the heavens. Thus in all ages arrogant reason has adulterated
and ruined what is good because of its aping and impertinence,
which impel it to imitate everything it sees and hears, just as apes
do. In the same way false prophets imitate true prophets, sancti-
monious hypocrites ape true saints, and sham scholars pretend to
be true real scholars. If we observe the world, we find that the
work of reason is no more than plain apishness; it desires to follow
after what is good and yet turns it topsy-turvy, misleading itself
and everyone else as well. Therefore these magi simply were what
the philosophers were in Greece, the priests in Egypt, and what the
university scholars are in our country today; in short they were
priests and scholars in rich Arabia. It is just as if nowadays we
were to send learned clergy from the universities to a prince with
gifts. For the universities are also proud of the way they teach that
natural knowledge which they call philosophy; this is not only a
farce but also poisonous error and a vain dream. For the knowledge of nature, formerly known as magic and now referred to as
physiology, is the knowledge which discovers the powers and
processes in nature, as, for example, that a stag forces a snake out
from a cleft in a rock by the breath through his nostrils, kills, and
devours it and then thirsts for a fresh spring because of the great
fever from the venom, of which Psalm 42[:1] speaks; or, that a
weasel by wagging its little tail in front of the snake's hole lures out
the snake, and the snake is annoyed and crawls out while the
weasel lies in wait at the hole, and when the snake looks up in
search of the enemy, the weasel buries its teeth in the snake's neck
just at the poison glands, and so strangles the foe in his very own
hole. These are the arts which the magi studied, and great wisdom
lies hidden in them concerning Christ and how man should conduct himself in his life. But this knowledge is no longer pursued in
the universities, and the peasants are better versed in it than our
magi of today, the masters of natural knowledge; thus they are not
unfairly called the fools of natural knowledge who, with eyes
closed to the world, pursue their learning with great expense and
industriousness and are the devil's mocking birds. If then we

should want to express this gospel in our vernacular, we would have to say: the masters of natural knowledge came from the East, or: those versed in nature came from rich Arabia.

Some express surprise that they should have been able to cover such a distance in so few days for it is commonly believed that they arrived on the thirteenth day after the birth of Christ. The geographers write that the distance from Sheba, the capital of rich Arabia, to the Mediterranean is a journey of sixty days; and from there to Bethlehem is just about three German miles.[3] But such and similar questions are of no great concern to me, and besides, it is not an article of faith to believe that they came on the thirteenth day. There is no compelling reason why they should have come from the capital city Sheba or from the furthest part of the country; they may very well have come from near the border in easy stages and by normal means. For like any other woman, Mary was compelled by law to stay in Bethlehem and remain indoors for six weeks as impure, so that she could well have been found there for twenty or thirty days.

On the other hand I do not want thereby to dismiss the common notion that it all happened in a miraculous way, as long as no one is compelled to accept it as an article of faith, as has been done and is custom in many similar matters. What divine Scripture does not affirm, cannot be required as an article of faith.

This, then, is what the evangelist means to say: When Christ was born in the reign of Herod, the first foreign king, and the time of the prophecies was fulfilled, behold, the great miraculous sign occurred that strange foreigners who had journeyed many days, sought him, whom his own people and the inhabitants and citizens of his own country neither sought nor wanted to know, that soothsayers and astrologers came to him, whom scholars and priests had no desire to visit and adore. That was indeed a most shameful thing for the whole Israelite land and nation, that Christ was born in their midst and they should first hear of it from alien and heathen foreigners who came from a far country, especially when they in the capital of Jerusalem should have been the first to know. So they

---

[3] The source of Luther's statement could not be established; cf. WA 10^I. 1, 563, n. 4.

were sternly admonished to recognize and seek Christ. But their forehead was brass and their neck iron, as Isaiah says of them [cf. Isa. 48:4].

> *"Where is he who is born king of the Jews? We have seen his star in the East, and have come with gifts to worship him"* [Matt. 2:2].

The text requires, and makes it necessary, that we should discuss somewhat further those men versed in nature, those masters of the knowledge of nature. For the magi recognized a king's birth from the stars, as they also confess. We must realize that everyone knows something of this knowledge of nature. Thus I know that dog's tongue is useful for the healing of wounds, that a cat catches mice when she has satisfied her hunger, that a hawk catches partridges, and so on; one person knows more about nature than the other, either because of his own observation or because he has been told by others. However, God has not revealed the whole of nature, only the smaller part; therefore reason is curious and wants to know more and more. And so the study and investigation of nature arose.

It is impossible after the fall of Adam that reason, blinded by that fall, should have a greater apprehension of nature than is given it by experience or divine enlightenment. But restless reason cannot keep still and be satisfied with such limitations; like an ape, it wants to know and see everything. So it begins to muse and to investigate more than it is commanded to do and it despises what it has received by experience or from God. Yet it fails to reach the goal of its search. Thus all its study and knowledge end in nothing but error and folly. And because men despised the knowledge of nature or could not attain to it, they split up into innumerable groups and sects; for some it was the earth, for some it was the waters, for some this, for some that, and so there was no end of the making of books and of study.

Finally, when they were tired of study here on earth, they ascended to heaven and wanted to know the nature of heaven and the stars, of which no one could possibly have any experience. So they decided to let their imagination run wild, to lie and deceive, and to say whatever pleased them about that innocent heaven. For as the saying has it, those who lie about distant lands, lie boldly,

164

because verification is impossible, and so refutation is also not possible. Since no one can get to the heavens and verify through experience their teaching or point out their error, they are free to lie with the complete confidence that no one will challenge them. Consequently they teach that he who was born under a certain star will be a gambler; he who was born under another will be rich or wise. Or they say: he will be killed; or again: he who builds or marries or goes out on a particular day, will say this or meet up with that. Such, they claim, is the nature of the stars in the heavens and such is the power they have over people who come within the sphere of their influence at any given time. God help us, how completely this art has everything under its sway! Reason has fallen prey to it and worships it with abject reverence, because in its blindness reason has greatest delight in coarse lies and petty, empty fables. Its taste is not so much for truth as for lies and fables.

Finally, the true heroes came on the scene. They really lifted up their eyes. They did not concern themselves with such puerile matters but began to investigate the world as a whole and in every detail; where it came from and where it is going; whether it had a beginning or whether it is from eternity and will remain for ever; whether there is a Highest Being above the world who governs all things.[4]

Here we find the most famous Aristotle, that noble light of nature, that heathen master, that archmaster of all masters of nature, who rules in all of our universities and teaches in the place of Christ. He taught and still teaches that a stone is heavy and a feather is light, that water is wet and fire is dry, likewise—and this is a special masterpiece—that the earth is above and the sky below, which he proves thus: the roots of the trees and of all plants are fixed in the earth and the branches reach towards heaven. Now, that with which nourishment is received is always above and that to which nourishment proceeds is below, as we see in man. So man is a tree turned upside down. Likewise when a feather flies, it flies beneath itself, and when the stone falls, it falls above itself. Further, when he speaks of the Highest Being, he decides that the earth has been as it is from eternity and will remain so forever and

4 E.g., Thomas Aquinas, *Summa theologiae*, I, ques. 46, art. 2.

that all souls die with the body. The Highest Being sits beyond heaven and sees nothing of what happens anywhere; rather, in the same way as blind fate is depicted, he shakes the heavens eternally, once every day, and hence everything occurs as it does.[5] The reason for this is that: if he were to see all things, he would observe much evil and wickedness and this would make him unhappy; so to retain his happiness, he must contemplate nothing but himself and govern the world blindly, like a woman who rocks her child in the cradle by night.[6]

This is the knowledge of the universities and whoever knows this and has learned it, is given a brown cap to wear and is addressed as Worthy Master of Arts and Philosophy. He who does not know this science, cannot be a theologian or understand sacred Scripture; indeed, he must be a heretic and can never be a Christian. Now tell me, what shall we call these people? They are neither magi nor sorcerers nor tricksters, but mad and stupid. Let us ask ourselves whether Christ has not given us our just due because we were so ungrateful to him for the gift of his grace and for despising the gospel. So he permitted us to become such terrible and awful fools of the devil that we are no longer able to see through all this, but pursue it as the ultimate in wisdom, at great expense to ourselves and with much industriousness and effort.

St. Paul spoke of all this when he said in Colossians 2[:8]: "See to it that no one makes a prey of you by the knowledge of nature and empty deceit, which are not from Christ." Likewise in I Timothy 6[:20–21]: "Guard what has been entrusted to you. Avoid the godless chatter and contradictions of what is falsely called knowledge, for by professing it some have missed the mark as regards faith." Here in explicit terms and in a way that cannot be challenged, the apostle truly condemns what the universities teach because he demands that everything not from Christ must be avoided. So every man must confess that Aristotle, the highest

---

[5] An illustration of this sort is found in Gregor Reisch's *Margarita philosophica*, VIII (*De principiis rerum naturalium*). This work, probably first published in 1496, with numerous reprints in the early part of the sixteenth century, was an encyclopedic summary of late scholastic learning. Written in the form of a dialogue between a teacher and his pupil, the book discusses the seven liberal arts as well as the *philosophia naturalis*, including alchemy, psychology, and ethics.

[6] Cf. Aristotle, *Physics*, I, and *Metaphysics*, IX, 9; also *Margarita philosophica*, VIII.

master of all universities, not only fails to teach anything concerning Christ, but also that what he teaches is idle nonsense, as has been said above. The apostle well commands us that we should guard the doctrine that has been entrusted to our care. He calls the natural philosophy of Aristotle un-Christian, idle words without substance; in fact, it is opposed to Christ; he says, it is "falsely called knowledge." He could not have assessed it more aptly than to say that it is "falsely called knowledge." There is no greater reputation than that which is derived from the knowledge of Aristotle in the universities. Yet that reputation is false, for that knowledge is nothing; it is simply opposed to Christ and has arisen to destroy him.

Therefore, dear man, give up this natural philosophy, even though you do not know what forces reside in every single star, stone, wood, animal or any creature, which natural philosophy seeks to uncover when it is at its best. Be satisfied with the lessons of your own experience and common knowledge. It is of little consequence if you do not know everything; it suffices that you know that fire is hot, water is cold and moist, that the work to be done in summer is different from that in winter. Know how to deal with your field, your animals, your house and child, that is enough natural knowledge for you. After that think about the way you may attain a knowledge of Christ, and he will expose you to yourself, who you are, and what you can do. So you will get to know God and yourself, which no master of nature nor any natural philosophy has ever discovered, as St. Paul teaches in I Corinthians 2[:14].

But let us return to our text. You say: Well, but does not this Gospel tell us how these magi learned of the birth of a king from the stars; so there is proof that the knowledge of the stars should be taught and known; after all, God himself encourages it by allowing a star to arise by which he attracts and teaches these magi? I reply: Indeed, stick to this as an example and note how these magi learned from that star, and you will do well and not err. For there is no doubt that the sun, moon, and stars are created, as Moses writes in Genesis 1[:14–18], to be signs and to serve the earth with their light. From the rising of the sun you learn that the day has begun; from its setting, that the day is at an end; when it reaches the center of the sky, that it is midday; thus it is set to be a sign and measure of time and of the hour for you; accordingly you regulate your work and activity. The moon and the stars function in the same way at night. In addition you need the sun to plow and cultivate your field, to tend your animals; depending on whether it is hot or not, you can do your work. Let that be enough. That is all you need to know of the sun and the heavens. Whatever else you would like to know is unnecessary and nothing but curiosity; furthermore, it is uncertain at that, and for the greater part error; as, for example, when fools want to know the size of the sun, its distance from the earth, its peculiar influence on gold, and that he who is born in the sign of the sun will be wise, and much more of such fools' teachings for which they have no proof. Or again, you are supposed to know that when there is an eclipse of the sun, it is certainly a bad omen, and a disaster will occur. The same is true when a comet, a star with a tail, shines. For experience teaches, and Christ too says in Luke 21[:25], that such signs will be in the sun, moon, and stars which will signify the final disaster of the world. So, too, big thunderstorms, lightning, floods, and fire in the skies and on earth are signs. But how this happens, or what natural powers are at work here, or what secret processes are active, these are questions that the magi investigate and juggle with; they are of no use to you and not necessary for you to know. It is enough that you should recognize God's wrath in these things and lead a better life. That is why there have been an unusual number of eclipses of the sun in recent years and many signs in many lands have been seen in the skies. Assuredly a big commotion is about to take place. Similarly the darkness that took place at Christ's passion signifies the disaster that clings to the Israelites to this day. These signs are certain and God has brought them to pass, but their meaning is uncertain and the tricksters devise their cunning answers.

This star was no more than a sign for these magi and they used it for no other purpose than as a sign, for which God also designated it. Therefore the star gazers and diviners may not boast, nor gain encouragement from this Gospel for their false knowledge. Even though these magi may otherwise have been ensnared in this same knowledge, they nevertheless did not make any other use of the star, except as a sign. They do not say what will be

Christ's future or what will happen to him, nor do they pose such questions. They are content that there is a sign that points to a great king and ask where he may be found. And that Christ might forever and completely silence the mouths of such garrulous fellows, he created a special, personal, and new star for his birth which was as yet unsullied and untouched by their idle talk. If they should say he was born under the influence of the stars, then he anticipates them and says: Yet this star is not that one about which your science muses. Though the fortunes of all men are foretold in the stars, as you teach, yet not one of these fortunes is to be found in this star, for it is a new and different star and unlike any other. You have never heard or known of it before. Further, if none of the other stars has any influence on Christ, and he has his own new star, it follows that the stars have no influence on any other man, for he is as much man as any other. Again, if this new star has no influence over other men since it was not in the sky for long, then assuredly it also has no influence over Christ who is man like all other men. Thus this natural science concerning the stars is idle quackery.

How these magi recognized this star to be such a sign which certainly signified a new born king, I do not know. Maybe they discovered in their histories and chronicles that in previous times the birth of a few kings was indicated in the skies, or by a star. For in Latin and Greek history we find that the coming or birth of some great princes or special people was announced with signs and miracles and by omens in the skies and heavens. So these magi certainly knew that the Israelites were a special, chosen people of God, for whom God was doing and had done much, above all other nations. Because this was such a lovely star, they surely thought that God had given them a new king. Some indeed say they knew the words of Balaam, Numbers 24[:17], "A star shall come forth out of Jacob," etc.[7] but this is not convincing, for this text refers more to the spiritual coming of Christ, and Christ himself is the star. Whoever is not satisfied with all this is free to think as he will. Perhaps they knew it by divine revelation.

At first, they did not consider this king to be God; rather

---

[7] Among those who maintained this position were Nicholas of Lyra, Origen, Ambrose, Augustine, and the Venerable Bede; cf. WA 10[I, 1], 573, n. 2.

they considered him to be the usual kind of temporal king, just as the queen of rich Arabia considered Solomon and came to him with gifts from her country. For this reason they came to Jerusalem, the capital. They hoped they would find him in splendor at the royal court. For the star which they saw above the land of the Israelites when they were still at home in Arabia, afterwards disappeared so that they did not see it on the way until they travelled from Jerusalem to Bethlehem, as the Gospel says. But when they say, "we have seen his star," they do not at that time mean that Christ created it, but that it is his own star because it is the sign of his birth, just as the masters of the stars call everyone's sign his own sign; they mean that he was born under it and not that he had created it. For the divinity of Christ remained unrevealed until his ascension, although it was frequently indicated. And when they desire to worship him, they do so, mindful of the fact that adoration, as Scripture points out, is customarily shown to kings in the East. This does not however mean that they are thought to be gods. Similarly, when Scripture refers to their falling down before him as "worshipping" him, as "adoration," it uses a term applicable to both God and man, as can also be seen from the use of the term "lord" or "king" and even from the name "God" which is used with a twofold meaning, as when he says to Moses, Exodus 7[:1], "See I make you as God to Pharaoh."

"When Herod the King heard this, he was troubled, and all Jerusalem with him" [Matt. 2:3].

Why should this trouble them? After all the Israelites were waiting for Christ whom God had promised them, as was said above in reference to Genesis 49[:10]. Simeon and Anna and many other pious people were doubtless in Jerusalem at the time and they foresaw the coming of Christ and were glad. There is an obvious reason why Herod was troubled: he feared for his kingdom since he well knew that he was a foreigner and had made himself most unpopular with the Israelites. Besides, he also knew that the Jews were waiting for Christ who should save them, as Moses had once done. Thus he was troubled in his conscience that a revolt against him might take place with the result that he would be ousted from his kingdom. On the other hand, the Israelites feared Herod and the

Romans and they were afraid that there would be much bloodshed if they had a new king. For prior to this they had instigated a most disastrous revolt against the Romans and Herod, and their experience was the same as the people of Israel in Egypt when Moses was commanded to lead them out of that country: they were more severely persecuted than ever so that they murmured against Moses. That was a sign of their weak faith, as also this panic in Jerusalem reveals a lack of faith. Their eyes were fixed on human might rather than on the power of God. But the pious people were not troubled; on the contrary, they rejoiced. When the evangelist says Herod was troubled and the whole of the city with him, he is not saying this of all inhabitants or of the citizens of the whole city, but he writes in keeping with the manner of Scripture. If Scripture refers to a town, and not to its inhabitants as well, it does not refer to all who live within, but rather to the larger and greater part of the population, as we often find written in the book of Joshua that he destroyed such and such a town, and then it adds: he killed all its inhabitants and whatever was alive in it.

> "And assembling all the chief priests and scribes of the people, he inquired of them where the Christ was to be born. They told him, 'In Bethlehem of Judea; for so it is written by the prophet: "And you, O Bethlehem, in the land of Judah, are by no means least among the rulers of Judah: for from you shall come a ruler who will govern my people Israel" ' " [Matt. 2:4–6].

Here we ask why Christ did not lead these magi up to Bethlehem with the star, but instead permitted his birth, which was now known, to be searched for in Scripture. He did this to teach us to cling to Scripture and not to follow our own presumptuous ideas or any human teaching. For it was not his desire to give us his Scripture in vain. It is in Scripture and nowhere else, that he permits himself to be found. He who despises Scripture and sets it aside, will never find him. We heard earlier that the angel gave a sign to the shepherds [Luke 2:12]; but to Mary or Joseph or to any other man, however pious they may have been, he gave no sign except the swaddling clothes in which he was wrapped, and the cradle into which he was laid, that is, the Scripture of the prophets and the law. In these he is enclosed, they possess him, they speak of him alone and witness to him and are his sure sign, as he says himself, in John 5[:39]: "Search the scriptures, because you think that in them you have eternal life; and it is they that bear witness to me." Likewise Paul, in Romans 3[:21]: "The righteousness of Christ has been manifested through the law and the prophets." Again, we heard above of Simeon and Anna that they signify the Scriptures which point to Christ and carry him in their arms. And Luke 16[:29–31]: Abraham did not grant Dives in hell his wish that Lazarus should be sent to his brethren; instead, he pointed them to the Scriptures and said: "They have Moses and the prophets; let them hear them. If they do not hear Moses and the prophets, neither will they be convinced if some one should rise from the dead."

In opposition to this true and godly teaching our learned scholars have devised all manner of ways to learn the truth. We must tell of some of them so that we may know how to protect ourselves against them. First, they have devised innumerable laws, statutes, articles, and doctrines, invented by men, as for example canon law and similar rules for religious orders, which doubtless are not the swaddling clothes and cradle of Christ, nor Simeon or Anna. Paul has frequently warned us against such doctrines that we should by all means cling to God's word alone. For all doctrines of men are dangerous and finally lead to the loss of faith, just as Solomon was led astray by foreign women. Paul refers to this danger when he says in Titus 2[:14] that the doctrines of men lead to the rejection of truth. Naturally if the doctrines of men were used in the same way as food and drink and clothes are used, they would be harmless. No one eats or drinks or clothes himself because he thinks that these things will make him pious and blessed. Such a belief and conviction would be sheer stupidity in the eyes of all. On the contrary, his belief and conviction about piety are based entirely on an unshakable faith in Christ and in this way he will be pious and blessed; such a belief is correct; such a conviction is good. So then, he who fasts, or does good works, or wears the habit of a monk or priest, observes the rule of his religious order, and looks on all these in the same way as he would look on eating and drinking, realizing that all these works do not make him pious, nor wicked if he does not do them, knowing that he is pious by faith alone—such a man fares well and acts rightly and the doctrines of men will harm him as little as eating and drinking and being clothed. But where are they who act in such a fashion? Among a thousand there is hardly one. Usually they say: If I should not attain piety and blessedness by such a life, by religious orders, rules, and works, why should I be engaged in them, like a stupid fool? So it is unthinkable that human doctrine should not lead to the rejection of truth, as Paul says.

For one of two things must happen: Either these doctrines are despised and cast aside when we hear that they do not make us pious and blessed, or they ensnare and strangle our conscience and belief when we think that they make us pious and must be observed. Then faith must perish and the soul must die, and there is no help or rescue: for faith will not survive, nor allow us to look to anything but itself, nor will it have the conviction that something else, and not faith, is necessary and useful to be pious. Therefore he who has faith cannot obey the laws of men, but he observes them how and when he will, and is completely lord over them. But he who is bound to the laws of men without faith, cannot know faith and forever remains a slave to the doctrines of men and never does a good work, as Paul says in Titus 1[:16]. So we must cling to the pure Scriptures alone which teach nothing but Christ so that we may attain piety through him in faith, and then do all our works in freedom for the benefit of our neighbor, as has been frequently pointed out above.

Second, they confront us with the lives and example of the saints in order to support and prove their human doctrines. Indeed this is most effective and destroys innumerable souls. So subtly are we drawn away from Scripture and faith that no one is aware of it. They set before us SS. Benedict, Gregory, Bernard, Augustine, Francis, Dominic, and many great saints.[8] No one can deny their saintliness, for they lived their lives in religious orders and in accordance with such human doctrines. Tell me, how shall a simple

---

[8] Benedict of Nursia (d. ca. 543) was the founder of the Benedictine Order; Pope Gregory I (590–604) was a key figure in shaping Latin Christianity; Bernard of Clairvaux (1090–1153) through the force of both his personality and his writings, helped to reform and revitalize the church in the twelfth century; Augustine (354–430) was Bishop of Hippo and the most influential theologian of western Christendom; Francis of Assisi (1182–1226) founded the Franciscan Order; Dominic (ca. 1170–ca. 1221) was founder of the Order of Preachers, commonly known as the Dominican Order.

heart withstand such an onslaught and retain its faith? You must have the spirit of an apostle or evangelist, if you are to hold your ground against them. Oh how sure they are, how they stalk about, when they have found examples in the lives of such saints which we should emulate. They think they have kindled the true lamp. If now I say to them: Of course, these saints also ate and drank and slept and wore clothes. Would it not be a good idea to found a religious order for eating, another for drinking, one for sleeping, and another for wearing clothes? To this they reply: True, nevertheless our dear fathers did not establish such orders as a means to piety, but they did establish those which they considered to be good and saintly. To this I answer: If you say that these dear fathers attained piety by observing such rules, rather than by eating and drinking, sleeping and wearing clothes, you obviously err; for God anticipated that argument, because he has never honored any one of the saints with a single miracle because of good works: rather, they were men and women full of faith and the spirit. If then you reject their spirit and faith and only choose their outward works, you act like a fool who spends his whole life sleeping, only because he heard that St. Bernard once slept and in this way wanted to become pious and blessed. Thus, we wrong the saints when we pretend that they observed such rules in the belief that thereby they became pious and blessed and we deceive the simple folk with the lives and reputation of the blessed saints.

You say: True enough, but they observed their rules and did not reject them, nor did they consider them as unimportant as you teach us to regard them. I answer: It is not for you or me to judge their intention and heart. But this we say: It is not impossible that they laid too much stress on these things. However, they erred as human beings; for everyone must confess that the dear saints erred and sinned. Therefore it is God's will that we should look to his word alone and follow the example of the blessed saints only insofar as they follow the word of God. But in those matters where as human beings they follow their own conceits or human doctrines, we should imitate pious Shem and Japheth who covered their father's nakedness and refused to join wicked Ham in holding forth and babbling about it [Gen. 9:21–23]. Likewise we too should keep silent about the weaknesses of those saints and not spread

174

them abroad, but rather take their strength alone as an example. It is no wonder at all that the saints stumbled and erred in this. Knowledge of Christ and faith in him are such a lofty and great matter, that God's grace alone must work them in us; flesh and blood can tell us nothing here, only our Father in heaven, as Christ proclaims, Matthew 16[:17]. Greater saints than SS. Augustine, Benedict, Gregory, and their like have here certainly erred. Already in the apostolic age such teachers existed, against whom St. Paul wrote his epistles, constantly emphasizing faith over against works and doctrines. You will be even more surprised to hear that the whole church erred in this matter when it was still new and at its best; SS. Peter, Paul, and Barnabas stood their ground alone and maintained that no law or work is necessary or useful to make us pious; St. Luke describes it all clearly in Acts 15[:2 ff.].

Now there were great saints present there, as for example the apostles and their disciples, and yet they insisted that the law and works are necessary for salvation; and they would have continued to insist if SS. Paul and Peter had not opposed them. Even they themselves would not have known it, if God had not given them the assurance by signs and wonders from heaven that they were right in their opinion that faith alone can help us and is necessary for our salvation, as it is written in Acts 10[:34 ff.]. Furthermore, even though St. Peter knew this and had himself helped to uphold it, he, too, erred in Antioch and failed to use such freedom aright, so that St. Paul alone withstood him, as he writes in Galatians 1[:11 ff.]. Not that St. Peter thought he must keep the law; rather he failed to use boldly that freedom for himself which he well knew; for he thought he should be cautious for the sake of the others, which was not right, and so he was castigated by St. Paul.

Therefore it will not do and is not right, if we urge as examples the lives which the saints lived, beyond or against the authority of Scripture. They deceive just as much as any heretic's or false teacher's error, indeed, much more, because true and authentic saintliness adorns such weakness too much; but God permits this to keep us close to his Scripture and teaching, beyond which there is no life or light, even though angels were to teach it.

Third, they adduce the saints' exposition of Scripture and say, this too is a light. They cling firmly to it and think they have something here which no one dares reject. So they prevent us from coming to the pure Scriptures. They tell us the Scriptures are dark causing many heretics to arise. Is that not the height of all blasphemy? But who tells them that the fathers are not also in darkness? Or who guarantees that the fathers do not err in their exposition? For it is apparent that they often erred and often contradicted themselves and one another, and very rarely spoke with one voice. God permitted this and made the exposition of the fathers uncertain and so takes care in every way that we will not escape him in his Scriptures, nor slip away and refuse to be caught. So we must know that it is not true when they say the fathers throw light on dark Scripture. They wrong the fathers and say of them what is not true. It is not the task of the fathers to throw light on the Scriptures with their own glosses, but rather to set forth the clear Scriptures and so to prove Scripture with Scripture alone, without adding any of their own thoughts. It is true they claim, that heretics are produced by the Scriptures. From where else should they come? For there is no book which teaches faith except the Scriptures. Therefore just as no Christian is born except by the Scriptures, so too no one can become a heretic except by the Scriptures. For if Christ is a sign of rejection over which men stumble, some falling, others getting up again, should we therefore reject him or set up another Christ alongside of him? If you abuse wine and bread, should fields and vineyards therefore go untended or others be cultivated instead? The evil spirit is an enemy of the Scripture and he has given it an evil reputation and made it suspect in this matter because of those blasphemous mouths which shout these things everywhere.

But what does this Gospel teach? First of all, the magi do not ask to see the High Priest. Nor do they say: Where is Annas or Caiaphas? Or: What kind of life has this man or that man lived? Rather they say: "Where is he who is born the king of the Jews?" Indeed, as an example to us, Christ permits them to run into difficulties and to fail, because they seek him in the holy city of Jerusalem at the doors of the spiritual leaders and scholars and rulers. He will not permit himself to be found in holy places, nor in holy guise; nor will the glosses of men yield an answer. The Scriptures alone and their word of Christ, these and nothing else, must be sought in holy places and at the doors of holy people.

This is a sufficient indication that we should not look to the works and teachings, the glosses and lives of men, but rather fix our eyes on the pure Scriptures and retain what is best from the lives and teachings of all the saints, so that we may not undertake to snatch up everything they do and say, but judge all things carefully and choose with discrimination what is born of the Scriptures. Whatever the saints have devised themselves, without the Scriptures, that we should consider human and abstain from, as St. Paul teaches us in II Thessalonians 3 [I Thess. 5:21]: "Test everything; hold fast what is good." Moses also indicated this in the law in Leviticus 11[:2 ff.] and Deuteronomy 14[:4 ff.], where he describes the clean and unclean beasts, and says that all beasts which are not cloven-footed and chew their cud, shall be unclean. This refers to people who are not cloven-hoofed, that is, those who rush aimlessly into life, and snatch up whatever crosses their path and follow it. But the clean beasts are they who act with the discrimination of the spirit in external matters and in things relating to doctrine. They retain what they observe to be in harmony with the Scriptures, but whatever has no basis in the Scriptures and is a valueless human trifle, they reject, no matter how great the saints. For there has been no saint so perfect that he did not also possess flesh and blood; no saint was uninvolved in a constant struggle with his flesh and blood. Thus it is impossible to consider his life purely one of the spirit and an example. Many a time human nature and reason will have intervened, yet these we may not obey at all. So Moses commands us to be cloven-hoofed, and Paul exhorts us to employ the discrimination of the spirit, and not to follow every work and manner of life.

However, they think, and everyone believes, that they fare well if they rely on these three things, the teachings of men, the examples of the saints, and the glosses of the fathers. In this no one may doubt or oppose them. They rule with self-assurance and imagine that they alone possess the Holy Scriptures which they have excellently and well caught up in these three vessels. Besides all this, they have fallen even deeper into the abyss of darkness, because they claim that natural insight and pagan knowledge are also a good means to discover truth. Our universities have bound-lessly erred in claiming this position when they teach that no one may be a theologian without Aristotle, the best of Christians! O blindness beyond all blindness! We could of course tolerate it, if they meant by natural knowledge that fire is hot, three and five are eight, and so on, all of which are well known to natural reason. But they outdo themselves and dream idle dreams and useless thoughts about things which do not exist, and about which they are ignor-ant. It is distressing to think of their mad and senseless zeal for study and the cost and trouble they expend on it, so that the evil spirit simply laughs at them. God plagues them as they have de-served, because they do not cling to the pure Scriptures. Conse-quently they are all condemned to devour such muck and stench of hell, and to perish. After this they fall into the hands of the devil and follow the examples of those who have visions of departed souls and pray to them for help; without fear or trembling they believe everything that those spirits told them. That is why the mass has fallen into such abuse, with masses for departed souls and the sale of masses, so that no complaint and pity could ever suffice, though all the world should weep blood day and night. The devil permitted himself to be adjured and compelled to speak the truth. So he has made a joke and game out of our faith and sacrament, just as he wanted it. This is our reward for our inquisitiveness, because we were not satisfied to have God's Scriptures alone and we treated our faithful God and Father as a fool and jester who had the presumption to teach us in his Scriptures, and lacked the knowledge and ability to tell us what we should know or what was necessary for us to learn. Since we despised his school, he deals with us justly when he allows us to become the devil's pupils.

You say: Should we not believe that wandering spirits lose their way and seek help? To this I answer: Let those wanderers wander further. You hear what your God commands. If you con-sider these spirits suspect, you do not sin at all. But if you consider only one of them to be upright, you are already in danger of error. Why? Because God does not desire that you should learn from the dead and seek the truth from them. He wants to be your living, abundant, and satisfying teacher himself. You must cling to his word. He knows well what he ought to tell you about the living and the dead, for he knows all things. What he does not tell you or refuses to say, you should not seek to know, but do him so much honor as to believe that he realizes it is neither necessary nor useful nor good for you to know. So you should happily and gladly cast to the winds all this swindle of the spirits and not be afraid of them; doubtless they will then also depart from you in peace. If you should have a poltergeist and tapping spirit in your house, do not go and discuss it here and there, but know that it is not a good spirit which has not come from God. Cross yourself quietly and trust in your faith. If God has sent him to punish you, as he did with pious Job, be ready and suffer willingly. But if the spirit has his own little game with you, despise him with a strong faith and courageously put your trust in God's word; he will not harm you or attack God's word. Do not doubt, for in my opinion none of those poltergeists are sent by God to punish us; of their own accord and for their own sport they vainly try to frighten us because they have no power to harm men. If that spirit had the power to harm, he would not be such a noisy fellow, but would do his mischief even before you had the chance to discover who did it. If it should be a good spirit that comes to you, his coming will not occur in that same noisy and wanton way. Test it, and manifest faith and you will see that this empty delusion is not of God, and it will cease. If you have no faith, you make it easy for that spirit, for God's word, which alone he fears, is absent.

The divine words on which you may take a courageous stand are in Luke 16[:29], where Abraham spoke to the rich man in hell after the latter had asked that dead Lazarus should be sent to his brethren who were still alive on earth and Abraham refused his request and said: "They have Moses and the prophets, let them hear them." From this text it clearly follows that God does not desire to have the dead teach us, but that we should cling to his Scriptures. Therefore, wherever a spirit crosses your path, do not ask whether he is evil or good, but make short shrift of him, despise him and push this word, *Habent Mosen et prophetas*, "They have Moses and the prophets," right up his nose, and he will soon know what you think. If he is a good spirit, he will like you all the more because you use the words of God, yours and his, so bravely and joyfully; if he is an evil spirit, as all of the poltergeists are, he

179

will soon say farewell. Then there is that other word of Moses in Deuteronomy 18[:9–11], where he says: "Israel, when you come into the land which the Lord your God gives you, see to it that you do not learn to follow the abominable practices of those nations that now inhabit it; there shall not be found among you any one who burns his son or his daughter as an offering, anyone who practises divination, or a soothsayer, or a medium, or a wizard, or a charmer, or an augur, or a sorcerer, or a necromancer," etc. Here you hear that in the eyes of God it is an abominable and pagan thing to consult the spirits and practise necromancy; it is strictly forbidden. Abraham is thinking of this word of Moses when he refuses to let Lazarus go to the living. You can confront the spirits with this text and say: *Non queras a mortuis, dicit dominus*, "God says, 'You shall not be a necromancer'" [Deut. 18:11]. God has so firmly stood by his command that there is no example, no story, in the Scriptures from which we learn that the saints sought information from the dead. This is the third blow that you can deliver to the spirits: no example of such spirits and their activity has ever been heard of or read of in the Scriptures, and so this must be despised and avoided, for it is surely the devil's phantom.

Therefore we may easily see that the bringing up of Samuel from the dead, I Samuel 28[:12 ff.], was trickery and deceit; the whole event is against this commandment of God. Accordingly we may not assume that the real prophet Samuel was brought from the dead by the medium. But when the Scriptures are silent and do not tell us whether this was the real Samuel or not, it demands from all of us that we should well know that through Moses God has forbidden necromancy. And he never recants what he has said, as Job says, and Balaam in Numbers 24 [23:19]. How should the sorcerers have power over the saints who rest securely in the hands of God? But if anyone says: in this way purgatory will also be denied, I answer: if you do not believe in a purgatory, you are not therefore a heretic. The Scriptures know nothing of it. It is better that you disbelieve what is not taught in the Scriptures, than that you reject what is found in the Scriptures. Let the pope and papists be as angry as they will. They have made an article of faith of purgatory because it has brought them the world's riches—and sent innumerable souls into hell, since they placed their reliance on

180

works and consoled themselves with the thought that works would bring them release. God has given no command concerning purgatory; he has commanded you not to consult the dead nor to believe what they say. Accept God as more reliable and truthful than all angels, and let the pope and his papists keep silence, the more so since their doctrines are lies and deceit which do little to inspire faith in purgatory. I will not stop you if you desire to offer prayers for the dead. In my opinion purgatory is not our common lot, as they teach; I think very few souls get there. Nevertheless, as I said, there is no danger at all for your soul if you do not believe in purgatory. You are not obliged to believe more than what is taught in the Scriptures.[9] If here, too, they should cite Gregory, Augustine, and other saints and their pronouncements, glosses, and examples concerning purgatory, I remind you of what you heard earlier,[10] namely, to what extent we should follow those dear saints and believe what they say. Who can convince us that they were not deceived in this matter or did not err as in many other matters? Our faith must have a foundation which is God's word, and not sand or moss, which are the delusions and works of men.

Isaiah 8[:19–20] agrees with this: When they say to you, "Consult the diviners and the sorcerers who chirp and mutter their formulas," then you shall answer: "Should a people not consult their God alone, not the living or the dead? Should they not consult his law and testimony? If they will not, they will never receive a dawn," etc. There, too, is a clear text, penetrating and compelling. We are to consult God's law and testimony in everything we want to know. He who will not do this, will be robbed of his dawn, which doubtless is Christ and truth itself. Note that when he says we ought to consult God, he also shows us where and whence we should do so. This prevents anyone from gazing at the heavens, expecting something extraordinary from God. He says: in "his law and testimony." If, then, he will not allow us to consult even God

---

[9] Luther treated the question of purgatory in a number of his *Ninety-five Theses* (1517); see *LW* 31, 25–33. He developed these ideas in his *Explanations to the Ninety-five Theses* (1519), especially Theses 10–19; see *LW* 31, 114–45.

[10] For Augustine's views on purgatory see, for example, *The City of God* (*De civitate dei*), XXI, 13 (*MPL* 41, 727–28); *Confessions* (*Confessionum*), IX, 12 (*MPL* 32, 776–77); *Enchiridion*, 110 (*MPL* 40, 283). For Gregory's views, see the *Dialogues* (*Dialogorum*), IV, 39 (*MPL* 77, 393–96).

himself outside of the Scriptures, how much less will he permit us to go elsewhere to consult others. For this reason Moses has so much to say about those who are generally consulted. He refers to eight of them: Those who practise divination, i.e., those who foretell the future by inspiration of the devil, such as stargazers and false prophets. Then there are the soothsayers, i.e., those who determined certain days as unpropitious and other days as propitious for travelling, building, marrying, dressing, fighting and for all other undertakings. Likewise there are the mediums; I do not know what else I should call those who invoke the devil by oath on a mirror, picture, stick, sword, glass, crystal, fingernail, circle, rod, and the like and desire to see hidden treasures and other matters and things. Next there are the witches, i.e., the wicked devil's whores who steal milk, influence the weather, ride on he-goats and broomsticks, travel on cloaks, shoot people, make lame and paralyze, torture children in their cradles, bewitch genitals, and the like. Fifth, we have charmers who cast a spell on beasts and men, charm snakes, charm away steel and iron, and have the ability to see much, to hypnotize, and to perform magic. Sixth, there are the diviners who have the devil at their elbows and in the manner of the Tartars and gypsies are able to tell people what has been lost, what they are doing or will be doing. Seventh, there are the sorcerers who can give things another appearance, so that what seems to be a cow or an ox is in truth a man. They compel people to fall in love and to have love affairs, and much else that is devilish. Finally, there are the wandering spirits of the dead.

Moses has not forgotten anything; he has stopped all gaps which might enable us to consult and seek knowledge outside of God's word. Therefore he has condemned our self-conceit and natural reason many times, especially in Deuteronomy 12[:8], "You shall not do whatever is right in your own eyes," and in Proverbs 3[:5], "Be not wise in your own eyes and do not rely on your own insight." He does this so that we may see that it is not the will of God that we should follow either what is in our reason or beyond it; rather we should follow his word alone, as Isaiah said so well above: We should consult neither the living nor the dead, but God alone in his law. St. Peter says the same thing in II Peter 1[:19]: "We have a firm, sure word. You will do well to pay attention to this as to a lamp shining in a dark place, until the day dawns and the morning star rises in your hearts." Does not St. Peter here agree well with Isaiah when he speaks about the word of God and the morning light? And when St. Peter says that the word alone is a lamp shining in a dark place, does he not conclusively indicate that anything that is not this word is plain darkness?

This digression was necessary so that we might know how to answer false spirits and human doctrines safeguarding the purity of the Scriptures. But we must return to our text and learn from the magi to ask: "Where is the newborn king of the Jews?" Let Herod ask for the priests and scribes, we shall ask for no one but for this newborn king. Let the universities ask: Where is Aristotle? Where is the pope? Where is natural reason? Where is Bernard? Where is Gregory? Where are the Councils? Where are the doctors? etc. Our question is: Where is Christ? We will neither be satisfied nor content unless we hear the Scriptures which speak of him; we are not troubled in any way when we are told how large and holy is the city of Jerusalem, how high and mighty is the city of Rome. We seek neither Jerusalem nor Rome, only Christ, the king, in his Scriptures. If we have them, we let go Herod, priests, and scribes together with Jerusalem and Rome and follow the Scriptures, till we find him.

Once again we note that the Scriptures and Christ have three kinds of disciples. First, there are the priests and scribes who know the Scriptures and teach them to everyone and yet fail to ponder them. Surely that is a great and stubborn hardness of heart and a contempt on the part of the ecclesiastical and learned people. They hear and see that great and honest people come from distant lands to seek Christ; they are told that a star in the heavens indicated the birth; and they themselves testify to what the Scriptures say. Being priests and most learned persons, they should have been the very first to run speedily to Bethlehem, full of joy and longing. Indeed, when they had heard that Christ was born in the East, they should have hurried to him with all their possessions, for their hope and consolation are based on Christ's coming. But they feared Herod who would certainly have killed them if they had confessed Christ with even a single word and accepted him as their king, just as prior to this he killed Hyrcanus and many of his followers for the same reason,[11] and he afterwards had the innocent children killed. Therefore, being afraid of death they forsook their lord and king and remained loyal in their allegiance to the tyrant Herod and the devil. Afterward, when Christ did not manifest himself and come forward with a display of worldly splendor, these things were pushed aside and contempt and oblivion took their place. They assumed that the magi had been deceived; hence Christ grew up among them quite unknown, so that they no longer knew where he came from, as it is written in the gospel of John [John 7:41–43]. These then are Christ's disciples who well know the truth, but dare not confess it or stand up for it, and so they are lost, as Christ says: "Every one who acknowledges me before men, I also will acknowledge before my Father; whoever denies me before men, I also will deny before my Father" [Matt. 10:32–33].

The second group of disciples comprises Herod and his people. For Herod searches in the Scriptures and believes them, regarding them as truth. He also believes that Christ is foretold in them and that now he is born; otherwise he would have shown contempt for all this and not taken it up so earnestly. Assuredly, he regarded the Scriptures as God's word, which must be fulfilled, and Christ's birth as God's work which here had reached its actual fulfillment. Yet he undertakes to run headlong, knowingly and openly, full tilt, against God's word and work. He believed he could change what God had said and done, even though he knew that it was God who was speaking and at work. Therefore with great diligence he searched and heard the Scriptures, and Christ too, but for the sole purpose of destroying it all and bringing it to naught. He was troubled that what God had said might be true, since God cannot lie. Is this not an incredibly foolish arrogance? Who can imagine that such a thought should enter a human heart? Yet the whole world is always full of such arrogance; so, too, are the best men of highest rank everywhere.

The third kind of disciples are the pious magi who left their land, their homes, their possessions, and disregarded them all so that they might come and find Christ. They are those who cour-

---

[11] Hyrcanus II was the aged grandfather of Herod's wife Mariamne and one of the few remaining Hasmonaeans, a family that had ruled Israel as priest-kings since 135 B.C. Herod murdered Hyrcanus II in 30 B.C. Cf. *IDB* 2, 134–35.

ageously confess Christ and his truth; but he who persecutes and destroys them is Herod, who nonetheless is God's servant, and goes to the temple and behaves like other pious people.

The question may also arise here: Why does the evangelist vary the words of the prophet and say: "And you, O Bethlehem, in the land of Judah are by no means least among the rulers of Judah, for from you, shall come the ruler who will govern my people Israel," when the prophet speaks in Micah 5[:2]: "But you, O Bethlehem Ephrathah, who are little among the thousands of Judah, from you shall come forth for me one who is to be a lord in Israel"? How do these two statements, "you are by no means least," as Matthew says, and "you are little," as Micah says, agree? A second inconsistency, when Matthew says, "among the rulers of Judah" and Micah says, "among the thousands of Judah," is easily harmonized. The little Hebrew word *alphe* means "rulers" and "thousand," so that you may interpret the prophet as you please, giving the meaning as "rulers" or as "thousand." It is the same as when I say in German: There comes a *Herzog*, which anyone may understand to mean a prince or an army, for *Herzog* in German refers to an army marching by, the progress of an army, the whole armed forces, even as it refers to the commander or ruler of that force. Any action, victory, or defeat of that force is said to have been the doing of that commander or ruler. Likewise the law of Moses has a regulation according to which a ruler was placed over every thousand men; Exodus 18[:21]. Consequently it is one and the same thing to say: among the rulers, or: among the thousands. For what he intends to say is: There are many groups into which the people were divided, each a thousand strong with its own commander. Among these rulers or thousands in the tribe of Judah, he speaks of the town of Bethlehem as humble and small, just as we might say that among the towns of Saxony Wittenberg is small. But the evangelist preferred to say: "among the rulers" rather than "among the thousands." For there was no need for the presence of literally a thousand men; it was enough if a particular regiment was present which could, if desired, be a thousand strong. At all times there was an authority there which had a thousand men at its disposal. Similarly we might call a town, mayor, or community an *aluph*, i.e., a thousand or a community, in which there might be approximately a thousand persons with an *aluph,* a ruler or mayor. We could translate the prophet and the evangelist thus into German: "And you, O Bethlehem, are a small community or town among the communities or towns of Judah." Indeed, in those days, it was a minor town in comparison with other towns like Hebron, Cariatsephre, and so on.

Also, it is one and the same thing for the prophet to call it "Bethlehem Ephrathah" and the evangelist "Bethlehem in the land of Judah." For both of them wanted to be exact in their reference and clearly indicate Bethlehem as the town which in ancient times was known as Ephrathah but at this time was called [Luke 2:4] Bethlehem, situated in the land of Judah. In the Gospel for Christmas Eve we heard why it was called Ephrathah and Bethlehem, for it is a land rich in corn.[12] It may also have something to do with the fact that Ephrathah, wife of the patriarch Caleb, lies buried there; this perhaps confirms the name. Bethlehem means "house of bread" and Ephrathah means "fruitful," indicating that it was a fruitful country with good food. Likewise we can readily harmonize the passage where the prophet [Mic. 5:1] says, "a lord in Israel," with the passage of the evangelist [Matt. 2:6], "a prince who will govern my people Israel," where the evangelist does not expressly refer to lordship and its usefulness for governing a people. But how can the two passages be reconciled when the prophet calls the town small and the evangelist says it is not small? Surely these statements are completely irreconcilable! One might indeed assert that the books were falsified.

We cannot understand this in any other way than to assume that the evangelist is thinking more of the spiritual greatness, to which the prophet also refers. As if he wanted to say: You, O Bethlehem, perhaps are small in the eyes of men, but in truth you are not the least in the eyes of God, since the Lord of Israel will come from you. Thus, the evangelist expressed and fulfilled what the prophet intended, but actually did not say. This figure and manner of speech, which is silent about something and yet suggests it, is commonly used in everyday language, as when I say: you are indeed my friend, but you associate with my enemies. That is tantamount to saying: You are not one of the least of my enemies.

---

[12] Cf. above, pp. 19 f.

186

Or again: beggars are poor, and yet they have much money; that is, they are, of course, not the poorest. Or as Paul says in Romans 2[:22]: you worship no idol, you merely are a robber of temples; that is you do not worship idols, so that you may rob the temples.

But enough of this. There is no joy in expending great energy on these questions. It is not necessary for a true believer who gives God the glory and does not doubt that everything in the Scriptures has been well and truly said, even if he has not the knowledge to prove everything. It is useful for scholars in order to defend the Scriptures against the blasphemers and perverters. We return to the matter of the sense and meaning of the Scriptures which do not speak here of a plain, common lord in Israel, similar to the many who were there prior to this, but they refer to one who must be unique and above all others, hailed and proclaimed so loudly by the prophets. The text in Micah [Mic. 5:2], in saying "from Bethlehem shall come forth for me one who is to be lord in Israel," suggests that before this time there was no lord in Israel. That is just as if he were saying: I will give the people of Israel a lord too, for once, so that they may also have a ruler of their own; till now the kings and rulers have been nothing but vassals and the nation was not their own. But this shall be a lord to whom the nation will belong. Hence the ancient fathers have always understood such texts to mean that Christ had to be not only man but also God, and his dominion should have no end and he should reign spiritually, not physically. For no human being, indeed no angel, has a people that is his own. Only God is lord among his people, as David says in Psalm 7[:8], "The Lord himself is judge." When Gideon was asked by the people that he should be their lord, he said: "Neither I nor my children will be your lord; God will be your lord" [cf. Judg. 8:23]. And so God also said, I Samuel 8[:7], when the people asked Samuel for a king: "They have not rejected you, but they have rejected me from being king over them." Their sin was not their desire to have a king, for after all God gave them one, but rather, that they set their trust on human help and government when they should have trusted in God alone. This was a grave sin.

If now Christ was to be lord of the nation, as of his own particular people, then his kingship could be neither temporal nor physical; rather it was necessary that he rule over the whole nation, past, present, and future. So it was necessary that he should be a lord forever; therefore his kingdom had to be a spiritual one. Since God gave him his very own dominion, he could not be purely man. It is impossible that God should give his honor, his dominion, his possession, his people to one who was not the real true God. As he declares through Isaiah 42[:8]: "My glory I give to no other." For that reason, too, the following is said in the prophet Micah immediately after the words that we have been considering: "And his origin is from of old, from ancient days" [Mic. 5:2]. It is as if he wanted to say: I announce the lord who will come from Bethlehem, but his origins do not lie there; he has been from the very beginning and since the foundation of the world, all the days, so that we cannot name any day, any beginning, that lies beyond his origin and dominion. Now nothing has ever been from of old, from ancient days, except the true, natural God. Therefore the origin from of old cannot refer only to one. An origin points to something from which it originates. So Micah compels us to infer that this lord must be God's born, natural son who with him is one true God for all creatures eternally. Again, when he is announced as having his temporal origin in Bethlehem, he must be a true natural man. That is the chief article of the Christian faith. His own people and the true Israel are they who acknowledge him to be a lord and permit him to rule and perform his work among them. But he is not lord of them who do not believe this: such are not Israel. From all this we may again easily infer that Christ had to die and rise from the dead that he might eternally exercise his spiritual dominion. Since this text compels us to acknowledge that he had to become a true, natural, human being, so it follows that he had to change that same life in the body into a spiritual, invisible life, and this all the more so since it was not possible that the extent and duration of his rule in the body should be such as the prophet indicates in the text when he continues: "Therefore he shall give them up until the time when she who is in travail has brought forth; then the rest of his brethren shall return to the people of Israel. And he shall stand and feed his flock in the strength of the Lord, in the majesty of the name of his God. And they shall be converted to him, for now he shall be great to the ends of the

earth" [Mic. 5:3–4]. These words clearly show that Christ's kingdom shall increase to the ends of the earth by preaching and
suffering, of which he speaks here when he says that he will preach
and feed his flock in the majesty of God's name. This indicates that
he will suffer persecution because of his preaching. For that reason
he also says that he will grant the Israelites an appointed time for
their temporal affairs and government until a new people is born. The
church of the apostles is in travail; she experienced the sufferings
of Christ and was in the anguish of birth, to bring forth a new
spiritual people for this lord of Israel, as he himself foretold in
John 16[:21–22].

> *"Then Herod summoned the magi secretly and ascertained with dili-*
> *gence from them what time the star appeared to them; and he sent*
> *them to Bethlehem, saying, 'Go and search diligently for the child,*
> *and when you have found him bring me word, that I too may come*
> *and worship him'"* [Matt. 2:7–8].

On the basis of this text we may assume that the magi were
not kings or princes but simple, honest people like the scholars and
clergy. Herod does not treat them like lords, but gets them to
travel to Bethlehem to attend to their business and commands
them to report back to him as if they were his subjects, which he
would not have done if they had been kings or great lords. He
would have invited them to stay with him, would have accom-
panied them on their journey and treated them royally. After all,
according to all historical accounts Herod was surrounded with
splendor and knew how to accord people honorable and magnificent treatment and wanted to be the center of public attention.
Therefore, since he called them into his presence secretly, without
any pomp or show, they must have been of a considerably lower
rank than he. Why does he call for them secretly? It was his
country, and he was lord of it all. He did it because he knew that
the Israelites hated him with all their heart and would gladly have
been rid of him. He was troubled and thought that if he called
them into his presence publicly and the Israelites heard of it, they
would anticipate him and instruct the magi not to pledge themselves to grant him his request, so that the new king might survive.
He was prompted by the very same fear when he asked them
about the time of the star's appearance, for within himself he had

189

already determined to slaughter the innocent children. His thoughts were as follows: If the new king is born, the Israelites will rejoice and hide him from me for a time, till he has grown up, and then flock to him, set him up as king, and destroy me. Therefore I must anticipate them and craftily discover the time of his birth. Even though he is hidden from me, I shall nevertheless catch him among them all when I have all children of similar age killed; all their attempts to hide him will be futile. Apart from this cunning plan, Herod goes to considerable trouble to know of the whereabouts of the new king and orders the magi to report back to him, pretending to be most religious and humble, as if he too would like to worship him. If human wisdom could help, his action was appropriate enough to achieve his purpose, to slaughter Christ. But Ecclesiastes speaks the truth when he says: "No wisdom, no counsel can avail against the Lord" [Eccles. 21:30]; and Psalm 33[:10] says: "The Lord brings the counsel of the nations to naught; he frustrates the plans of the peoples"; and Psalm 37[:32–33] says: "The wicked watches the righteous and seeks to slay him, but the Lord laughs at him and will not let him fall into his hand." Such texts Herod must involuntarily prove true. For our comfort he becomes an example of their fulfillment, that we may be free and secure and fear no one except God; if he is for us, neither cunning nor might can harm us.

> "When they had heard the king they went their way; and lo, the star which they had seen in the East went before them, till it came to rest over the place where the child was. When they saw the star, they rejoiced exceedingly" [Matt. 2:9–10].

He does not say that they promised to do as the king demanded, rather he says they "heard" him and his demand to bring back word to him. Yet the answer which they received later on in a dream suggests that they intended to return to Herod in all innocence; they were not aware of his wickedness and plan and considered him to be a simple and upright person. From this we should learn that even the saints are duped and may be led astray by the fine gestures and the outward show of unbelieving saints, so that they consider good what is not good. But they are not caught forever; instruction and salvation come down from heaven for them. The evangelist's remark that they "heard," may also be in-

190

tended to refer to the fact that they heard from him the Scripture of the prophet which told them that the new king must be in Bethlehem, the very thing about which they had enquired and were most anxious to hear.

This example shows how the enemies of Christ are also useful sometimes and teach others the truth, even though at times they do this involuntarily and unwittingly. So for example, Caiaphas teaches correctly in John 11[:50] that one man of necessity should die for the people, and Balaam speaks many fine words concerning Christ in Numbers 24[:17 ff.]. Thus Christ taught the people, Matthew 23[:2–3], that they should follow and listen to the scribes and Pharisees when they sit on Moses' seat and teach, and yet he forbade them to follow them in their works.

So the magi acted rightly and gave us a good example when they heard Herod, not for Herod's sake, nor as if the words he spoke were his very own, but because of the Scriptures which he proclaimed to them and which they followed rather than Herod's works. From this we may well learn that we should listen to the evil bishops and priests as much as to the pious, and pattern our lives according to their teaching, not according to their lives, always provided their doctrine is completely scriptural and not mere human vanity. For in the same way as we should listen to the teaching of the Scripture, even though it be a Herod who proclaims it, who all the while is engaged in plain murder, so in like manner we should not listen to human teaching, even though a St. Peter or Paul or an angel proclaims it and inundates us at the same time with a flood and storm of miracles. As was said earlier, the saints frequently err and are a stumbling block with their human doctrines and works. So it is not the will of God that we should fix our eyes on their example, but rather on his Scriptures alone. For this reason he ordains that the saints often confront us with human doctrines and works; likewise he disposes that the impious often teach the pure and clear Scriptures, so that he may better preserve us on either side against both offenses, on the left hand from the evil lives of the impious, and on the right hand from the fine and ostentatious lives of the saints. For if you do not look to the Scriptures alone, the lives of the saints are ten times more harmful, dangerous, and offensive than those of the impious. For the wicked sin gravely and their sins are easily recognizable and must be avoided. But the saints present a subtle and fine show with their human doctrines and this is likely to lead astray even the elect as Christ says, in Matthew 24[:24].

Now such offense of the saints is directly against the main article, namely, faith and its doctrine. However, gross sins are not opposed to faith or its doctrine, even though they depart from it, for they do not assault it. Human doctrines are nothing but assaults on faith and its doctrines, for they induce men to rely on themselves and their works, when it is Christ who preserves his saints in the midst of human doctrines and works, just as he preserved the three men, Hananiah, Azariah, and Mishael in the midst of the fiery furnace in Babylon [Dan. 1:6; 3:20 ff.]. Therefore the lives of the saints should not be followed as an example in these things, but should be avoided as sheer miracles, which merely deserve praise and honor. For he does not desire to perform miracles in the fiery furnace for every single one of us; nor is it his will to make a Bernard, a Francis, a Gregory, a Benedict, or an Augustine out of each one of us.

The evangelist has taken care not to mention Herod by name, saying: "they heard the King." He refers to him by the name of his majesty and authority, just as according to John 11[:51] Caiaphas prophesied, not because he was called Caiaphas, but because he was high priest. The offices of king and priest are good and instituted by God, even though wicked men terribly abuse them, just as gold and silver and all creatures are good, even though they may be rightly used or terribly abused. So here, too, God used Herod, because he is God's creature, in a situation where he could be of real service. He offers him to the magi too, for their service in the same situation. Hence it was not Herod, but the king whom they beheld and heard; it was of no concern to them that he himself was wicked; they selected that in him which was of God and good, just as the bee sucks honey from the flower and leaves the poison to the spider. They listened to him when he bade them go to Bethlehem to inquire diligently after the child as the prophet had foretold. He did not have this knowledge from himself but from the priests. However, they were unable (or did not desire) to know either his evil counsel and purpose, or his wicked life. So we, too, should learn to hate the vices of men, and yet to love the person, so that we may separate honey and poison from one another.

It is also suggested here that this star cannot have been high up in the heavens like the other stars, but it must have hovered close above them in the air; otherwise it would have been impossible for them to tell whether it was above Jerusalem or Bethlehem. The astronomers and experience clearly show that it is not easy to discern over what town the stars in the heavens actually are because they are up so high. Thus two towns that are ten or more miles apart each thinks the star is above it. It is also impossible to know the courses of the stars by sight, for they travel more quickly than a moment of time or a flash of lightning. Actually they did not see this star move rapidly; rather it went before them slowly, as they proceeded on foot or on horseback. A star in the heavens moves much further in one moment than the distance of ten journeys from Jerusalem to Bethlehem; every day and night they travel once around the earth and heaven.[13] Thus all stars move from east to west, and again from west to east. But this star, because it was moving with them, moved from Jerusalem to Bethlehem, moved from north to south. This clearly proves that this star differed from the stars in the heavens in nature, orbit, and position, and was not a fixed star, as the astronomers call them, but a movable star, able to rise and descend and turn in any direction.[14] The mouths of the star gazers are once again stopped; this star clearly had no special influence on the birth and life of Christ. It cannot have been as large as the stars in the heavens above, even though it seemed larger because of its proximity. In short, it was a servant of Christ and had no dominion or power over his birth.

Yet it is strange that the star should appear just when they had no further need of it and knew the town where the child was, while before it hid itself when they needed it and were ignorant of the place. This happened that their faith might be strengthened by a twofold witness, as is written in the law of Moses: All matters shall be determined on the evidence of two or three witnesses. So

---

[13] Cf. *Margarita philosophica*, I, 1 (*De principiis astronomiae*), esp. chaps. 19 and 27.

[14] *Ibid.*, chaps. 19–20.

these magi first of all heard the written word of the prophet at Jerusalem, as one witness to the birth of Christ. The star, the second witness, agrees with the prophet and points to the same birth so that they proceed with inner certainty. The prophet says no more than that Christ is in Bethlehem and similarly the star goes no further than to where the child was in Bethlehem, where it remained. That truly filled them with exceeding joy.

"And they went into the house and found the child with Mary his mother, and they fell down and worshipped him. Then opening their treasures, they offered him gifts, gold and frankincense and myrrh" [Matt. 2:11].

These magi were carefully prevented from finding Christ by their own efforts or with the aid of men. They found him solely because of the prophet, written word, and the star that shone from heaven, in order that all natural knowledge and all human reason might be rejected and every enlightenment repudiated except that which comes through the Spirit and grace. For human reason boasts and claims arrogantly to teach truth and show the proper way, just as the blind men in the universities, of whom we spoke earlier, at present claim to be able to do. Here is determined for all time that Christ, who is the truth that brings salvation, will not permit himself to be taught or found through the teachings or aid of men. The Scriptures alone and the light of God must show him, as he says, Matthew 16[:17]: "Blessed are you, Simon Bar-Jona. For flesh and blood has not revealed this to you, but my Father who is in heaven." In this way Christ clearly condemns flesh and blood and revelation through them, that is, men and all human reason, which certainly cannot reveal Christ and therefore are surely nothing but darkness. The universities, those schools of the devil, continue to rave and not only extol the natural light, but also establish it, claiming that it is good, useful, and necessary for knowledge of Christian truth. Therefore clearly no one but the devil himself invented universities, in order to destroy and darken the Christian truth, as has indeed happened, sad to say. Also, in John 6[:44] Christ says: "No one can come to me unless my Father draws him." In these words the presumption of our own reason and of all human reason, even as its ability to lead us aright, is condemned; all who follow it must of necessity go astray. God diligently and powerfully resists our natural pride everywhere; he wills us to recognize that we are blind and that we despair of our own light, giving only him our hand and letting him lead us on ways which reason can neither know nor follow.

Thus the magi teach us true faith. After they had heard the sermon and the word of the prophet they were neither slothful nor slow to believe. Note the obstructions and obstacles they faced: first, they were off the mark; they came to Jerusalem the capital, and did not find him; and in the meantime the star disappeared. Would we not expect that their thoughts, if guided by human reason, would have been as follows: "Alas, in vain we travelled so far; the star deceived us, it was a phantom. If a king had been born, we would easily have found him in the capital city, lying in the royal palace. But upon our arrival, the star disappears, and we find no one who knows of him. Should we foreigners be the first who speak of him in his own country and royal city? Ah, it must all be a mistake. Besides, the news frightens them; his own people do not like hearing it, show us the way out of the royal city and direct us to a tiny village. Who knows what we will find there! They behave so coldly and act so strangely; no one accompanies us to show us the child. They themselves do not believe that a king is born to them, and we come here and hope to find one? How desolate and confused everything appears for the birth of a king! If a young pup had been born, at least there would be some shouting. A king is supposed to have been born here, and yet everything is so quiet. Should not the people sing and dance, light lights and lamps, and decorate their streets with green branches and roses? What a poor king do we seek. We are fools for allowing ourselves to be so deceived and duped!"

Without a doubt these magi were partly still flesh and blood and harbored such kinds of thoughts and ideas within themselves, and their faith had to endure a sound and mighty struggle. Natural reason would in no way have survived this test; it would have opened its big mouth at once and puffed itself up upon failing to find the king where it expected him, and would have said: "The devil has led me here. What king can have been born here where everything is so quiet and dull? Why, there is more noise and shouting when a child is born to our shepherds; the cow that calves is better known than this king." See reason and human nature always act in this way; they never go beyond what they perceive, and when there is no perception, they immediately deny God and utter the words ascribed to them, Psalms 14[:1]: There is no God in this place; the devil must be here. Such is the light in our universities; it ought to point the way to God; alas, it points into the abyss of hell. The natural light of man and the light of grace cannot be friends. Human nature wants perception and certitude as a condition for faith. Grace wants faith prior to perception; that is why human nature will not proceed beyond its own light. Grace happily steps out into the darkness and follows nothing but the word and the Scriptures, no matter where or how it shines; it clings firmly to that word, whether it seems true or false to human nature.

Therefore because those dear magi battled and struggled to hold on to the word of the prophet, following it into such uninviting and confusing external circumstances of a royal birth, God met them and gave them strength through the star, which went before them and was indeed more kindly disposed to them than on the first occasion. Now they see it close at hand; it is their pilot; they are certain about all things and there is no need for queries. At the onset it had been far from them and they were uncertain where they would find the king. Such is always the experience of the Christian when he has successfully withstood trial and temptation. He feels that God is so wonderfully sweet and so close to him, clearly recognizable, that he not only forgets his anguish and affliction, but also desires and longs for more affliction and continues to grow in strength, so that he is no longer easily angered by the uncomely and despised life and manner of Christ. For he has tested and experienced that this is the way it must be: He who would find Christ must know that it will seem that he is destined to find nothing but shame. For the magi here would have felt ashamed if they in their failure had said openly, what they may well have secretly said in their hearts: "Ah, how well we have managed to reach our goal, let us journey some other time and seek new kings." That, I believe, really amounts to being led up the fool's path, as Dame Folly, human nature, is accustomed to do with every work and word of God. From the fact that they rejoiced so greatly when they saw the star, we can infer that these magi were sorely tried and depressed because of the uninviting circumstances they had found. Their joy indicates that it was not a small burden and displeasure which they carried in their hearts, and unbelief was a great temptation. For there was sufficient cause for that, if one considered human nature. So Christ rightly says in Matthew 11[:6]: "Blessed is he who takes no offence at me." Yes, blessed indeed; nevertheless the struggle is hard and close, for appearances do not indicate that Christ is there.

After the magi had passed through their trial and were newly born because of their great joy, they were strong and no longer offended by Christ; they had passed the test. For when they arrive at a poor hut and find there a poor young woman with a poor little child, they meet once again with appearances so utterly out of keeping with a king, that even their domestic servant is more honorable and more noble; they do not allow this to make them waver, but with a great, strong, and full faith they dismiss from their eyes and senses whatever human nature in its vanity might question and undermine, and follow the word of the prophet and the witness of the star in all purity of heart, take him to be a king, fall down on their knees, worship him, and give him gifts.

Ah, what a mighty faith that was, how many things it despised which would have moved human nature. How many here present who thought: Why, these are the greatest of fools who worship such a poor infant; surely they are under a spell if they make the infant a king! But here we have the kernel of the gospel which teaches us the manner and quality of faith, namely, that it is *argumentum non apparentium*, "the conviction of things not seen" [Heb. 11:1]. Faith simply clings to the mere word of God and follows things which it cannot see, except that they are indicated by that same word. Faith sees many other things besides, which challenge it as if the message of the word were empty and in vain. From whatever human nature recoils and describes as being led up the fool's path, that very thing faith describes as the right way and pushes on. Faith lets human nature be wise and clever and is willing to remain the fool and knave. In this manner faith comes to Christ and finds him; here the word of St. Paul, I Corinthians 1[:19

ff.], applies: The fools of God are wiser than men, and the weak people of God are stronger than men. Feeling and faith are not compatible with one another.

When, however, it is said that they gave three gifts and worshipped him, we should not understand this to mean that each of them singly gave something, but, as was said above[15] there was one common gift from the products of their country with which they confessed the child. The adoration, too, was not the same as worship of God. In my opinion they did not yet recognize him as God, but they acted in keeping with the custom mentioned in Scripture, according to which kings and important people were worshipped; this did not mean more than falling down before them at their feet and honoring them, in the same way as nowadays we bow, which is done without a word of mouth and expressed entirely by the bearing of the body.

What may have been their conversation with Mary and Joseph I leave to idle minds. The languages of the East are not so strange or far different from Hebrew, so they may have easily understood one another. They would have talked to Mary and Joseph in the same way as they talked to Herod and to the priests and citizens at Jerusalem. Even if they spoke a different language, the people would have been conversant with it because of their business connections and their knowledge of the area around the Red Sea, so that at all times both languages would have been known in both countries, just as in Germany, we find Italians and in Italy Germans. The one side of the Red Sea is entirely an Arabian kindgom from which these magi came.

"And in their sleep they received an answer from God not to return to Herod, so they went home to their country by another way" [Matt. 2:12].

Here we see that they who trust in God are under his special protection; for he watches over these magi so closely that he also cares for their journey home and informs them about it in their sleep. But why does he not permit them to return to Herod, for he could easily have protected the child against all violence even if Herod had received information and discovered the child? The

---

[15] Cf. above, p. 160.

reason for this is that we should learn not to tempt God; we should not despise what can reasonably be achieved with the aid of his created gifts. We should say: Yes, I will trust in God; it will surely take care of itself. Just as if you do not want to work and say: I will trust in God; whatever is meant to grow, will certainly grow. What is the use of the gifts of creation, if you will not make use of them? According to Genesis 1[:1 ff., 28], he created and ordained all things, each with its own works, and determined how man should use and work with them; he will never rescind that and ordained a special order for you. You may well ask how can I act rightly and trust in God and yet not tempt him? For you praise and preach nothing but faith; increasingly you praise it to the skies. To this I answer: The word of God is decisive for you; it determines when and how far you may believe. For it is the nature and essence of faith that it builds and relies on the word of God, and where there is no word of God there can and shall be no faith. Is that not a clear and precise statement? That is why the words of God in Scripture are referred to as testament, *testimonia, pacta, federa,* because they demand faith; he has never yet demanded faith in any of his works without a word. On the other hand, he has well confirmed his words with works and miracles, so that we might believe the words. That is what Christ also speaks in John 10[:38]: "Even though you do not believe me, believe the works." If then you have no word of God you must carry on and use your strength, your goods, your friends, and everything God has given you and remain within the ordinance instituted in Genesis 1[:28]. For he has not given this to you without a purpose and he will not change wine to water and bread to stones for your sake; rather you are to accept and use everything as he created it, until he forces you by his word to use it otherwise.

But when the hour and time are at hand in which the gifts of creation are no longer able to help and all your strength falls short, look to faith, for at that very moment God's word applies. God has commanded that we should let him be God, that is, look to him and trust in him for all good things. There is a word and text, valid at all times, but in time of need, when nothing can help us, its meaning is especially clear and applicable. It is the word he speaks in Psalm 50[:15]: "Call on me in the day of your trouble; I will help you and you shall praise me." This clearly shows that we cannot tempt God in time of trouble; for all his words and promises point to the time of trouble, when he alone is able to help. Thus we read in Matthew 4[:7] when the devil tempted Christ to let himself down from the temple, he said: It is written: You shall not tempt God, as if to say: I can very well go down by way of the steps, there is no need to seek signs and wonders. Likewise we read in the lives of the ancient fathers that two brothers were on a journey and the one died of hunger for God's sake (that is: he went to hell).[16] They met cruel people who gave them food, and one refused, saying, he would not take bread from those people, but wait for food from heaven. The other, however, took bread, ate, and survived. What else did that fool do but despise the ordained order of God in his creation and tempt him? No matter how wicked, people still are God's creatures, as much as are thistles and thorns. If a thorn can serve you to prick open an ulcer or in some other way, will you despise it because it comes from an evil prickly bush? We read that Abraham and Isaac gave away their wives and allowed them to be taken, so that God might not be tempted [Gen. 12:10 ff., 26:1 ff.]. They permitted what they could not prevent, and did all in their power. Therefore God also preserved them, so that no harm was done to them or their wives; yes, in fact, as a result of this he punished powerful kings. From this we learn that to tempt God except in time of need is to oppose God and is blasphemy.

Besides this form of temptation, there is another one which also occurs in time of trouble. It was sternly punished among the people of Israel and unfortunately, compared with the other, occurs commonly and is equally irrational. For the former kind of temptation occurs before we have God's word, the latter after we have the word of God. It occurs in this way: Even if we know that God has promised help in every time of trouble, we are not satisfied, and take up the matter and will not tarry or wait for the fulfillment of the promise, but prescribe and set the goal, the place, the time and the manner of his help. If he does not come in the way we expect and desire it, our faith lapses. In the former case faith is too long, in the latter it is too short; there, it is too early,

---

[16] Cf. *The Lives of the Fathers* (*De vitis patrum*), IV, 44 (*MPL* 73, 841).

here, it is too late; in both cases they fall away from the word. The former have faith without the word, which is not valid; the latter have the word without faith, which is of no avail. The middle way is good and blessed: to have both, word and faith together, united, even as God and man are one person in the one Christ. He who clings to nothing but the word and puts his trust in it and waits, never doubting that what the word says will surely come to pass, and sets no goal, determines no time, chooses no measure or manner, but freely resigns it to the will and pleasure of God and so honors his word to do its work when, how, where, and through whom he will: such is a free and right faith which does not and cannot tempt God. We must learn what it is to tempt God; we may easily recognize it, as it is truly a lack of authentic faith. Faith, above all, needs the word of God as the foundation and rock of faith. To tempt God is nothing else than to deal with God without his word, that is, to believe in something which he has not commanded us to believe in, and for which he has not determined a word. It is not to believe in that in which he has commanded us to believe, and for which he has determined a word. Now he has not commanded you to believe that he will feed you when you either have food with you or can find it without a miracle. But where you cannot find it, he has commanded that you should believe he will not leave you. But you must not determine time or manner for him. For it is his desire to be free; that is his right; and yet he will not forsake you, as is fitting for God. What more could you desire?

Such too, was the lot of Christ on this occasion; God could well have protected him against Herod's might, but because help was possible without any obvious need of miracles, he made use of his created gifts in an ordinary way, as an example for us, and led the magi home by another way. It would probably have cost him many an unnecessary miracle, if they had returned to Herod and informed him of the house in which they had found the child. But quite apart from this, this story has its own particular meaning, and about this more will now have to be said.

Concerning the Spiritual Meaning of This Gospel

The natural birth of Christ in every way signifies his spiritual birth, his birth in us and ours in him; concerning this Paul says in

Galatians 4[:19]: "Dear children, I am again in travail with you, until Christ is formed in you." For this birth two things are necessary, God's word and faith, and in these two the spiritual birth of Christ is fulfilled. Therefore the spiritual interpretation of this Gospel simply shows us the nature both of the word of God and of faith, how those do who are thus born, and the trials and struggles of faith.

First we note that Herod, the foreigner, was ruler over the people of God. Thereby God indicated what manner of government they exercised within themselves, in their souls. They had cast God aside so that he no longer reigned within them by faith. In every way they had become a Pharisaic, Sadducean, hypocritical people, torn apart by factions, and with doctrines of men and outward works they made righteousness and eternal life their own achievement. No faith was present, as is shown by the whole gospel and the life of Christ. In the same way as in their spiritual unbelief they had set Herod on the throne in place of Christ, so in an outward way they put up with a bodily Herod in place of the natural royal line of David, so that in two realms there was Herodian rule. In the Greek language the great people who are loudly acclaimed because of their deeds are called heroes, as for example, Hercules, Hector, Achilles, and others like them; in German they are called "giants," in Saxon "churls" from which the name Charles is derived. Therefore for us he is much the same as Heros or Herod for the Greeks; for Herod is derived from Heros and means churlish or manly, giantlike, famous for his deeds, such as a Dietrich of Berne, Hildebrand, or Roland, or whatever other name we might call these great murderers and devourers of people. They existed before the flood and Moses referred to them in Hebrew as *Niflim*, which means "those who fall," because they fall upon others and suppress them by force [cf. Gen. 6:4]. The people of Israel slew many of them in the Promised Land, such as Anak, Rephaim, Emim [Deut. 2:10–11]. Anak means "golden chain"; they were called the Anakim, because they were the aristocracy of the country and wore golden chains. Rephaim means "saviours," because they were thought to have the power of saving the land and its people. Emim means "the horrible, terrible ones," because they were feared. There always have been Herods, only in different ways and called by different names. So, too, Herods will be found among us before the Last Judgment; Christ will destroy them, when he comes again. Today these are known as pope, cardinal, bishop, priests, monks, spiritual lords, and holy fathers. They have to suffer the grave injustice that they carry the name of shepherds of the sheep of Christ, when in truth they are ravening wolves, who fleece and devour the people of Christ in body and soul and goods. They are the ultimate and mightiest churls, giants, devourers of people, and Herods, whom only Christ from heaven will destroy.

Christ and Herod are quite dissimilar and completely opposed to one another. For Christ's manner is not made manifest by large and great clamor and deeds; he is no giant, no hero's deeds are found here, only pure humility, in order that man may not think highly of himself, but be despised and let God alone be all things and do all things and have the glory. On the other hand it is the characteristic of a Herod to do big things, to be able to do all things, and to receive the applause, as if he were the one who lacks nothing. Since the Israelites were real Herods in their hearts and thought highly of themselves and their works, and sought public regard because of their seemingly good moral life, therefore the manner of Christ meant nothing to them. So God sent them a King Herod, who physically treated them in the same way as they treated souls spiritually. They cast out Christ and the godly life and so he cast out their royal house. Because he did not rule in their hearts, he also did not allow one of their own flesh and blood to rule over their bodies and goods; just as they killed and suppressed the people spiritually by their government and human doctrines, so he permitted them to be killed, suppressed, and martyred by Herod. Thus Herod in the flesh was a chastisement and a sign pointing to their own Herod in the spirit. As is the case with all sins, that we feel and hate the punishment, but like the sin and do not feel it, so also the Israelites very keenly felt Herod in the flesh and were hostile to him. But their spiritual Herod, their unbelieving, spiritual tyranny was precious and good in their eyes. Because of their Pharisaic and exclusive manner they arrogantly claimed much merit before God with their human doctrines and works of the law. Yet they did not see that thereby they deserved the rule of Herod which they were unable to shake off much as they would have liked to do so. On the contrary, they saw themselves as worthy, because of their great, spiritual, and holy life. Likewise we today feel our Herod keenly, the way he fleeces and throttles us in body and goods. But we cannot rid ourselves of him and there is no hope for us, because we are not good Christians and will not let Christ be our king with a pure and free faith; we prefer our own works and the spiritual government that now rules us. So we have to permit ourselves to be devoured and destroyed. We cannot prevent it. A physical and a spiritual Herod must equally rule us.

Let this then be our first basic notion: Herod signifies a government; not an ordinary government in the way in which secular lords rule, for Herod was himself a secular ruler. Therefore his government cannot signify itself, a secular realm, it must point to another, a spiritual realm. Thus this government cannot rule over secular people and goods, but it must rule over spiritual people and possessions, that is, conscience and all things that belong to our salvation, such as: good works, a good life, doctrine, the sacrament, and God's word. Further, the rule in this spiritual realm can be exercised in only two ways: either for salvation, when Christ alone governs, by pure faith and the true gospel; or for destruction, when a human being governs here by works and human doctrine—just as the people of Israel were at one time governed by their own kindred and their own kings, and at another time by Herod, a foreign king. Herod cannot signify anything other than a spiritual government which does not rule people by faith and the gospel, but by works and human doctrines; yet it has the name and appearance of showing the way to heaven and teaching people what is right, when, in fact, it is none other than the gate and wide road to hell. In short, Herod is the pope and his spiritual realm. For here is no faith, no gospel, nothing but doctrines of men and works, and yet there is a real, mighty Herodian power and noise. Consciences want to and may be led, fed, and kept by God's word alone; so he leads and feeds them with his own snot and slobber, with indulgences and religious orders, with celebration of masses and prayers, with fasting and the like. So we have here in the one person a mighty giant, a saviour, and a churl. They say that the Christian church is preserved by this government; that it would otherwise be overwhelmed in the floods, if faith alone and Christ should rule. Hence it is as the peasants say: Cuntz Hildebrand, the great whale, carries the world on his tail;[17] in other words, if the pope were not actively present with his realm, God would be far too weak, and the world's orb would assuredly glide out of his hand and neither faith nor the gospel could avail. But the pope comes to his aid and lays the foundation with so many tonsures, caps, cords, wooden shoes, bishops' and cardinals' hats, peal of organs and smoke of incense, ringing of bells and snuffing of candles, bawling in the church and rumbling of bellies, especially of those who fast and abstain from milk, eggs, meat and the like, in which the pope's holiness consists; and so everything is sustained. If such spiritual, orderly, holy government were done away with (may the pope forbid!) what would become of the world? This then, is what Herod and Christ are: two spiritual realms, one unbelieving, the other believing.

What is the star? It is none other than the new light, preaching and the gospel, oral and public preaching. Christ has two witnesses to his birth and his realm. The one is Scripture, the word comprehended in the letters of the alphabet. The other is the voice or the words proclaimed by mouth. St. Paul and St. Peter call this same word a light and a lamp [II Cor. 4:4, II Pet. 1:19]. We cannot understand Scripture unless the light shines. For by the gospel the prophets are illuminated, so that star must rise first and be seen. In the New Testament, preaching must be done orally and publicly, with the living voice, to produce in speech and hearing what prior to this lay hidden in the letter and in secret vision. For the New Testament is nothing but an uncovering and a revelation of the Old Testament, as is shown in Revelation 5[:3 ff.], where the Lamb of God opens the book with the seven seals. We also see this in the preaching of the apostles. All their preaching was simply setting forth Scripture and building on it. That is why Christ did not write his doctrine himself, as Moses did his, but transmitted it orally, and also commanded that it should be orally continued giving no command that it should be written. Likewise the apostles wrote little,

---

17 The German *Cuntz Hildebrand* is a corruption of *concelebrant*. The *concelebrant* is the assistant at the celebration of the mass. The name was also used by the common people for the legendary fish which, like Leviathan, surrounds or carries the earth. Cf. WA 10I, 1, 624, n. 2 and LW 13, 56.

and not all of them at that, but only Peter, Paul, John, and Matthew. From the hand of the other apostles we have nothing except James and Jude, and many do not consider them apostolic writings. Those who did write, do no more than point us to the old Scripture, just as the angel pointed the shepherds to the manger and the swaddling clothes, and the star pointed the magi to Bethlehem. So it is not at all in keeping with the New Testament to write books on Christian doctrine. Rather in all places there should be fine, goodly, learned, spiritual, diligent preachers without books, who extract the living word from the old Scripture and unceasingly inculcate it into the people, just as the apostles did. For before they wrote, they first of all preached to the people by word of mouth and converted them, and this was their real apostolic and New Testament work. That is the right star which points to Christ's birth and the angelic message which tells of the swaddling clothes and the crib.

However, the need to write books was a serious decline and a lack of the Spirit which necessity forced upon us; it is not the manner of the New Testament. For when heretics, false teachers, and all manner of errors arose in the place of pious preachers giving the flock of Christ poison as pasture, then every last thing that could and needed to be done, had to be attempted, so that at least some sheep might be saved from the wolves. So they began to write in order to lead the flock of Christ as much as possible by Scripture into Scripture. They wanted to ensure that the sheep could feed themselves and hence protect themselves against the wolves, if their shepherds failed to feed them or were in danger of becoming wolves too. Therefore St. Luke says in his preface that he was moved to write his Gospel because of some who had dared to write the story of Christ, doubtless because he saw that they did not manage it too well [Luke 1:1–4]. Similarly the epistles of St. Paul make the point that the purpose of his writing is to preserve what he at first preached; without a doubt he preached far more fully than he wrote. If wishing could help, we could wish nothing better than that all books might simply be abolished and nothing but the pure, simple Scripture or Bible remain throughout the world, especially among Christians. There is more than enough in it about all manner of knowledge and doctrine which is useful and necessary for a person to know. But wishing is in vain now; would to God there were few books besides Scripture.

Let it suffice for the present that this star signifies oral preaching and the bright revelation of Christ, which shows him as hidden and promised in Scripture. Therefore whoever sees the star will assuredly recognize the King of the Jews, the newborn Christ. For the gospel teaches nothing but Christ, and therefore Scripture contains nothing but Christ. Whoever fails to recognize Christ may hear the gospel or he may indeed carry the book in his hand, but he lacks understanding, for to have the gospel without understanding, is to have no gospel at all. And to possess Scripture without knowing Christ, is to have no Scripture, which is nothing else than to let this star shine, and to fail to see it.

Such happens to these Herodists and to those who dwelt in Jerusalem: the star is above their country and above their heads, and they fail to see it. Similarly when the gospel arose over the Israelites as Isaiah writes in the Epistle [Isa. 60:1], they let it shine and yet did not recognize it. St. Paul speaks of this in II Corinthians 4[:3–4]: "If our gospel is veiled, it is veiled only to those who perish, among whom the god of this world (that is, the devil) blinds the hearts of the unbelievers, so that the light of the clear gospel of Christ may not shine in them." From which we clearly see that unbelief alone is the reason for a blindness which fails to see the gospel, even though it shines and is preached without ceasing. For it is impossible that Christ and his gospel should be recognized by reason; faith alone is recognition here, and the seeing of the star signifies that same faith. These magi signify, and in fact are, the first fruits of heathendom, converted to faith by the gospel. For the magi and Gentiles were people who lived their lives according to reason and did not have the law and the prophets like the Israelites, but went their way according to the laws of nature without the law and word of God.

The masters of natural knowledge, like these magi, generally deviate from their accepted path and change natural knowledge into sorcery and magic formulas, as was pointed out above. Where human nature is left to go its own way and receives no help from the doctrines of God, it will certainly deviate from the right path and of itself fall into sheer error and blindness and become a veritable sorceress full of all manner of superstition. St. Paul, in Romans 2[:14–15], says that although the Gentiles did not receive the law of God, they do have the natural law of the conscience and so they do the works of the natural law which they find written in their hearts. But just as they were far away from the law and without the law of God, so also they came sooner and much closer to the gospel than the Israelites. The reason is this: the Israelites had the law and relied on it, thinking that by works they satisfied its demands. They despised the gospel as something which they did not need and which was false because it damned the works in which they gloried and praised faith alone. The Gentiles had no need for such inflated self-importance, because they were without the law. Therefore they easily came to the gospel; they realized its worth and their own need.

The coming of the magi to Jerusalem and their quest for the new king signifies nothing else than that the Gentiles are enlightened by the gospel and come into the Christian church to seek Christ. Jerusalem prefigures the Christian church and is its birthplace. Here God's people are gathered together. In German, Jerusalem means a vision of peace, because peace is found in the Christian church; a good conscience and a calm assurance of the heart are the possession of all who are in the Christian church and are good Christians by the grace of God through the forgiveness of sins. But now Herod the devourer of people rules and continually seeks to rule in this peaceful place. For all men, especially those who teach merit by works carry within themselves the sickness that by their nature they seduce, destroy, and suppress the true Jerusalem, take captive good consciences and pious simple hearts, teach people to trust in works and in themselves, so that faith dies, peace and the good conscience are destroyed, and a Herod's dominion remains, a great external show with noise and works, which actually is without solid foundation. Precisely that is the point this text of the evangelist wants to make, when he says that Christ was born at the time of Herod and was sought in the very city where Herod himself ruled. For the truth of the gospel is locked in battle with Herod's holiness, and whenever it comes to us it discovers Herodists who rule among the people with doctrines of men and works. And it comes to condemn them, and it teaches us the pure grace of God instead of works, pure faith instead of the law, and saves God's people in Jerusalem from the rule of Herod.

Herod, hearing this, is troubled and all Jerusalem with him. Why? Herod fears the other man who is the true king, because he himself wants to be king alone, by force. This fear is realized when the Gentiles are led by the gospel to praise Christ and faith in opposition to works and the doctrines of men. Then the Israelites became angry, for they clearly saw the outcome. Their religion would be regarded as worthless and the seeming splendor of their traffic in works and doctrines would be set entirely at nought. They were not prepared to suffer that and began to rave, as the history of the apostles in Acts clearly shows. Their superiority, honor and wealth, which they derived in abundance from the reign of their Herodian hierarchy, would receive a powerful blow, inasmuch as works and doctrines of men always bring much revenue and many possessions. On the other hand, the doctrine of God and the work of Christ bring with them a cross, poverty and shame and much calamity which the Herodian holiness cannot endure. Hence those who have imprisoned and suppressed poor folk with erring consciences and doctrines of men, do not like to hear that poor, miserable consciences are receiving a right understanding and instruction and are looking only to the pure word of God and faith, and are spreading the news that having seen his star, they want a new king. For pope and bishop, holy fathers and spiritual lords could not well fill their bellies with that new insight. Therefore, their Herodian dominion does not consider it opportune or useful that the magi, the unlearned, and the laity, who must remain ignorant, should begin to speak of the light of the gospel; without any regard for the spiritual pomp surrounding them, they demand an essentially new manner of life in the midst of Jerusalem. That must frighten Herod and his servants, for his purse and his belly are at stake. Indeed, like him, all Jerusalem receives a shock. For although many just people are enemies of the Herodian rule and wish it did not exist, they nevertheless fear that the truth could come to light at an inopportune time, leading to a rebellion and misguided action in the world, so that hands are laid on a realm which in all probability could not be overwhelmed without causing considerable chaos. So they think it advisable to withhold the truth for a time or to present it in such a way that Herod will not be frightened or be incited to cause greater damage. But the magi show no concern for his fear or anger, and in Jerusalem speak openly of the star and the new king. They are not troubled that the heavens might fall. For we must not deny or fail the gospel because of any person; it is God's word, and Herod must give way to it and obey it. If he rages, let him rage; Christ will yet continue to be his lord.

But observe that at first Herod does not plan to deal with the new king by force, only by cunning. He convenes the scholars and diligently searches in the Scriptures, as if he really wanted to know the truth. And all the while he intends that not Scripture but his will and schemes shall triumph and be fulfilled. So here we come upon Herod's character. We see the pope and his followers truly portrayed. But to prevent anyone from being offended by my application of all this to the pope and the comparison of the ecclesiastical estate above all others with Herod, I want to submit the following as my reason for doing so. It is a matter of Christian duty and loyalty which I owe and must show to everyone because my conscience compels me; but I do not compel anyone to believe me. If truth and experience do not prove everything I say as true, then anyone whom it pleases may call me a liar; I at least want to satisfy my duty of brotherly love and to stand excused before God. If anyone rejects my faithful warning, he must answer for that; I at any rate have told him that Christ and his doctrine will not and cannot be compatible with the pope and his ecclesiastical estate. Therefore everyone must be on his guard against him, as against his eternal destruction, and must cling to Christ alone; if that does not bring much to the pope by way of possessions or honor, it is none of my concern. My task is to preach Christ, not the possessions and honor of the pope or the clerics. And what has been said of the pope and the clerics applies to all those who oppress the people with works and doctrines instead of proclaiming pure faith, the pure Scripture, the one and only Christ, as the Israelites also did, but, compared with the pope and his servants, in a far lesser degree. He who will allow himself to be led astray, has heard my thought. I am innocent of his blood and destruction.

Herod's convening the rulers from among the priests and the

scribes of the people, searching for information about the birth of Christ, is the same as is done by our ecclesiastical rule and the unbelieving teachers of works. They want to have Scripture on their side and what they teach must be in Scripture, but in such a way that their own opinion has priority; Scripture must be twisted to fall in line with them. For their intention in using Scripture is merely to suppress the truth and to confirm their own actions, just as Herod searched the Scripture only to kill Christ. Herod does the same through his Herodist, the pope, who searches Scripture and uses it, but understands its meaning in such a way as to enable him to destroy the right sense and read his own understanding into it. Even the elect are seduced by such pretence. No greater pretence frightens and deceives every conscience than that which sets forth the name of God and claims to seek and obey nothing but divine Scripture and God's word, while in actual fact the exact opposite is intended, namely, to suppress Scripture with all its contents. Therefore these magi do not see the star in Jerusalem and do not know where they should go. All who come to such fine and flittering men lose their way and the proper Christian understanding, because of the dazzling show of greatness among the unbelieving saints, until they grasp the pure Scripture rightly and fully, just as here both Herod and the magi received the Scripture from the priests, Herod, however, with a false and wicked intention. The magi received it with a right and good intention and so their sight is restored and they see the star again and are rescued from the Herodian hypocrisy which was to blame for their loss of the star. Hence what took place between Herod and the magi signifies the struggle which takes place between the true and false saints concerning Scripture. The true saints may err slightly and lose the true light for a little while, but not for long. In the end they grasp the true sense of Scripture, return to the clear light and let the Herodists glory in their false understanding of Scripture.

St. Paul spoke of this in II Timothy 3[:1–9]: "the last day will be dangerous, for men will come who will be lovers of self, misers, proud, arrogant, blasphemers, disobedient to their parents, ungrateful, unholy, inhuman, dissocial, slanderers, profligates, fierce, indifferent to good works, treacherous, reckless, swollen with conceit, blind, lovers of pleasure rather than lovers of God, who hold the form of a godly life but deny its power. Beware of such people! For among them are those who make their way into houses and take captive weak women who are burdened with sins and are easily swayed by various impulses, always learning and never arriving at a knowledge of the truth. As Jannes and Jambres opposed Moses,[18] so these men also oppose the truth, men of corrupt mind and incapable of faith; but they will not last the distance because their folly will be plain to all, as was that of those two men," etc. It seems to me that here St. Paul did not mince words but, as it were, pointed at our ecclesiastical lords and Herod's holy servants. To the very last letter of the text, everyone can see a patent and powerful application to the ecclesiastical estate. But they have a hard skull and think that nothing here refers to them; they opine that they are wronged if one applies this to them, because the pope supports and confirms them with his parchments and leaden seals.

So we must consider and examine this rich word of Paul a little, that we may truly recognize Herod. Paul says that people will come in the last days, which have been with us for many years already; those days will be dangerous, since few will be saved because of the corrupters who with human doctrines and their own babble destroy faith and strangle souls. We should not understand the apostle as speaking of the simple people whom we now refer to as the secular class or laity. On the contrary, his words are clear and force us to apply them to the persons with tonsure and cap, the ecclesiastical estate. Among their other noble virtues, the apostle candidly mentions the one that is eminent: they follow the form of a godly life or religion but fall short in their deeds. Who does not know who they are? Where are spiritual life, worship, and holy orders, except in religious institutions and monasteries? Likewise, when the apostle says that they maneuver their way through houses and take women captive and continuously teach them, this clearly is applicable to the teachers and preachers, in particular to the mendicant friars and vagabond monks. And the statement that they oppose the truth as Jannes and Jambres opposed Moses shows sufficiently that he speaks of those who preach and rule among the people. Let us examine each point in turn.

---

[18] Jannes and Jambres were the legendary Egyptian magicians who opposed Moses and Aaron and tried to discredit them; cf. Exod. 7:11–12, 22.

First of all we have the *Philauti,* those who are lovers of self, who are pleased with themselves; they claim that everything they do is done well and correctly. They consider heaven their exclusive privilege; they alone have identified the right way of life; they alone constitute the Christian church; they alone sustain heaven and earth. Compared with them, all other people are poor sinners, in a perilous condition, who must purchase from them intercessions, good works, and merit. They have brought it about that all other Christians are referred to as secular, but they are spiritual; one can hardly find words to express how this label tickles their fancy and how they consider themselves to be superior to all the other classes. Indeed no people has been found on earth to whom the name *Philauti* applies more nearly than to these; the apostle has hit the mark very well. Especially, their chief lord, the pope, stinks of pure self-conceit and self-esteem throughout the world, even they have to confess that his spiritual claims are nothing but *philautia,* nothing but pure self-esteem. God help us, how highly this abomination thinks of himself, how well he loves his position, how arrogantly he makes a distinction between himself and other Christians, not only the secular, but also the spiritual; he does nothing but tickle himself and virtually laughs himself sick out of sheer devilment. Anyone who examines his life, his dominion, his bulls, his laws and teaching, has to admit openly that this is true. Then the others, each in his own position, draw this poison from him; he helps them with privileges and immunities, with benediction and praise. The laity in turn learn it from them, each with his own fine little prayer and in his own special way. As a result the Christian faith perishes. For it takes pleasure in and praises Christ alone, and considers all other beings as equal, giving none a special priority over the other.

Second, they are proud; that follows from the first. Because they esteem themselves highly and in their minds rank themselves above all others, they think themselves better than everyone. This may be seen abundantly in the pope and clerics, indeed in such extreme fashion, that they themselves quite unashamedly say and boast that the ecclesiastical estate is better than the secular one, even though there are Christians in the latter and the Christian estate alone is good and tolerates such a distinction only at the cost

213

of its own existence. Truly, this poisonous pride is the foundation for their entire rule. For if they were not accorded a higher status, their whole power and dominion would collapse. These two great horrible and radical vices are so subtle and so completely spiritual, that they are not able to catch even a glimpse of them; indeed, they consider them to be the truth and thoroughly right, and so they cheerfully proceed in their devilish holy life and expect others to call them holy, spiritual, and blessed, indeed to honor them for such terrible vices.

Third, they are arrogant. This follows from the previous vice, pride. After all pride is not satisfied with exalting itself in its own eyes. It breaks out and wants to soar to heights that are equal to its lofty opinion of itself; it wants to have pre-eminence; it looks for pride of place, and determines its outer bearing in keeping with its inner self-understanding. For pride and arrogance may be distinguished in this way: Pride resides in the heart, arrogance is the outer, overbearing manner and attitude. Who does not observe this in the pope and in the entire spiritual estate? Do they not, in fact, ride roughshod over the emperor, over kings and princes, and over everything small or large on earth? They set themselves over the possessions, the body, and the soul of all men and rule with an arbitrary outrageous power as if they had the best right and reason. If one tells them that Christ forbade such arrogance by saying to his disciples: "He who would be the greatest among you, let him be as the smallest" [cf. Matthew 20:26], "You shall not rule as do the princes among the heathens" [cf. Matthew 20:25], then they take the sting out of this text and give us an interpretation which of course only they are entitled to offer, which says: Here Christ has not forbidden positions of authority and a superiority over others; he prohibits the inner attitude of heart which would exalt itself and esteem itself more highly than others. They tell us that there may very well be a prelate who is humble and does not exalt himself above others in his heart, even though outwardly he must move in high places. In support of this interpretation they cite words from the sacred fathers with which, however, they merely blind and fool themselves and everyone else. The apostle is speaking here of outward arrogance knowing full well that he who has to teach others and have authority over them must be a spiritual

214

superior. But they turn the external into the internal, make spiritual what is physical for they want to have pre-eminence; their possessions, their honor, their manner, their person, their affairs, their rights, their power must be over all possession, honor, persons, affairs, and dominions. That is their aim and towards it, these dear noble masters of ours move. They turn material possessions, honor, persons, manners, clothes, etc., into spiritual things before our very eyes. While on earth, Christ was also spiritually superior to everyone, for he taught everyone as a teacher and master. Nevertheless he never put his person above that of any man; on the contrary, he served others with all his might and to the utmost of his ability. The prophets and apostles also were without a doubt spiritually superior to everyone on earth, for they were lights in the world and teachers. But when did a single one of them ever put his person, his possessions, his affairs above those of any man, let alone above those of any king or prince? The opposite was the case. They were subject to them in their body and with their possessions, and also commanded the people to be subject to them, even as Christ was subject to caesar, Matthew 17[:27]. Dear Herodists, we cannot see the spiritual dominion, nor does it exercise rule over possessions or persons, but it rules over souls and spirits by the word of God. You, however, make of it a dominion of this world, and call it spiritual, merely to cover up and adorn your accursed arrogance when you say you may not be a subject, need not pay interest, tolls, or taxes, are exempt from every duty, and all this in order that you may be greedy and rob.

I forgot and overlooked that I should have included the love of money in my second section; so I must say something about it now and make this the fourth section. This vice is so crass in the case of the pope and in the ecclesiastical estate that sticks and stones cry out to heaven. But this is nothing in comparison with what few people see, namely, that the ecclesiastical estate rests almost entirely on usury, because of the accursed and damned *Zinskauf*[19] which the pope has instituted as support and patron of avarice and with which he manifestly devours the world. Also

---

[19] Luther dealt with *Zinskauf* in his *Long Sermon on Usury* (1520), WA 6, 36–60. This *Long Sermon* was incorporated into a larger treatise, *Trade and Usury*, in 1524; see LW 45, 245–310. The section on *Zinskauf*, dating from 1520, is in LW 45, 273–308. For a definition of *Zinskauf* see LW 45, 235–37.

hardly one of a thousand is aware of the secret avarice which is rampant among them, namely, that they join the ecclesiastical estate for the sake of physical nourishment and care. Truth invented the proverb: Despair makes a monk. Who knows the number of those who enter holy orders simply because they are afraid they might not be able to feed themselves or might have to do it with labor and toil. Even now some become bishops and canons for that reason. What is this but avarice which will not trust that God who created us can also feed us? Some join the ecclesiastical estate because they despair of attaining eternal life in any other way. These, however, are the smaller group; besides, their reasons are not good and hence also not convincing.

Fifth, they are blasphemers. This vice is bound to follow the previous virtues. If their pride, arrogance, avarice, and self-conceit are to be preserved and to continue, they must assuredly equip themselves with armor to ward off those who condemn all this with the words of Scripture, as it should be condemned, since it is incompatible with Scripture. For that reason the pope must issue bulls and laws and must curse, damn, condemn, and ban all who attack his rule. He must declare it to be the word of the devil and not of God that opposes his holiness and his clerics, which should be avoided like the worst heresy. In II Peter 2[:2], St. Peter prophesied that such people would revile the way of truth and say that it is all for the sake of God's glory and spiritual goods, and that his faction, his Herodian servants, would adhere to him and spread such curses and slander in every region over which their avarice and pride and arrogance hold sway, so that the world would be submerged with blasphemy and curses. O God, heavenly Father, how awful is thy anger, how terrible thy judgments against the world in these dangerous and miserable times; no one, alas, is ready to acknowledge it. Surely thou hast not created all men in vain?

Sixth, they are disobedient to parents. Next to obedience to himself, God has commanded us to obey our parents, before and above all else. But what do the pope and his ecclesiastical dominion teach? If a father has a son who is a priest or a bishop, he has reared a lord over himself, in no way bound to be obedient to him, because of the great worthiness of the all-holy Herodian ecclesiastical estate. For that reason people today live free and permissive lives, as we can observe. God's commandment that we should obey parents is torn to shreds, as they claim that they are bound to God and to a higher obedience, even though God has not given a single command concerning their estate. Of their own accord they chose to enter it. Now God does not abrogate his commandments for his own sake, far less for the sake of man's choices and preferences. The monasteries have also been caught up in the fashion to do away with this commandment. If a son or daughter runs away from his or her father and enters the monastery without permission, the most holy father, the pope, and his Herodists, judge that this is a right, goodly deed and so they virtually compel people to tear God's commandments to shreds in order to serve God. Hence the whole ecclesiastical estate is entirely free from obedience to this highest and first of God's Commandments of the Second Table.

If, however, you decide to follow me, let me give you advice out of the fullness of my spirit and in the name of our Lord Jesus Christ: If your child enters the ecclesiastical estate, whether as priest, monk, or nun, you may, if you please, grant your permission afterwards, and let the disobedience pass. But if you refuse permission, troubled perhaps that your child will not be able to observe the rule of chastity because of weakness, or may otherwise lapse into a perverse and licentious life, or may possibly put on a false show of piety, or if you need your child, then do not engage in long disputes, but take courage and remove your child from that monastery, out of habit, out of tonsure, and out of whatever else is worn. Do not be concerned even if a hundred thousand vows were made and all bishops gathered to give their blessing. God entrusted your child to you to be subject to you and will call you to account if you allow your child to be destroyed when you might have given help and good advice. If they say anything to you, show them God's commandment that children are to obey their parents, especially when parents are concerned about danger and are not prepared to grant permission. There is even a paragraph in the pope's law which grants a wife the right, without hindrance, to withdraw her husband from a monastery or the priesthood. Now the Fourth Commandment that we should obey our parents in

217

those matters which are not against the will of God, has always been as much a divine commandment as the commandment that husband and wife may not be divorced. So I say: It is sheer blasphemy when the pope deprives parents of the right to remove monks and nuns from the monasteries; he has no authority for this. Parents do and they may leave their children or take them out, when and how they please, according to what in their judgment is best for their children.

But if the Herodists declare that in this case obedience to parents is no longer necessary, because the First Commandment commands service to God in precedence over the Fourth Commandment, then take courage in hand and answer: service to God is not identical with the ecclesiastical estate. He has not commanded this anywhere; therefore they lie and what they call service to God is their own little invention. Service to God is simply obeying his commandments. His commandments in the First Table demand faith, and love of God. They who become clerics do not thereby walk in faith and in love of God, but they adopt an external and peculiar way of life in which there is less of love and faith than in any married or secular estate.

Unfortunately, however, many people are pleased when their children join the ecclesiastical estate, for they do not see the dangers that lurk within it. Some even vow that their children will enter the ecclesiastical estate. All this is nothing but ignorance about faith and the Christian estate. If parents should command something against God's commandment and against faith and love of the neighbor, we ought not to obey them; here Christ's word applies: "He who loves father and mother more than me, is not worthy of me" [Matt. 10:37]. But apart from this, the commandment of obedience must retain its validity. However, parents may, and indeed should, be ready to grant permission and to yield to persuasion where this is possible and beneficial for the soul of the child.

In this connection another point arises which is also of importance, namely, the matter of child marriages. Of course no one is so foolish as to compel his child to marry, and he should not do so. But if it does happen, a child should place obedience above virginity, or else ask the father to release it from the need of obedience.

Likewise a child should not be compelled to take a particular marriage partner; marriage should be arranged subject to the child's willingness, as was done with Rebecca, Genesis 24[:57]. But if obedience is, after all, the decisive factor, then, in my opinion, it must be done. The question arises whether a father has the authority to tear apart a marriage when his child was betrothed without or against his will. The pope answers negatively and releases the child from obeying the father. My opinion is different. I do not release the child from obedience to its father; I also think no person has the right to grant such a release before cohabitation has taken place. If there was cohabitation, or there is a pregnancy, or they like being together, it is inhuman if a father intervenes to separate and tear them apart, even though he has the authority. However great his authority, he is nevertheless in duty bound to show love and kindness, to bend a little for the sake of his child whose wishes he should take into account, lest he separate them out of sheer arbitrariness and rebellion. For parents, too, at times are inclined to look more to their own arbitrary will than to the advancement and need of the child. Even though a child must accept it, it is not right of the father to act in such a way, for he is in duty bound to be kind to his child, to help it to the best of his ability, and to exercise his authority for its well-being, just as Manoah and his wife permitted their son Samson to plead with them to get him a woman as wife who pleased him but not his parents, Judges 14[:3]. But if the girl is secretly engaged and her father or guardian has given her to another man, she should reject the pope's bonds that tie her and, without burdening of her conscience, renounce the first husband and go with the second. The pope has authority neither to act against God's commandments nor to confirm the first betrothal as valid and to tear apart the second. By doing so he confuses consciences and pronounces such a girl to be an adulteress if she lies with the second man; yet he compels her to go to this man and tells her she must suffer it, not lying with him willingly, and not demand her conjugal rights. Oh, you murderer of souls, how you comfort consciences, how you confuse one thing with another, leaving no room for salvation and causing our times to be so dangerous. If, however, the girl is able to get her parents' consent to stay with the first man because she desires him greatly, then she may indeed do so; otherwise obedience must have precedence and demands that conjugal obligations be fulfilled and acts as if she had never been betrothed. With this rule and custom, all secret betrothals would have disappeared long ago and the great and false bonds of papal law that bind consciences would never have been devised.

I think you will be able to appreciate the depth of St. Paul's insight into an ecclesiastical dominion which teaches children to be disobedient to their parents, allows them the choice between the secular or ecclesiastical estate, and encourages them to remain in that estate without parental consent after they have made their own voluntary choice. In this way God's commandment which requires obedience has been completely abrogated and torn to pieces; at the same time consciences have been so sadly confused that they no longer know what to do. In the same way they teach disobedience to parents and emancipation from God's commandments by their spiritual holiness, so they also teach young secular people to act in the matter of matrimony. But a pious child should learn to honor its parents, to be pleased with all their plans, and gladly to accept them, provided they are not against the commandments of God. And even if it could raise the dead or heaven stood open before it, a child should engage in none of these things knowing that this was against the parents' wish. For whoever obeys parents will also obey God who commands us that we ought to obey our parents. Therefore a child should gladly allow to be nullified whatever is done in disobedience to parents, provided it is not demanded by God, no matter how good it is, or how much it is service of God. God can have no pleasure in anything that is done against the will of parents, provided the parents do not make demands that oppose the will of God. Hence God speaks to parents in Jeremiah 29[:6]: "Take wives for your children, and give your daughters to men," etc., so that the children may not act independently but that the parents may have the authority to give them away themselves. There is probably more I could say about it, but I consider it sufficient for this time.

Seventh, they are ungrateful, not only to God, which necessarily follows when they blaspheme his word and destroy his commandments, but also to men. They receive great possessions and honor from the princes and the whole world, even as all of their sweet life is the fruit of the sweat and blood of others. Yet in no way do they acknowledge this. Thus, when a town or country was threatened by ruin, they would not make a single contribution or offer help from the abundance of their riches and treasures. They know nothing but: into my money bag! In addition, if their dues and possessions are diminished or interfered with, they know no mercy, but excommunicate, exert pressures, and inflict torture. Not one of them says to himself: Very well, we have received these possessions and our abundance of riches from this and that family, or country, and because they have now fallen into decline and ruin, we will requite them with love and give them a helping hand. Rather what they say is this: These are ecclesiastical possessions, they cannot be used to help secular people. Indeed, they regard it as the greatest of all vices if they should show such gratefulness. They say that he who acts in such a way is squandering the possessions of the religious foundation, of the monastery, of the holy church. In other words, Christian love and natural gratefulness must disappear so that the possessions of the church may remain intact. Nonetheless they are the holy and spiritual people who alone will go to heaven—as likely as the cow into the mouse hole.

Eighth, they have no regard for holy things. The apostle here does them considerable injustice when he calls them *anosios*. *Osios* means, "that which is set apart, holy, spiritual; those who have the duty to deal with sacred things and have been ordained for this purpose," just as by consecration men become spiritual or holy men. *Anosios* means, "not set apart, unspiritual." But surely that is a blaspheming apostle who in straightforward, unadorned language calls consecrated men unconsecrated. Why, they have tonsures, are anointed with oil, have white gowns, celebrate mass, sing with a high voice and read with a low voice, play organs and pipes, ring and tinkle bells, consecrate churches and chapels, burn incense and sprinkle water, wear the cross and carry banners, and clothe themselves in silk and velvet. And what is most important: they carry the golden chalice and the silver monstrance. If these things are not holy and spiritual, what is? Accordingly, pope and bishops must be wrong. Surely St. Paul is under the pope's ban, for his words contradict sacred canon law which considers only such

221

spiritual matters as were just mentioned. No cow, ass, or swine is so completely stupid as not to realize that these are physical and external things which make no one spiritual or holy; but in this Herodian realm these things must all be called spiritual and consecrated. Hence St. Paul rightly calls them the unspiritual clerics because of such unspiritual spiritual behavior. Furthermore, they neglect the true spiritual things. Paul's eye penetrated their falseness; he saw how these men in holy orders puff themselves up, and so he changed their name into its opposite, as if he wanted to say: they claim to be the spiritual estate and say that they are handling spiritual things; but they are actually unspiritual, and are engaged in foolishness and neglect the things that are truly spiritual. For he is *osios* or spiritual who works with and offers God's word and the sacraments, so that he might lead himself and his people to God; that actually is the spiritual office. But they do neither of these things, and through their abuses of the sacraments, especially of the mass, they lead everyone, including themselves, farther away from God. They preach no gospel and perform no spiritual office properly. Much could be said about this. The apostle has included in this word everything that concerns their true office from which they take their name and says: they do none of these things, and so they are rather the unspiritual estate.

Ninth, they are merciless. They love no one with their heart, that is, they befriend no one. They let everyone fare as he will and go where he pleases; if they themselves have enough, they are satisfied. I just said that the task of the spiritual office is to wait on people in spiritual matters. But they must also see to it that no one suffers bodily need because of poverty. Now it is evident to all, that no one on earth is less concerned about people, or cares for them less, than the ecclesiastical estate. This is the result of the vices that were previously mentioned: greed, ungratefulness, and unspiritual life. They are a people bent upon their own advantage and gain in secular and spiritual things, unless, of course, someone would care to speak of kindness and concern when the pope and his servants shed much Christian blood, drive the whole world into war, and suck dry and milk and skin the world with indulgences and wickedness. It is a particularly fine virtue in rulers if they show sympathetic concern for their subjects and take to heart their problems and needs in secular matters. It is an even finer virtue when those in holy office act in such a fashion in spiritual matters, as indeed they should if they were *osii*. As things are, they are *anosii* and *astorgi*, that is, they are both unholy and inhuman.

Tenth, they are antisocial, devoid of all social commitment. With that remark St. Paul surely rushed headlong against the wall of the sacred canon law which teaches so much about privileges, liberties, and exemptions. He hits the very core of the holy *scrinium pectoris* at Rome.[20] Both nature and God's ordinances teach that since people have to live together as a community, they must pool their interests and carry common burdens on a common back, undertake common work with common hands; in this way they are bound together by the common needs of a common life. Contrary to this, the pope and canon law uphold *privilegia, libertates, immunitates, indulta, gratias,* and obvious exemptions, and he and his servants avail themselves of the advantages of the goods, but let others undertake the common work and shoulder the common burdens. They would consider it the greatest sin if someone wanted to obey St. Paul, give up the *privilegia*, and bear with the community the burdens and responsibilities, even though they see that their liberties cause anger and disgust and for very good reasons make hearts bitter and so are contrary to brotherly love. In addition the most holy father, the pope, decreed that even though some clerics might want to become members of a community or indeed had taken that step, any contract that was should be torn up and they should consider themselves released from all oaths and vows, for these had been made to the detriment of ecclesiastical possessions. It is a result of their lack of social concern, that they adopt the attitude that only they themselves should be free and rich, have enough and all the pleasures, live without worry, and have every security. They want to be socially uncommitted and to have special privileges, and so St. Paul calls them *aspondos*, those who refuse social commitment, those who are antisocial, those whose possessions no one can enjoy but who nevertheless desire to enjoy those of everyone else, who desire all the advantages but will

---

[20] According to a decree of Boniface VIII (1294–1303), the Roman pontiff has all the law in *scrinio pectoris*, "in the chamber of his heart." This statement was incorporated into canon law and meant that the pope claimed authority over canon law. Cf. *LW* 44, 202, n. 215.

have none of the disadvantages. All this is intolerable in any community. It is not only against Christian love but contrary to natural fairness and all human reason.

Eleventh, they are slanderers and defamers. What a huge vice St. Paul touches on here. Generally it is more prevalent among clerics than among any other class, even among those who in the eyes of men have a reputation for self-discipline, honor, and an upright life! Just take note of the attitude such people adopt concerning the sins or weaknesses of other people, how they blow up their love and desire for discipline, honor, and uprightness, the seriousness with which they propagate the cause of justice, so that no tinge of mercy or love is left for the neighbor. To help us to understand this more clearly it will be necessary to speak about it at length and in greater detail.

In considering the previous vices, I showed how this group conducts itself in relation to the person and possessions of its neighbor. Here St. Paul speaks in particular of their attitude towards the sins of the neighbor. Oh how blind and ignorant they are in this matter, how greatly they are influenced by their self-conceit and pride! Scripture teaches us to adopt the following attitude toward the sins of our neighbor: first, we should not be filled with mistrust, but, whenever possible, put the best interpretation on everything we see in the life of our neighbor, provided it is not public sin. For thus St. Paul writes in I Corinthians 13[:5]: "Love does not think the worst," this is, it assumes the best in everyone and bears no ill-will towards anyone, believes that others think and act in the same way as love itself thinks and acts; even when love acts in a way that appears to be evil, it has good intentions, and so puts the best interpretation on the deeds of everyone else, however evil they may seem to be. Second, where the deed of the neighbor is obviously evil, so that a good interpretation of it is impossible, love acts as follows: if the deed is done in secret and love alone sees it or hears about it, it will keep silence, keep it buried within itself, say nothing about it to anyone, and, wherever possible, cover it up so that no one hears about it. In this way love preserves the honor of the neighbor. However, love will quietly take him aside, tell him his fault, pray for him, have patience and mercy, and think

as one of the ancient fathers thought who said:[21] this man fell
yesterday, today I might fall; or: if he sins in this matter, I sin in
others, both of us are in need of the same grace. So love forgives
and helps, even as it prays that it too may be forgiven and helped.
Christ teaches this in Matthew 18[:15]: "If your brother sins
against you," (that is) secretly, so that you alone witness it, "go
and tell him his fault, between you and him alone." And St. Paul
says in Galatians 5 [6:1]: "If a man is overtaken in any trespass,
then teach him in a spirit of gentleness and look to yourself, lest
you too be tempted."

Third, when the neighbor's sin is public so that it cannot be
covered up and certain people know about it, love will act as
follows: it will keep silence, not tell anyone about it, and go and
report it to his superior whose duty it is to punish him; he will let it
rest at that, pray for him and show him mercy, as in the previous
case. Thus we read in Genesis 37[:2] that Joseph reported to his
father Jacob that his brothers were in ill repute; he did not report
their secret deeds, but merely their evil reputation; as the text has
it, that is, their deeds were no longer secret but public, so that
people were talking about them.

Now compare with that the attitude of the lovers of discipline
and honor. First, because secretly they hold themselves in high
regard and are conceited, they think that no person acts and thinks
as well as they. They are the most mistrusting people on earth, full
of unnecessary anxiety and pedantic fear that no one does the right
thing; they put the worst construction on all things and even
though the deed is good, they think the intention was evil and so
they search and dig to discover the intention and do not rest until
they hear something about their neighbor that is evil. Oh what
fine, honorable people are caught up in this vice; at times they just
seem to be cautious, lest they be deceived! But caution concentrates on possible dangers and goes so far as to satisfy itself that it
is not being deceived. It openly says: I believe your intentions are
not evil, but we are all human and your attitude could change and
you might err, in the same way as it might happen to me, etc.
Mistrust, however, concentrates entirely on the present deed, has

---

[21] Cf. *The Lives of the Fathers* (*De vitis patrum*), VII, 16 (*MPL* 73, 1039).

no good opinion about it. It is not concerned about possible, unforeseen dangers. It thinks that that is already evil which caution judges to be good and which it undertakes to prevent from becoming evil.

Second, when mistrust secretly observes or hears about the evil deed of the neighbor, it rejoices, for then it can show how good it is, and how wicked other people are, how it loves justice, discipline, and honor: Then our poor publican is at the mercy of the Pharisee, then Noah in his nakedness is exposed to the eyes of his son Ham [Gen. 9:21 ff.]. Ah, they say, what an honorable, good man he is, and so everyone must know of the wickedness of the neighbor. There are some who like nothing better than to be informed about the sins of others and to hear them being discussed. It is true indeed that this vice exercises a wider and more horrible influence than anyone is likely to believe, in particular among seemingly honorable and chaste people. There is no covering up here, no admonition, no reproof, no intercession, nothing but defamation and slander, and yet they who do this are the saintly, spiritual people.

Third, if they do admonish or accuse, they do so in such a merciless way, that it would appear that they themselves were in no need of grace and had never committed sin. Instead of reporting a man to his superior, they scold him publicly, so all can hear it who did not know about it before. Love with justice is at a premium and therefore they destroy the neighbor's good name, and heap upon him every calumny. It is of no concern to them, if as a result he should lose heart, give up body and goods, and end as a desperate man. As good and honorable people they have reproved the sin; let someone else take care of improvement. They cast him from their midst and treat him as one who can never again be a useful member of society. Oh what a senseless people these saints and honorable folk are. But all this does not burden their consciences; they go and pray as if they had done well. Behold, the previously mentioned vices of pride and self-conceit have led them into this one, together with the other two most recently mentioned ones, namely, that they are merciless, hard-hearted, and dissocial people who care for no one, are useful to no one, and seek only their own honor at the expense of others by defaming them and damaging their good name.

For this reason St. Paul calls them *diabolos*, slanderers, and defamers, because they do not know how to deal with the sins of their neighbors in any other way than to defame them and publicly deprive them of their good name; they do all this merely to make a big show of themselves so that everyone may see how good and fine and honorable they are. If they were merciful or kind, they would simply be concerned about betterment and neither defame a person nor condemn him, but wipe out the sin. St. Paul truly describes them well, for we know from experience how insanely keen the clerics and their like are to hear of the sin and shame of others, to laugh and talk about it and spread the news; they are fittingly called *diaboli*. St. Paul always uses the word *diabolus* in this sense, even though some also call the devil by this name, and indeed it is characteristic of him to uncover, reproach, spread, and magnify the sins of men. But when St. Paul wants to refer to the devil, he generally speaks of Satan. He does this in I Timothy 3[:6-7]: "A bishop must not be a recent convert, or he may be puffed up with conceit and fall into the condemnation of the devil, that is, of the slanderer, lest he have cause to reproach him," etc.

Twelfth, they are unchaste. What else can we expect of those who lead such arrogant, free, secure, indolent, jolly, and wanton lives? How can they possibly remain chaste, when they are entangled in the vices mentioned above; when those who struggle courageously and live virtuously can hardly withstand? It is common knowledge that this vice is found among them, in fact, it is rampant, and yet they are blameless. No one but the pope is to be blamed for this lack of chastity, because he has forbidden marriage for those who belong to the ecclesiastical estate. If marriage were permitted, many would give up their former vice and be obliged to enter another estate. The evil spirit was well aware of this; therefore, so that such vices would increase he whispered the thought into the pope's ear to forbid marriage. So the clergy entered a special and unique life and this pleased them. Finally he so blinded them with outer appearances, that they could not recognize the eleven vices mentioned above or feel sorrow or repentence for them. On the contrary, they consider them to be virtues and right, for which they will enter heaven. But this twelfth vice is so crude that it is easily recognized. They cannot deny it, and so they rue it and confess it and are made as white as snow, just like a sow which lies in the mud with its whole body and just manages to keep clean one ear or several bristles on its back.

Thirteenth, they are fierce. That is, they are completely untrained, untamed, unrefined people who cannot take criticism. The moment you touch them, they break apart. This follows of necessity from the free way of life in which they were brought up. Just like a child that is permitted to have its own way, and becomes coarse, vulgar, and rough, so they are inflexible, unpliable, intolerable people. They are accustomed to receive honor, to receive plenty, to have their way, and to go unpunished. Therefore, they will not tolerate anything that runs counter to this. If, however, they were disciplined, as others are, they would often have to suppress their desires and refrain from that which they freely do now, and so they would probably become more pliable and gentle, so that one could associate with them more easily. This vice is rather common, particularly in the monasteries. They even call themselves *passionatos*, that is, people who easily become angry.

Fourteenth, they take no pleasure in the good, that is, they pay no attention to the good or are quite careless about doing good works. They live their lives as if no good works were necessary and they knew of another and better way to heaven. They think that through their celebrating mass and observing the *horas* for prayer, they are so superabundantly rich in good works that they are able to sell them to others. They simply do not know of any other good works than their own self-imposed and self-chosen little deeds, for which God has given no commandment. The most pious ones make their last will and testament when they die and endow masses and vigils, increase the fees of officiating clergy, and make increased provision for the possessions and worship of the holy church. These are their good works, but apart from them they do no one a good deed all their life, and bestow no benefit on anyone, unless you call it a good work that, like the Israelites, they impose dues on poor people, extort usury everywhere, and levy taxes on lands and estates. But do not imagine for a moment that they will give something for nothing or lend without interest. Why, they must gather it in for their last will and testament and the requiem masses. Hence, the saying, that the last wills and testaments of a priest are all one and the same sausage, the same today, and tomorrow, for the same testament continues to pass through the hands of the executors, as the one priest transmits to the next what he received from the one before him; such possessions are not worthy of use for the poor. The same applies to other good works such as visiting the sick, clothing the naked, comforting the sorrowful, and so continuing to serve the neighbor and helping him. They show no concern for their things; in their eyes they are not a service to God. They prefer their masses and their howling in church; they make mass a good work and sacrifice, since it costs them no money or exertion, but brings wealth and assures leisure and fine days. Moreover, they divide works of mercy into two classes: spiritual and external.[22] They say the spiritual ones are better than the external ones and so they despise the latter as inferior, and concentrate on the spiritual as the superior. Hence they subtly and imperceptibly depart from Christ's way and commandment. They interpret spiritual works of mercy to mean the mass and their own commandments, and so anything which is not a mass or a vigil stinks in their eyes. So completely and thoroughly they have lapsed into oblivion and disregard of good works. Tell me, in what better way could the devil have blinded them than to suggest that they should call their masses and prayers spiritual works which are superior to the external works which Christ—who knows nothing concerning their spiritual works—commands?

Therefore the apostle truly hit the mark when he scolds them as being indifferent towards the good. He does not say they are ignorant of good works, but that they show no concern for them, even though they well know that Christ has commanded them, and they themselves admit that there are external works of mercy. But they successfully evade them with this distinction, and so destroy them with their own spiritual good works. Dear friends, look at all the religious foundations and monasteries and tell me: Who derives a single penny's worth of benefit from these people? Whom do they serve? Whom do they help? They claim that their idola-

---

[22] Cf. Thomas Aquinas, *Summa theologiae*, II², ques. 30.

trous masses and foul bawling and murmuring in their churches are all spiritual works of mercy. But they, not God, call all these good, spiritual works, for certainly they are nothing but a fiction of the devil. All this could be endured, if only they went to hell with all these works. But these accursed people lead the whole world astray, drag it along into condemnation, because the whole world has learned to despise good works, and to follow them and fall in after them in pursuit of masses and vigils and prayers and making endowments and similar good works of the devil. So we find them having fine and lazy days, not being permitted to do good to anyone, but getting everyone to give them gifts and do good to them; in this way everyone joins them in doing spiritual good works while the external good works go begging. No one helps his fellow man, rather everyone saves and scrimps and is bent on these spiritual works. Of course they are spiritual good works, yet they do not proceed from the Holy Spirit, but are devised by the evil spirit. Oh how many thousand times more blessed is the estate of matrimony or any secular estate! For the estate of matrimony compels us to do good works to children and servants. A married person has to be physically useful to others rather than serve himself, and a secular government has to serve its subjects in some way. Servants and maids and all subjects must be useful to others and serve them. But these miserable people do not benefit a single person on this earth; rather they oblige everyone to serve them and so are drowned in their unconcern for all that is good. Meanwhile they pray for others and celebrate masses for them, as if prayer and the mass were their possession and not entrusted to the whole congregation. O Lord God, what an accursed way of life and perverted worship![23]

Fifteenth, they are treacherous. St. Paul, where are you going? Will you never stop? How you bite, how you needle! What a terrible attack you levy on this delicate crowd with its soft ears! You say they are traitors of the band of Judas who sold Christ?! What have they done to deserve that name? A traitor takes money or receives favors sweetly, leading his master or friend to death or

---

[23] For a fuller treatment of Luther's position on the mass at this time, see, for example, *The Babylonian Captivity of the Church* (1520), *LW* 36, 18–57, and *The Misuse of the Mass* (1521), *LW* 36, 133–230.

into danger, just as Judas took money and led our Lord with a friendly greeting and a kiss into the hands of his enemies. The pope certainly does this to his people in a spiritual way, without ceasing. He takes treasures from people everywhere and gives them indulgences while his servants preach his lies about indulgences and false works to the poor people. Thereby they encourage them and lead them from faith to works, so that they depart from Christ and fall into the devil's snare. This is a huge and awful betrayal of souls throughout the world. But this betrayal is merely spiritual.

St. Paul must also be interpreted here as speaking of a physical betrayal. We read of the number of times popes hounded kings and princes with sweet words to fight against the Turks and against each other, promising them eternal life and so depriving them of body and soul and filling the world with the blood of Christians. Even now the popes do not cease to betray poor people in this way as often as it pleases them. They preach (or they have men preach) about holy wars which are waged for the sake of spiritual possessions and for the good of the church, and it is nothing but lies and all for the sake of their bellies. From history books we have more than adequate proof how the pope has always and in his own interests resorted to treacherous devices in his dealings with emperors and kings. Bishops and priests join and help him in this; otherwise he could not have achieved it. Thus, treachery is their common practice. With good reason the apostle calls them treacherous. Even in our day they do not cease to betray and sell emperor and princes, wherever the opportunity presents itself, for otherwise they are unable to suppress and overcome them. So they ally themselves now with the one, now with the other, in order to suppress them, one after the other, so that they may assert their superiority. They have no scruples in this matter but regard it as a real achievement. He who agrees with the most holy father, the pope, is no traitor, but an obedient son of the Christian church. In the same manner in which they betray a king, a country, and its people in a physical way, so they betray one another in spiritual things, and with fine words allow themselves to be initiated into the practice of treachery as if it were a service of God, while as reward they receive papal benedictions and grace and so help to betray the whole world. Do you see how clearly St. Paul foresaw everything and how much he is to the point in assessing what has been going on in our own day and for a long time? Truly, he never misses the mark, not even by a hair's breadth!

Sixteenth, they are reckless. They practice treachery and all their other vices boldly, unblushingly, insolently, without any sense of shame towards their fellow men and without any fear of God, as if it is impossible for them to err, and there was no one who will judge and punish them. They are a mad, rash, brazen, impudent people in all their undertakings. Since they have renounced all obligations and norms, they dare to carry out with insolence and brazenness whatever occurs to them, wherever place and opportunity are favorable. This vice is particularly apparent in the pope who calls it *plenitudinem potestatis* and *proprium motum et certam scientiam*. But it is present in others as well who define it as *zelum veritatis et iustitie, reverentiam Ecclesie* and so on. Beware if you find yourself confronted with any one of these pretexts; you may be sure that it is plain recklessness and brazenness.

Seventeenth, they are swollen with conceit. Theirs is a large pompous heart, which necessarily follows from the previous vice of inordinate recklessness. When they have practiced treachery and done all manner of evil in the most shameless way, they arrogantly boast and brag and say: Who will rebuke us for this? Who will hinder us? Who will judge us? We are free and independent of everyone; we must judge and rebuke, but no one shall judge or rebuke us. They not only claim absolute immunity to practice every villainy, but they defy those who want to hinder them and demand that no one judge them; in fact everyone is to keep his silence as well, call them gracious lords, and allow them to do as much damage as they like to body and soul, possessions and reputation throughout the world. St. Peter, also speaks of this vice in II Peter 2[:18], and says they will want to be above the law, will utter loud boasts of folly as if their throat was swollen. Many provisions in the papal law are like this. The pope puffs himself up like a viper, defies the whole world, and protests that everyone should mind his own business, judging neither him nor his servants.[24] The

---

24 Cf. *Decretum Magistri Gratiani*, I, dist. 40, chap. 6 (*MPL* 187, 215): "The pope is to be judged by no one."

clerics follow him, all defiant and swollen with conceit. They demand that no one judge them, and threaten with thunder and
lightning and twenty-four hells, as we can prove from experience.
Everything St. Paul says of them is openly practiced by them, so
that everything they do is virtually a full and superabundant fulfillment of St. Paul's word.

Eighteenth, they are blind. Come now, be careful, be careful
holy apostle, these are the learned men, the lights of the world who
have the authority to make new articles of faith, and without them
no one may expound scripture! Do you want to cause an uproar
and have the laity rise up against the clergy? Why, worship would
be perverted, and the heavens would fall, for they rest on them.
You should be silent or else only scold the laity. For to scold the
clerics will do no good; it will incite the people to rebellion and to
defiance of ecclesiastical authority; it will not make them any
better. They will fly into a temper and become angry and may
indeed excommunicate you, and condemn you as a heretic to be
burnt at the stake. But why are they blind and engaged in this
folly and make such a show of it that even children and fools can
see its emptiness? They do not see even a tiny beam of the true
light of faith and of the gospel. Egyptian darkness covers them and
is in them, so that we can virtually grasp it with our hands; neither
do they possess all the virtues. At present the greatest virtue of the
bishops is that they are big, coarse, ignorant asses' heads, and they
consider it a disgrace if they are educated.

Nineteenth, they are lovers of sensual pleasure rather than
lovers of God. Here the apostle says the very thing that is expressed in a common saying among us: The clergy have an easy
life! If any life on earth is full of sensual pleasure, it is theirs, for
they feed on the labor of the sweat and blood of others. Without
working, they are idle, eat and drink the best, clothe themselves
lavishly, have the best lands and houses, as well as the prettiest
girls, or some other pleasure and amusement, so that there is a
common saying among us: If it is good the clergy own it. But they
have betrayed in a masterful way the holy cross which Christ has
laid upon all his disciples and which will not tolerate a life of
sensual pleasure. They have set it in silver, making it easy to bear
without hurting. They even sell its kisses and blessings; it has

become a useful servant for their sensual pleasures. But that dear cross cannot enter their hearts, nor can it associate itself with their lives, because their license, brazenness, defiance, and swollen conceit have put a bar in the way. Yet they honorably wear the cross in silver to the Lord's glory so they will enter heaven when they breathe their last. Now if the Lord says to them, "I carried my cross myself and did not command that you should carry it; let each carry his own cross and follow me," [Matt. 16:24] then they will perhaps again outwit him and invent two kinds of crosses, as they also invented two kinds of works of mercy, and say that Christ's cross was better than their own, and so they preferred the best and discarded their own in order that they might honorably wear his— yes, honor it and revere it like an idol. Unfortunately this is the way they are directing the poor people now and teaching them to pray to wood, silver, or gold. They pretend that one can relate and look to God through that cross, as if the mind of the poor, ordinary man could also devise such subtle foolishness when he prays to the holy cross. They are the enemies of the cross of Christ, that is the sum and substance of it all.

Twentieth, and finally, they hold the form of a godly life but deny its power. The apostle does not deviate from his line of thought and so he anticipates the serious question and objection that someone might raise: How can all this be? After all, they pray and sing much daily, they celebrate mass and conduct worship with great embellishment and pomp! Do not the clergy lead lives of obedience, poverty and chastity in keeping with their holy order and rule? To this objection, and any other that one may want to raise, the apostle gives a concise answer: It is all outer form, glitter, and glamor behind which these terrible vices are hidden, cultivated, and given a fine facade. Their whole way of life is of their own choosing; it is devised by men and not commanded by God. They discard God's commandments and cling to their own empty splendor; they are the fine cathedral canons who do what they choose to do and not what God commands. When our Lord Christ wanted to give a concise definition of all these vices hidden behind an outer splendid form, he referred to them as sacrilege, Matthew 24[:15], "When you see the desolating sacrilege standing in the holy place," etc. It is a sacrilege from which everyone rightly shrinks back, that behind such a small outer form such huge, nasty, stinking vices should breed and reign. He also stresses that they deny the power or strength of a godly life, which is saying considerably more and putting it more severely than if he had said that they lack the power or the deeds of a godly life. The emphasis is on the denial and the opposition. We shall see later what this implies when we proceed with our consideration of Herod and his worship. Let it suffice for the present that we realize how much these words of St. Paul agree with the words of this Gospel which tells us both how the magi searched the Scriptures and of their right attitude towards them. Herod also had the Scriptures, but only apparently, for his attitude towards them was wrong, inasmuch as he sought to hinder them for the sake of his power, in the same way as the papists do. Therefore we must examine St. Paul's word more thoroughly and completely.

He says: Beware, "avoid such people." In this way he warns us to beware of the ecclesiastical estate and its rule. To those who are entrapped in it because of the rule that is imposed on them, as we shall hear later, he gives permission to leave. Indeed, he commands them to do so, thus unlocking all nunneries and monasteries and releasing every priest and monk. Similarly Christ commands us, Matthew 24[:23, 26], that we should flee from them and avoid them. Furthermore he describes some of them more particularly and says: "Among them are those who make their way through houses and take captive weak women who are burdened with sins and are easily swayed by various impulses, always learning and never arriving at a knowledge of the truth." This cannot be interpreted in any other way than as pointing to the mendicant orders which the apostle here clearly foresaw. They are always making their way through the houses. What St. Paul refers to here as houses, we nowadays call churches, for in his time there were no churches; Christians assembled in a house, just as if today ten or twenty neighbors assembled in the house of one of them, heard the word, prayed, and received the sacrament. Nowadays the mendicant orders pass through all the parish churches which do not belong to them and preach their sermons there. The pope gave this privilege out of sheer impudence and power.

The other aspect is the fact that they are virtually in control of

235

confession; the pope has granted them this privilege too, by virtue of the same authority by which he permitted them to make their way through the houses. This is truly the devil's game and the women fall for it, especially those who are secretly tormented by serious and grievous sins, or, as St. Paul says, are burdened with sins [II Tim. 3:6]. For as soon as their consciences plague them and they do not know where to seek help and advice, these foolish women run and disgorge their troubles into a cowl and think they have succeeded in getting rid of them. But they become really enmeshed and keep on bringing and donating whatever they can and own. The holy fathers then arise and preach about the need to confess sins and cite many examples of women who were eternally damned and appeared after death and stated that they were damned because they had failed to confess something. Thus the greatest of popish lies so surround us, that the stones might well tremble and sweat.

Observe the examples cited in their sermons and you will notice that usually it is only women, not men, who were damned because of failure to confess something, so we might clearly realize that it was an archrogue who invented these examples. For he was curious to know the innermost heart and the secrets of women. Noticing that womenfolk are by nature fainthearted and bashful, more so than men, he thought: I will give them good advice and extort the innermost secrets from their hearts through the terrors of confession. With the help of the devil he succeeded in this. But in this manner he also bound and condemned the consciences of many who had failed to confess because of sheer unconquerable bashfulness and timidity, and so they sinned against their consciences because they believed it was necessary to confess and yet did not do so. God will judge you according to your faith; if you believe that it is your duty to do a thing and you fail to do it, it is a sin. In my judgment this rogue who by such examples binds consciences in a false faith and condemns them, deserves to have not only his body but also his soul torn apart by all devils and pulverized into a hundred thousand pieces. What a horrible murder of souls is perpetrated throughout the world by these hellish traitors and popish liars! Oh weep whoever can weep, over such lamentable destruction of poor souls!

When poor, fainthearted women who are naive and credulous by nature and want to be pious and devout, hear such preaching, they fall for it and are caught and seek advice and help from their spiritual father. But this coarse ass and blind leader of the blind knows nothing of faith or of Christ and proceeds to teach them to do penance for their sins by works and satisfactions. And so the martyrdom begins of which St. Paul speaks here when he says that they always learn and never arrive at the knowledge of the truth. But this is not the way to pacify women's consciences. Their sins burden and torment them and they would gladly be rid of them, but do not know how, and so they reach the next stage about which St. Paul speaks here when he says that they are swayed by various impulses. They then begin to fast with bread and water, go on pilgrimages in bare feet, want to visit the saints. Some whip themselves until they bleed, some make gifts to the church, others donate a chalice. There is no end or limit to the various impulses that sway them. They fall on anything they hear as being good for the expiation of sins, and with utter seriousness they are anxious to emulate it and yet they cannot find peace. Meanwhile the spiritual, holy father sits tight, for he has trapped the poor animal and its value for him far surpasses the possession of so many cows that can be milked. Once the women are trapped, their men are soon caught too and must accommodate themselves to the extortions of secret confession. But where the true royal road to freedom is preached, they will say: Dear women, if anyone among you is burdened by sin, let her confess it, if she so desires. But whether she confesses or not, let her have the firm faith that Christ forgives her sins, and let her secretly confess to him with a full and hearty trust in his grace which he has promised to all who seek it and do not doubt it, and so her sins are most certainly forgiven. Let her thereafter avoid such sins and practice good works towards her neighbors who are in need of them; let her invite the poor, wash their feet, and humbly serve them. Behold, that would be the right way to restore a sinful woman, and all of it would be done with joy and good will, without burdening the conscience, and so would be well pleasing in the sight of God.

But were this to happen, the murderers of souls and the torturers of the spirit would lose their confession money and the cow would run dry, and consciences would be free and no longer under the tutelage of their incessant teaching and preaching. That would hit the holy ecclesiastical estate in their innermost being, and they might die of hunger. For not without good reason has the apostle mentioned women who are burdened with sins. They will not plague others who are innocent, with such devilish examples, teaching, and bondage. Their chief concern is that the source of their milk should not dry up, and so they inject fear into consciences, concentrating especially on those of women who are easily misled, most of all when they labour with an evil, sinful conscience. There is no counsel that they will not follow, no imposition that will satisfy them. They become wavering and, finally, despairing souls who have learned to comfort themselves with their own works and not with the grace of God. They desire to be rid of their sins not through faith alone but through satisfaction which is quite impossible. They talk much about sparing the clergy, that we should not scold or accuse them, but excuse and honor them. Yes, if they were merely evil in themselves and destroyed only themselves, I would gladly be silent. But their rule destroys the whole world! Whoever is silent about all this and does not risk body and life to expose it, is not a true Christian, nor does he love his neighbor's salvation as his own. If only I could be more moderate in my attacks on them. But they set the town on fire and then tell me not to shout "Fire, Fire" or extinguish the blaze. "Cursed is he" (says Jeremiah,) "who does the work of the Lord with slackness, and keeps back his sword from bloodshed" [Jer. 48:10]. It is God's will that we should use his sword courageously and that blood should flow; he who does his work with slackness is cursed. They, however, demand that we merely pluck some feathers and lightly brush them over with the fox's tail. Not so, my dear man!

St. Paul continues: "As Jannes and Jambres opposed Moses, so these men also oppose the truth" [II Tim. 3:8]. He does not merely refer here to the mendicant friars but to all the clergy mentioned above. Everyone can see how they oppose the truth and will not permit people to escape from their terrifying power and come to the knowledge of free faith for they fear that their rule and tyranny will pass away. In the same way the people of Israel were suppressed by Pharaoh in Egypt, and Moses was sent by God to rescue them. At first he performed two miracles to prove that he had been sent by God. Whereupon the two sorcerers of Pharaoh, Jannes and Jambres, performed the same miracles, thereby restraining the king and bringing to nought the miracles of Moses, so that the people had to stay [Exod. 8:19]. But when it came to the third miracle, they were no longer able to perform it, and clearly they were wrong and Moses was right. It is always the same: the tyrants over God's people have always the appearance on their side and act like real saints; in this way they hinder and restrain the simpleminded so that they cannot escape from their bondage. Theirs is a weak conscience, and they are unable to distinguish clearly between appearance and reality, between pretense and truth. Thus the poor people are always taken captive by show and pretense and are hindered and kept back from attaining the truth. It is the same with these magi in Jerusalem. They are kept back by Herod, who pretends to be searching the Scriptures. The spiritual pomp in our time achieves no more than that it hinders people from coming to faith and truth, because the outward appearance is so fine, and it is so very much like service of God.

St. Paul continues: They are "men of corrupt mind and incapable of faith" [II Tim. 3:8]. There you have it, now you know what they are in reality. Their thoughts and their judgments are perverted, for they claim that their attitude is right and that there can be no other. They know nothing of faith. Faith alone produces a blameless mind and spiritual virgins, it teaches a right judgment and a proper mind which insists that God's grace alone is our comfort. He who is without such a mind is a Christian in the same way as a harlot is a virgin, even if he performs the works of all saints. Where thoughts are so perverted, there is little hope that true faith will ever be attained, particularly if people have come to be so far removed from it that they fight against it, even though they were once implanted into it in baptism and later allowed themselves to become reprobate. Further: "but, they will not last the distance, for their folly will be plain to all." Thus the pope and our clergy will fare, truth will endure and prove to be too strong for them, their villainy and hypocrisy will be revealed, and neither rage nor fury will help them—even if they had four thousand Turkish emperors on their side. Dissimulation and lies will not endure in the end; that is impossible, even though for a time they maintain themselves and persist. Let that suffice as comment on the passage from St. Paul. We now return to the gospel and its interpretation.

Herod's secret request to the magi to come to him and his discovery of the time the star appeared, signify that the spiritual Herodists do not outwardly deny the gospel. They learn what it is from the true Christians, but with the mental reservation that they will arbitrarily use it for their own purpose, just as Herod proposed to make use of the time of the star in order to kill Christ and stabilize his kingdom. Again, it is just as when we hold up the gospel before the eyes of our clergy and they do not deny that it is the gospel, hear, and accept it, but tell us that our understanding of it is not correct and a gloss and an interpretation are necessary. This we cannot expect to get from anyone else but them, and everyone must agree with their interpretation. They do not thereby deny the gospel, but they rob it of all its power and offer their own dreams in the name and under the appearance of the gospel. This is what St. Paul calls "having the form of a godly life, but denying its power." He does not say that they do not have the power of the godly life, although that is also true; he puts it more forcibly and says that they also deny it. So he shows clearly that it is not simply their lives and deeds which are wicked, but also their doctrine and spiritual dominion, so that they lead themselves astray from the way of the gospel by their lives, and others by their doctrines. That is what the pope and the clergy are doing in all their sermons. The gospel, the gospel, they cry, and then they deny and condemn and curse everything that is in the gospel and all its contents. They are just like Herod, who learns everything about the star and yet wants to destroy that which the star signifies. We shall show this by way of example from a few of their doctrines so that we may guard ourselves against them.

The gospel teaches that salvation depends entirely on faith. They hear that and do not deny it. But then they deprive it of all its power and assert that faith without works is useless, and so they secretly move from faith to works, publicly condemning faith and ascribing all benefits to works. Thus they retain the little word "faith" only in outward appearance and deception, and deny, condemn, and curse everything that belongs to faith, and proceed to divide faith into many parts. Thus they distinguish on the one hand between natural faith and spiritual faith, and on the other between general and particular faith, and further, between explicit and implicit faith. Yet these blind leaders of the blind themselves understand this juggling less than a natural simpleton. The gospel knows nothing of these manifold distinctions; it proclaims the faith which puts its trust in nothing but God's grace, without any merit of works. They do not even have an inkling of this and yet condemn it as the worst heresy. Still they claim that it is their desire to defend the gospel and Christian faith.

Further, the gospel tells us that Christ is our Savior. They hear this, but set aside and nullify all of Christ's works, qualities, and attributes because of their public teaching that man can merit God's grace by his own natural powers and works. So they condemn Christ and all his works as St. Peter said of them when he declared, in II Peter 2[:1]: "There will be false teachers among you who will deny the Master who bought them." If human nature can of itself acquire the grace of God the universities, religious foundations, and monasteries teach and maintain in complete agreement with the pope, then Christ was born and died in vain and to no purpose. Why should he shed his blood to obtain grace for us, when we can obtain it by our own natural efforts? Nonetheless they desire to be Christians and raise high the name of Christ, and under this guise they revile and condemn the whole Christian religion as heresy.

Further, the gospel teaches that God's law is spiritual and that it is impossible for human nature to fulfill it; God's Spirit must fulfill it in us through faith, Romans 8[:3–4]. They deny neither the Spirit nor the law, but deprive it of its power and teach that man can fulfill the commandments of God by his own natural efforts and by his own works, without the help of the Spirit, even though he does not thereby merit eternal life.[25] This simply amounts to a denial of the power of the law and of the Spirit, and retains nothing but the name. Then they proceed to dismember

[25] E.g., Gabriel Biel, *Epithoma pariter et collectorium circa quattuor sententiarum libros*, II, dist. 30, ques. 1; dist. 28, ques. 1; dist. 27, ques. 1, art 2; and Duns Scotus, *Quaestiones in IV Libros Sententiarum*, III, dist. 27, ques. 1.

God's law. Wherever they think it too difficult to fulfill, they change it into counsels and superfluous, unnecessary things. They teach that it is neither a necessity nor a command that we should love God with all our heart, or give our cloak to him who desires our coat; likewise they deny that we ought not to engage in lawsuits, that we ought to lend to everyone without profit or charge; that we should not resist one who is evil and do good to our enemies, etc. Thereby they have undermined the whole, true nature and substance of the Christian life which simply consists of suffering evil and doing good to everyone. In place of such a life they have set up their own commandments which require them to wear tonsures and caps, prohibit eating meat, eggs, milk, and butter, and make them bawl in churches, so that nothing remains of God's laws.

Further, the gospel praises God's pure and simple grace because it remits and wipes out all sins. They do not deny that little word "grace" and seem to estimate it highly and greatly. But in addition to this they teach all manner of satisfaction for sins, set up orders, procedures, and stations of penance in order to purchase forgiveness of sins from God with these things and to pay for grace. In this way both substance and purpose of grace are completely destroyed and condemned. For grace wants to be pure grace, or nothing at all.

The gospel also teaches that because of original sin all men are children of wrath and disfavor, and all their works are sinful. Once again, they do not deny the word "original sin," but they deprive it of its force and argue that human nature is still good, that its works are not sin, and that it is able of itself to prepare for grace. They also say that the damage of original sin to human nature is not such that it merits damnation; it merely caused a weakness in regard to good works and a propensity towards sin. If human nature does not give way to this propensity, as indeed it is able to do of itself, it does not merit hell and can in fact earn the grace of God. Surely that is tantamount to saying: Original sin is not original sin. The concept is retained, but the nature and the works of sin are denied.

Further, the gospel teaches that love does not seek its own, but seeks to serve the neighbor. They retain that little word "love"

242

but deprive it of its whole substance by teaching that true love begins with itself and loves itself first and most of all.[26] They say that to love is enough, provided one wishes one's neighbor well; the accompanying deed and service is not required. After all, it would be dishonest for the pope to humble himself before an inferior; he should rather permit him to kiss his feet; it is enough that he harbors within himself the thought: I wish every man well, except my enemies. Truly, thus the very nature and power of love lie prostrate; nothing remains but the empty, bare, poor name.

Further, the gospel teaches that hope builds entirely on the promises of God and on nothing else. They, too, confess the little word "hope" but teach that hope does not rest on God's promises but on one's own merits.

Further, the gospel teaches that God's predestination is eternally certain. But they teach that it rests on free will and is uncertain. In short, they confess God and his name, but everything that God ordains, wills, does, institutes, and creates, they tear apart, destroy, and condemn as extreme heresy, so that it is manifest that the sufferings of Christ are now manifestly fulfilled in a spiritual way under the pope's dominion. Behold, in this way they have the outer form of faith, hope, love, grace, sin, the law, Christ, God, and the gospel in their doctrines and yet they deny their nature and power, condemning them as the greatest heresy. Therefore the apostle uses such harsh words when he says: They deny the power of all service of God and all godly life, they have nothing but the outer form. O Lord God in heaven, where are the streams of water, yes the bloodstreams which our eyes should truly shed as tears in these last, horrible, terrible times of the unspeakable and immeasurable wrath of God which he has poured out over all people because of their sins and ungratefulness?

To continue: Herod sent the magi to Bethlehem and commanded them to search diligently for the child. He pretended that he, too, wanted to go and worship him. Here we find the other aspect of the attitude of our Herodists, namely, that they practice what they preach. Their preaching and practice are mere outer form and deny the truth. Practice must agree with preaching. The pope and the ecclesiastical estate act the same way. They do in-

---

[26] E.g., Thomas Aquinas, *Summa theologiae*, II, ques. 26, art. 4.

deed allow Christians to be pious, exhorting them to see Christ and the truth, but that they should betray Christ and in seeking him, serve the pope. For the pope makes this plain to all the world when he unashamedly and brazenly declares: It is good if anyone seeks Christ and lives a godly life; but if he does not also keep the pope's orders and commandments, if he does not serve the pope, if his good life is not at the same time a life of obedience to the pope, he cannot be saved. So he makes people believe that obedience to the pope is more important than, or just as important as, God's commandments. Truly, that is the significance of Herod's additional command. He not only sent the magi to Bethlehem, but kept them subject to himself and in duty bound to practice nothing but treachery and thereby destroy Christ. What else do they do, who in this way obey the pope, as if it were necessary for salvation and worthy of damnation if they refused this allegiance to him, but betray and surrender Christ so that Herod may find and kill him? Christian faith cannot exist alongside of such allegiance or duty-bound conscience, as has often been pointed out. Faith alone must help, and such allegiance must be regarded as useless for salvation; but if it is held to be useful and permissible, faith must die. Then Herod will reign in Christ's stead, a matter surely tantamount to surrender and the betrayal of Christ and faith.

However, Herod clearly lies and his words are empty and utter pretence when he asserts: "I too, will come and worship him." Behind it all he harbors completely different thoughts, namely, to kill Christ and to destroy his kingdom. Here you have the archetype of all unbelieving saints, depicted in Herod in a fine and concise way. First, Herod does not say that he intends to do a wicked work. He does not say that he wants to give him gold and myrrh, nor that he wants to help him or be his good friend. He chooses the finest and best work in the service of God: humility and prayer. He says: I will go as a humble man and do him the greatest honor, namely, adoration. The Herodists, the clergy, do likewise nowadays. They choose no inferior work, but the very best, the service of God. This they appropriate to themselves, in this they exercise themselves and say openly that the lives of other people are temporal and secular lives, while they serve God day and night and when others work, they pray and serve God on behalf of the poor people. Do you not believe that? Well then, go, ask the bells; they are always ringing for their worship. They walk with humble mien, have themselves publicly proclaimed as servants of God, and behind it all fatten their bellies, grab everyone's possessions, and build houses, as if they wanted to live forever.

We must consider the proper distinction between the true and false worship of God so that we may recognize the heart and thoughts of that wicked Herod—and avoid them. No better distinction is possible here than that taught in God's word. The worship taught there must naturally be true worship. And whatever is established alongside and outside of the word of God, and therefore devised by men, must certainly be the false, Herodian worship, mere outer form. Worship of God is determined nowhere else except in his commandments; without a doubt only he serves God who keeps his commandments, just as a servant is said to serve his master when he is prepared to carry out what his master bids him. But if he does not do so, he cannot be said to serve his master, even though he acts in obedience to the will of a whole town. So he who does not keep God's commandments does not serve God, even though he observes the doctrines and commandments of all men.

This, then, is worship of God, that you know God, honor and love him with all your heart, place all your trust and reliance on him and never doubt his goodness, in life or in death, in sin or in well-doing, as the First Commandment teaches. Such worship we can attain to only through the merits and blood of Christ who has purchased such a heart for us and gives it to us when we hear his word and believe. Human nature cannot of itself have such a heart. Behold, this is the chief service of God and its foremost part, namely, an upright Christian faith and love towards God through Christ. In this way we fulfill the First Commandment through the blood of Christ, and serve God truly and rightly.

Second, if you honor God's name and call on it in time of need and publicly confess it before tyrants and the persecutors of this true worship of God, if you do not fear them, if you rebuke the Herodists and prevent them to the best of your ability from dishonoring God's name with their false life and teaching—which they present under the guise of God's name and which is a serious matter for it burdens them with the responsibility for the whole world—if you do all this, then, that truly is the second part of service of God and bidden in the Second Commandment.

Third, if you bear the holy cross and must suffer much because of such faith and witness, so that you have to risk body and life, goods and honor, friends and favor, then this is the true way to observe and sanctify the sabbath, for what you do is not of yourself, but entirely God's work within you, inasmuch as you are merely a suffering, persecuted person. This, then, is the third part of the service of God, bidden in the Third Commandment. And this is the First Table consisting of the first three commandments which are summed up in the three parts: faith, witness, and suffering; in this way you renounce this present life and the world and live for God alone.

Fourth, we come to the Second Table, and the first commandment here is that you serve God by honoring your father and mother, being subject and obedient to them, helping them whenever they are in need and before you help anyone else on earth; this means that you do not become a cleric without their permission, especially if they need you or want to make use of you in some other way. Fifth, you must harm no one in his body but do well to everyone, including your enemies, that you visit the sick and the prisoners, that you stretch out your hand to all who are in want and maintain a good, sweet disposition towards all men.

Sixth, that you lead a chaste and temperate life, or preserve your marriage and help others to do the same. Seventh, that you do not deceive or damage or defraud anyone in material things, but lend, give, and exchange wherever you can help anyone, and protect your neighbor against damage. Eighth, that you watch your tongue, do not defame anyone or damage his reputation, or lie to him, but grant him your protection, excuse him, and spare him. Ninth and last, that you covet no one's wife or goods.

These are truly the parts of a true and proper, godly service; this God demands from you, nothing else. Whatever else you do beyond that, he will not esteem. In addition, everyone can clearly and easily understand it. You see that this true worship of God must be a common worship, observed in all estates, among all men, and it alone, and no other, should be found among God's people.

Where any other worship of God is found, it must be false and will lead astray, as for example, worship which is not common among all, but is reserved for particular groups and estates of men. Let that suffice as far as the one, true, common worship is concerned. Now let us look at the false, particular, sectarian, manifold worship which God has not commanded, and which has been devised by the pope and his clergy.

There you see many different religious foundations and orders and monasteries, none of which has anything in common with the other. The one has a large, the other a small tonsure; the one wears grey, the other black, the other white, the other woolen, the other linen, the other coarse hairy clothes; the one prays on certain days and at certain times, the other on other days and at other times; the one eats meat, the other fish; the one is a Carthusian, the other a Franciscan; the one observes one kind of ceremonies, the other another; the one prays on a stool at Rome, the other on a bench at Jerusalem; the one celebrates mass this way, the other in another way; the one is bound to this monastery, the other to another; the one bawls in this choir, the other in another, and like swarms of bees they fill the churches with the hum of their mumbling. They also observe the celibate life and are subject to manifold disciplines. Who can list all the innumerable, sectional, particular, sectarian parts? Now this worship has grown beyond measure and has given birth to an immoderation that is even greater. There is no limit or moderation to the churches, chapels, monasteries, building of altars, founding of masses and vigils, establishing of hours, vestments for mass, choir caps, chalices, monstrances, silver images and precious stones, candlesticks, candles, tapers, incense, memorial tablets, casting of bells—what an ocean, what a forest of such things we have here! All this fully absorbs the religious fervor of the laity; they give dues, money, and possessions, and so worship of God is increased and the ministers of God are cared for, as the pope states it in his sacred decrees.

Compare these things with the true worship of God and tell me: Where did God ever command one single letter of all this? Do you still doubt that the whole ecclesiastical estate under the pope is clearly Herodian, outer show and deception which hinders and turns people away from true worship of God? Those are the altars and groves about which the prophets complained to the children of Israel when they said that there was no town which had not erected its own grove and altar and given up the one temple of God. This idolatrous, unbelieving, popish, Herodian worship has penetrated all corners of the earth and has driven out and destroyed the true and right worship of God. But perhaps you look around and think: Come now, should so many people be in error? Beware and do not be deceived by numbers, but cling to God's word, for he does not speak falsehoods even though all men may be liars, and as Scripture says: "All men are liars" [cf. Ps. 116:11]. Do not marvel that so many err now; remember that in the days of Elijah only seven thousand men among the whole people of Israel retained their faith. Tell me, what were seven thousand men compared with all Israel, which numbered more than twelve thousand men at arms, not counting wives and children? Or what would all the people have been, compared with a whole world in error? Should it be otherwise today, when we know that Christ and the apostles foretold such terrible things about our times and Christ himself says: "When the Son of man comes, will he find faith on earth" [Luke 18:8]? No, the prevailing error will be abominably great and multitudes will err and the Antichrist will rule most of all over those of whom one expects it least, and he will lead astray the world. But we like to feel secure and not remember God's judgment and not take to heart his wrath. So it would not be surprising if he hardly kept one single person on earth in the true faith. We are in the last and worst times which all of Scripture has foretold with terrible threats. Let us thank God that you see his word which tells you what is true and false worship, and beware that you cling to that and do not follow the masses which proceed without God's word. If they who have God's word and cling to it will hardly stand, how will they stand who follow their own noses without God's word? So let those doubt who will, God's word and true worship amply prove that the pope is the Antichrist and the spiritual estates are his disciples who lead astray the whole world.

But see the superb regulation of the Herodian worship. It has bronze bells which are large and numerous to lure the people to that worship. And these bells and inducements are like the worship itself. But God has given different and proper bells to true worship, namely, preachers whose task it is to let this worship sound and resound among the people. But where are they now? The bells of the Herodian worship are dead and senseless and would be more useful as pots and pans; that worship is also dead and useless and it would be more fitting if the whole business were transferred to the theater stage. See, such is Herod's worship; he pretends to worship Christ and serve God and there is nothing in it. He offers a fine outward show and so he has often seduced and daily leads astray many saintly and pious people, just as Christ says, Matthew 24[:24], that they would lead into error even the elect, as in fact happened to SS. Bernard, Francis, Dominic and others like them, although they were neither overcome by the floods of error nor did they stay there. Their true faith preserved them blameless on their path through error and led them out of it. So it was too with these good magi; theirs was a true and proper faith and good intentions, yet they did not doubt Herod but they considered his pretense to be honest faith, believed his lies, and would have been ready to follow and obey him. They had not received other heavenly commands. Likewise today, as in the past, many obey the pope and believe in simple faith that he and his church are true and good— and so they go their way in error; however, their Christian faith helps them and prevents them from taking harm from such poison, as Christ says, Mark 16[:18]: "If they drink any deadly thing, it will not hurt them, if they believe in my name." What draught can be more poisonous than such lies and the external glamor of false teaching concerning wrong worship?

Now that we have recognized Herod's worship for what it is, and have seen through his false, subtle outer show, we must also consider his pernicious intentions and wickedness and his plan to destroy not only true worship, but also Christ the king and his whole kingdom. The pope dares to undertake this in three ways: first, by means of that same showy pretense of false worship, Without the gift of special grace such pretense of worship is a strong and unconquerable inducement to depart from true worship, and so St. Paul rightly calls it *energiam erroris*, that is, the "powerful force of error." The common people are unable to withstand this temptation unless valiant bishops and preachers take their stand and rightly proclaim true worship, hold the people to the pure word of God, and do away with false worship just as the prophets did among the people of Israel, and were killed for that reason. Such preaching is a matter of life and death and will not be tolerated by Herod, the pope, and the holy clergy. It damages their purse too much and promotes the salvation of too many souls which is more than the devil, their teacher, will suffer.

Second, the pope destroys him by means of his doctrine, about which we spoke above. He teaches works instead of faith contrary to the First Commandment. He suppresses God's honor and works contrary to the Second and Third Commandments. He teaches his own works and arrogance and foolish faith and the confession of God's name. He teaches disobedience to father and mother contrary to the Fourth Commandment, as was pointed out above. He teaches that it is not necessary to love one's enemy and to treat him well, in opposition to the Fifth Commandment. He destroys marriage in opposition to the Sixth. He robs and steals illicit goods and permits others to do the same in opposition to the Seventh. He also teaches it is not necessary to lend or give. In short, he teaches it is not necessary to love God and the neighbor with all one's heart.

Third, he is not merely satisfied with his poisonous example and fatal doctrine, but proceeds to do violence to Christ in two ways: he lays a spiritual ban and curse on the souls who will not obey him, burns them on the stake, expels them, and persecutes their bodies, goods and honor, in a most terrible way. What more wicked thing can he do? I think he is a Herod. Yet he is compelled to let Christ be, and is unable to fulfill his own plans. He destroys many, but faith will remain till the end of time, no matter how hidden and in flight and unknown.

But some may ask what should those do who are in spiritual bondage and trapped in the erroneous worship of Herod in monasteries and religious foundations. I answer: You can only do this: you must put aside that erroneous worship, cling to God's word and seek the true worship, or do as the magi and take the poisonous draught believing that it will not harm you. You will find no other remedy; God's word will remain unchanged forever. Although I spoke about this above in the previous gospel, I must speak about it here once more. Let us assume someone challenges us, tenaciously arguing and debating that a priest, monk, or nun, indeed anyone who has entered an order and taken his vows, is in duty bound to keep these vows and cannot under any circumstances break or vary them all his life. All this is based on Scripture which says [Ps. 16:12] we should keep the vows which we make. But we are thinking of the vows which God has not commanded and which are made voluntarily by men. When in baptism we promise God to serve him and keep his commandments, that is the kind of vow which God desires all men to keep. Scripture speaks of such vows in Psalm 22[:26]: "I will pay my vows to God"; and Psalm 116[:14]: "I will pay my vows to the Lord in the presence of all his people"; etc. But the vows of the clerics God has not commanded.

We will deal with this challenge in two ways. First of all we will show conclusively that there can be neither doubt nor dispute about the matter. Second, we will debate with our opponent and search and seek for the truth. No one can or should ever doubt that everything that is contrary to God's commandment, whether life or death, taking or breaking of vows, speech or silence, is damnable. It is our duty to give it up by all means, to alter it, and to keep away from it. For God's will must have preeminence and shall be done on earth as it is in heaven, as we pray, even though a man might have the power to work every conceivable miracle. This is crystal clear and fully certain. There is therefore no doubt or dispute in this matter, and the conclusion is inescapable. If any priest, monk, nun, has entered an order contrary to the word of God, that priestly and monkish business is altogether worthless and damnable, and such a person is in duty bound to depart from it all and to change the situation. For example, if someone became priest or monk simply because he wanted to steal chalices and precious stones, he certainly became a cleric against the will of God and sinned in this matter; his vows in no way bind him. He should freely return to a secular life, or he must renew his vow with a sincere heart and with a pious intention. For his intention was never really to be a cleric, and if his urge to be a thief had not impelled him, he certainly would never have taken vows or considered holy orders. So God cannot accept those vows and the man himself is not bound to keep them.

Among men the matter is treated differently; vows that have been made must be kept, even though they were not made with a sincere heart. For man cannot tell what is in his neighbor's heart and consequently accepts a vow as honest and assumes it was made sincerely. Therefore a man rightly demands that a vow be kept; he will refuse to acknowledge that he who took a vow has, with regret, changed his mind; he is not bound to believe him. If the latter lied once before, let him suffer the consequences. But God cannot be deceived as he judges according to the innermost thoughts. Therefore a false vow has no validity before him and he will not demand that it be kept; rather his wrath is kindled because men should so tempt him.

If someone entered holy orders against the supreme First Commandment of God of the First Table, he would be more bound to give up his vows than a thief who made his vows in opposition to the Seventh Commandment of the Second Table; for the First Table and the First Commandment are greater than the Second Table and the Seventh Commandment. He who steals and transgresses the Seventh Commandment merely robs earthly goods, the least of God's creatures. But he who transgresses the First Commandment robs and denies God himself, the highest good and Creator of all creatures. Priests and monks who sin against the First Commandment are therefore immeasurably more wicked than a thieving rogue who sins against the Seventh.

What now if we could prove that almost all priests and monks enter holy orders in opposition to the First Commandment, that probably few become priests in a truly God-pleasing way—fewer perhaps than the number of those thieving, false rogues who enter holy orders? Why, that would open the doors of convents and monasteries, telling monks and priests to get out! Come then, watch and listen: The First Commandment is a concise summary of the Christian faith, for he who does not believe refuses to accept and honor God; unbelief is idolatry. Christian faith is the utter submission to God's grace which is purchased for us and granted to us by the blood of Christ, so that no work is useful or good to attain to the grace of God. For whatever is conceived and born in sin, lives and works and dies in it (unless Christ comes to its aid), is beyond human nature. God's mercy is won for us by his works, not through our deeds, and so we fulfill the demands of the First Commandment through him and have a God on whose grace we may rely with the complete trust that in Christ he forgives us all our sins without any merit on our part and grants us eternal life, as was pointed out earlier. Therefore it is impossible that such a faith should tolerate alongside itself any trust in works, as if by these anyone could receive grace and forgiveness of sins and become just and be saved. This is possible only through Christ who achieves all this by his work. We must only believe that and look to him with complete trust. Consequently there is no repentance, no satisfaction for sins, no grace, no eternal life, except by faith alone in Christ, faith that he has given full satisfaction for our sins, won grace for us, and saved us. Only then can we do works freely and gratuitously, to his honor and for the good of our neighbor, not in order to become just and receive eternal life and rid ourselves of sin. That must remain Christ's prerogative and be preserved intact by faith alone. He will grant this privilege to none of the angels— much less to any of our works—that they should abolish sins, purchase grace and grant us eternal life. That is his privilege, he has achieved it and continues to achieve it all alone, and desires that we believe it. When we so believe, it is ours, even as he offers it to us. St. Paul speaks of this in Galatians 2[:21]: "If anyone can be justified by the law and his own works, Christ has died to no purpose." In other words if we can do so much that God forgives us our sins for the sake of our deeds and grants us grace and eternal life, we have no need of Christ. Why else did he die, except to pay for our sins and to purchase grace for us so that we might despair of ourselves and our works, placing no trust in them, so that we might, with courageous defiance, look only to Christ, and firmly believe that he is the man whom God beholds in our stead and for the sake of his sole merits forgives us our sins, deigns to look upon us with favor, and grants us eternal life. That is the Christian faith, of which Christ says in Mark [16:16]: "He who believes will be saved; but he who does not believe will be condemned."

Now let us look at those in the ecclesiastical estate and consider them from the perspective of the First Commandment and the Christian faith. Anyone who desires to be priest or to take vows and enter a religious order in a Christian way so as neither to transgress the First Commandment nor deny God, must have both a sincere heart and a clear intention and say unequivocally: Yes, I want to be a priest, a monk, a nun. I want to take a vow and I do so knowing that priesthood or monasticism is not a means to attain eternal life, nor do I hope to become just or do penance for my sins or win the grace of God through such a religious life.[27] May God preserve me from such thoughts which would be an insult to Christ and his blood, indeed, the destruction of all his merits and honor and the greatest blasphemy. In true faith I look to him for these benefits and trust that he has done all this for me. I will not doubt this and because I must be active in some way in this life on earth, I will enter the religious life, observe its rules, mortify my body, and serve my neighbor, in the same way as some other person might work out in the fields or in a garden or perform some trade without any show of merit or goodness based on works. Whoever is without such thoughts and intentions, cannot but deny Christ and transgress the First Commandment and become involved in altogether unchristian, unbelieving, Israelite, heathenish practices. The powerful and fundamental word of Paul, Romans 14[:23], speaks to this situation: "Whatever does not proceed from faith is sin." Without faith no one can be saved, as Mark says in his last chapter. Without faith, in other words, there cannot be righteousness or truth.

Now tell me, how many priests and monks do you hope to find who enter holy orders and live the religious life with such Christian thoughts? Do not almost all of them say: Come now, if orders are not more helpful to me for doing penance for sins, for becoming just, for receiving eternal life, than is the plough for a peasant, or the thimble for a tailor, why am I in this order and in the priesthood? Not so, I will do good works, celebrate many masses, pray for myself and for other people, and do penance, etc. What language is that? Are these not the words of an unbelieving heart which has denied Christ and which attributes to its order and works what it should expect solely from Christ through faith? In addition, as was shown above, it is the understanding and teaching of all who are in the ecclesiastical estate that we may win the grace of God and abolish sin by our works. They are so brazen about this

---

[27] Luther expressed himself fully on this subject at this time in his treatise *On Monastic Vows* (1521), *LW* 44, 251–400.

that they sell and promise their good works, merits, and fraternities to others, and share them and have the gall to do for men what is exclusively Christ's very own prerogative, namely, to abolish the sins of men and to obtain righteousness for them. Christ particularly prophesied this in Matthew 24[:23–24], and said: "Many will arise in my name and say, Lo, I am Christ." Dear reader, take note of those words! Are they not true? Do they not support what has just been said that our priests and monks make themselves unto Christ? Of course not one of them says explicitly: "Lo, I am Christ." But they do say: "I help others, I give them my merits, I obtain grace for them, I free them from their sins," all of which are solely Christ's work and office. In this way they are Christ, even though they do not call themselves Christ. For Matthew 24[:23] does not prophesy that they will say: "I am called Christ," but, }"I am Christ." It is not the name but the office and work of Christ which they usurp.

Therefore we conclude without dispute, query, and doubt, that all in holy orders who are not priests, monks, or nuns with that inner Christian conviction which we mentioned have most certainly taken their vows against God's First Commandment, and their religious life must be evaluated accordingly. They are ten times worse than that thieving, wicked rogue, of whom we spoke above. Like heathens and Jews, they certainly belong to that mass of perdition which is the devil's own, they, and all they are and possess. Actually St. Peter says of them, II Peter 2[:1]: "False prophets will arise among you who will deny the Master who bought them, and in their greed they will exploit you with false words." They are certainly good at that. All goods and dues have been channeled to the clergy because of their wicked, unchristian spiritual life which they support with false words. Therefore, they should all be advised to give up tonsures and cowls, get out of convents and monasteries, and cease keeping their vows. Or they may begin anew and take vows for such a life with Christian faith and conviction. For a vow taken with an unchristian intention has no more significance in the eyes of God than these words: "Look here, God, I vow not to be a Christian all my life, I recant the vows given at my baptism, I desire to take and keep a better vow without Christ, aided by my own life and works." Is that not a terrible, nay a horrible vow? But that is how it is, as has been thoroughly proved above. Now this refers to people who, we generally assumed, enter holy orders with the finest possible intentions. For that mad and large mass of men who choose to be priests and monks for the sake of their belly, in order that they may have security in this life—and this at present comprises the greater number—is not worthy of any consideration, to say nothing of the fact that their vows cannot have any validity. Let them go back to a secular occupation if they so desire, for they never truly entered holy orders nor lived the religious life. They should stop blaspheming God with their tomfoolery and leave their benefices, tenures, and livings, and give up their nuns' and monkish business. O Lord God, how utterly blind this world is, how topsy-turvy! The secular is now spiritual and the clergy are the world. How powerful is the realm of Antichrist!

Second, we shall inquire whether someone, who honestly entered holy orders with Christian conviction, might not be permitted to return to a secular occupation in the face of cogent reasons. I ask that only men with a just and honest mind, who are not quick to judge but anxious to hear basic considerations should follow this debate. You cannot tell those mad, popish adherents or the Herodists anything; no one can debate with them. They can hold their ears, gnash their teeth, and cry: heretic, heretic, heretic, the stake, the stake, the stake! We bypass them for they are crazy, and we speak to those who would like to have consciences instructed. It is irrefutable, that a Christian intention to enter the ecclesiastical estate consists in this (as we said above) that it does not do so as if that estate were useful and necessary to abolish sins, earn grace, become just, serve God in a special way, and obtain eternal life. All these things are only attributes of the common Christian faith, which looks to Christ and nowhere else for such treasures. On the contrary such a decision must be devoid of that unchristian error; its only purpose must be to submit to a good bodily exercise for this life here on earth. It is also equally irrefutable that God will not acknowledge a vow or the ecclesiastical estate unless the Christian intention is presupposed. This must be so, because of the strong stand St. Paul takes when in Romans 14[:23] he says: "Whatever does not proceed from faith is sin."

God will not acknowledge sin; Psalm 5[:5] and Habakkuk 1[:13]. If God will not acknowledge such vows and estate unless they are seen as free and not necessary nor binding to obtain eternal life, and if Christian conviction does not approach this matter or the vows in any other way, I would gladly listen to him who could thoroughly and honestly deny that a clergyman could take up a secular occupation without harming his soul and with a good conscience towards God, especially if he does so for valid reasons. Frequently it is argued that this would be unusual and that the sacred fathers also acted and wrote differently. But this is no conclusive proof at all. We are not asking what was traditionally done or what the writings of the sacred fathers say, but what is right and pleasing to God. Who can guarantee us that tradition is not wrong and that the fathers never erred? This is particularly so, since Christ prophesied in Matthew 24[:24] that even the elect would be deceived by false Christians, which the clergy are. Say what you will, an agreement is simply impossible here between the two positions, namely, that something should be undertaken or vowed before God and our conscience freely and without necessity for the salvation of our soul, and yet that there can be no release from such vows and that they must be kept till we die, if we are not to suffer the loss of our soul's salvation. These two positions are diametrically opposed to each other. Think about that.

A Christian vow to enter holy orders must be made in the following way before God: Behold, God, I vow to observe this life which is free by nature and not a condition for obtaining eternal life. Will not God answer: What is it you are vowing here? What is it that you intend? Do you not have enough essential things to observe? You are vowing simply that you may keep it or leave it. Fine, go then, I do not object. This vow has the natural conclusion in the eyes of God that we are free to observe the religious life and free to leave it, just as when your servant vows and says to you: Master, I promise to serve you voluntarily for this extra day; it is a service I may do or omit while the other days I am in duty bound to you, etc. It is my opinion that this servant will have honored his vow whether he did the service or not, as it may transpire. According to my understanding the vows of all clerics are similar, for the simple reason that faith makes all things free and that it is impossible that anything but faith alone should be necessary or be made necessary by us or by angels or by any creatures for our salvation. That is the liberty which Christ has won for us, concerning which St. Paul teaches in Galatians 6 [5:1], where he opposes every doctrine of men: "Stand fast in the freedom for which Christ has set us free." Therefore the vows of all clerics must naturally presuppose the liberty to leave religious life again and must be made as follows: I vow chastity, poverty, and obedience to God and to you according to the rule of St. Augustine and to keep this vow or leave it, until I die.

Someone may now start to laugh and say: What a foolish, ridiculous vow, what obvious tomfoolery and swindle! I reply: Do not be surprised if men do ridiculous and foolish things when they depart from God's ordinances and follow their own blind ideas and do what pleases them rather than what God's word teaches. Such a vow is ridiculous, foolish and empty, but thereby God's wrath is kindled and innumerable souls are led astray, so that even the elect hardly manage to escape. Men have invented these vows and this religious life and that is why they are and will continue to be a mere human nothing. Long ago when the Christian education and upbringing of young people was begun (the very thing that ought to be done in our schools today), the youth were voluntarily placed under a discipline for a time. Some were happy to stay there for the rest of their lives and so a tradition arose that only few left the fellowship and usually all remained in the community till death. In this fashion convents and monasteries came into being. When the masters became lazy and the young people uncontrollable, they invented these cords and chains, these vows; with them they ensnared consciences and rid themselves of trouble and supervision. Each one had to discipline himself, to remain chaste and good, because he was bound to do so by his vow, much in the same way as we have the cursed practice at our universities of restraining and governing everything by oaths and vows and quite unnecessarily and shamefully entangle our poor youth. Thus free Christian schools became reformatories and monasteries, faith was transformed to works, and freedom was bound and destroyed by vows. Therefore it is not surprising that at a time when Christian freedom is again shining brightly, human vows should be

regarded as ridiculous and foolish. Christian liberty is never compatible with the scrupulous vows of external works. The one must
give way to the other, one of the two is useless. Faith grants
freedom in externals, while vows make externals mandatory. How
can the one be compatible with the other? Thus faith is of God,
vows are of men. It is impossible that God should cast faith aside
and look to our vows. Therefore whoever returns to a secular life
when he pleases, being a priest, monk, nun only as long as he
desires, certainly neither sins against God nor breaks his vows.

Let us consider this matter a little more, so that consciences, in
misery and bondage and suppressed by this Herod and Antichrist,
may be comforted. I shall assume that vows were taken in the
Christian way and that they are both binding and necessary to
keep. What shall we say, if it should become impossible for someone to keep any one of them? We may look, as an example, at one
of the most obvious cases, namely the vow of chastity, which
many, as all can see, find impossible to keep, particularly in the
virtual absence of the special natural gift for such a life. Moses
wrote extensively about natural discharges in men and women,
while awake and asleep. These are matters which nowadays one
does not discuss openly, for our ears have become so very much
cleaner than the Holy Spirit's mouth, and we are ashamed of
things about which there is nothing to be ashamed, and are not
ashamed when we ought to be ashamed. There is probably a need
for everyone, particularly the youth, to be informed and educated
in this regard. Where that high, heavenly gift is absent, there will
be discharges, according to the laws of nature. Where man and
woman do not come together, nature will nevertheless, take its
course and cannot be restrained, so that it would be better that
men and women lay with one another, in accordance with God's
creation and nature's demands. Much advice has been given and
many books written about all this. Would to God they were of
some help and all of them were well written! But I ask: What
advice will you give to a person who is unable to restrain himself?
You say: Restrain him with prohibitions! Very good, but one of
three things is bound to happen: because that high gift is absent,
men and women will get together wherever they can, as is now the
case among the priests; or nature will relieve itself; or, where

259

neither occurs, there will be a continual burning, an eternal sexual desire and a secret suffering, and you will have made a devil's martyr of such a person, with the result that a man will snatch the ugliest woman on earth, and a woman will take the most repulsive man on earth, and all this because of a raging, evil desire of the flesh.

All who have chaste ears should, and I am sure, will pardon me, but if I am to give any advice at all I must get to grips with this sickness of souls, like a doctor who has to examine the excrement and private parts. Now God does not desire a forced, involuntary chastity. Indeed in his eyes, unless it is voluntary, it is no chastity at all, just as any other service we offer God must be voluntary, if he is to accept it. What do you achieve if you keep such a poor person all his life in unchaste chastity so that without ceasing he sins in his heart against his vows? Might it not perhaps be better if the man sometimes had a girl in his room, and the girl a boy? Some teach that it is enough if a person is willing to take upon himself the vows of chastity and to enter upon such a life and that it will stand him in good stead if later he becomes unwilling; in view of his voluntary entry into that life, this will not harm him.[28] O you deceivers and blind leaders of the blind! You judge service to God according to works and not according to the spirit! Everything that is done unwillingly is done in vain and it were better to leave it. For it may well happen that men and women who come together have less sexual passion and desire than such a single man and single woman. But the greater the desire, the greater the sin of unchastity. So there is no help or advice for these three kinds of people. The pope lets them manage as best they can with their discharges, their flaming sexual desires, their sufferings, so that in my opinion, they are the children who were sacrificed and burnt as an offering to the fiery idol Moloch among the people of Israel.

You answer: What else can I do? It is not right to permit them to marry because of their vows, inasmuch as scripture says: *Vovete et reddite*, "Make your vows and perform them" [Ps. 76:11]. I was waiting for that answer. Now you must give me an answer as well. You say, it is not right to allow them to marry; but is it right to let

---

[28] E.g., Thomas Aquinas, *Summa theologiae*, II², ques. 88, art. 6, ad 2.

them fornicate and have their discharges and ardent sexual desires? Is this not a worse breaking of vows than if they were honest? What a fine way to support their vows, by prohibiting marriage, when you see that you cannot prevent fornication and discharges and ardent sexual desire! In my opinion that is a case of leaving the beam in the eye and pulling out the splinter.

Yes, you say, but the man can leave the concubine and lead a chaste life, which he cannot do if he is married. My dear man, give me some examples to prove that. Married people will sooner stay apart and voluntarily practice abstinence than such folk. But let us overlook that point. Now give me an answer to this: In his rule St. Augustine demands that his friars do not go anywhere alone, but always two by two. I once vowed to observe that to the end of my life. Well now, what if I am captured and am forced to be alone? Tell me, what happens to my vow? If I am to keep my vow in this situation I must rather have myself killed than permit myself to be alone. But what if they do not want to kill me but keep me in solitary confinement by force? There is no other way, my vow must be broken, or it must always have included this qualification. I vow to observe this rule in this and this, insofar as I am able.

Or again, I vow to pray, to wear certain clothes and other similar things according to the rule. Well now, I get ill and I have to lie in bed and am neither able, nor do I care, to observe any of these things. What about the commandment, *vovete et reddite*, "Make your vows and perform them"? My illness is no excuse, for God's commandments must be kept absolutely, without exception, in life as in death, in sickness as in health. What will you say to that? There is no point in thinking up lame, idle, unfounded excesses. We are dealing with serious matters on which depend the salvation of souls, where honest, correct, and solid answers are necessary. So if you were going to say: if I should be captured and forced to be alone and if I should be ill so that I were unable to observe those other requirements, then it is sufficient that I have the intention to keep my vows and that I am breaking the rule against my will. Let God see my intention, whenever fulfillment is not possible. My dear man, that is no help; when I took my vow, it was made in reference to deeds. It is not concerned with the will only, but includes those deeds that are described in the rule. Consequently, if deeds do not follow, the vow is broken, unless the vow excludes the case of inability. Otherwise I, too, could take a woman and say: I really have the will to observe the rule of chastity and what I do is against my will, but I find it impossible to act otherwise; nature compels and its attractions are overpowering me. Who in all the world would not rather live in chastity, without a woman, if only he could as he would? You will have to submit a better argument.

Now, if in the case of the vows of the clergy in some matters the impossibility [of keeping them] is taken into account (as no one can deny that it is), and no one sins even if he does not fulfill the vow all his life because of impossibility, then I would like to hear an honest reason why the vow of chastity must be singled out and kept, no matter whether this is possible or not; why could the vow of chastity not presuppose the following qualification: I vow chastity insofar as it is possible for me to keep it. If we speak openly and avoid all lame and frivolous trickery, we will have to admit that either impossible chastity, like all the other impossible things, is never vowed, or there never has been a true monk on this earth. After all, there never was a monk who was not sick at least once or was in some other way hindered so that he had to overlook some parts of his rule, which is actually against his vow. In all these matters it is common practice among them that such aspects of the rule are voluntarily submitted to the jurisdiction of their superior, who determines any matter, to grant exemption to the petitioner, not simply because of impossibility, but also for reasons of convenience or any other reason. But all this is contrary to the vows, because they must be understood without any qualification. No creature will relieve you of your obligation to keep what you have vowed to God. You vow to keep the whole rule, yet your superior excuses you from your obligation in whatever part he thinks fit or you need help, so that truly the vows of monks appear to have the following content: I vow to keep the rule insofar as I am able and my superior determines. If such are not the content and intention of the vow, all orders and monasteries are once again dishonest and damned, or there never has been a monk on earth. Not one of them has ever understood or viewed this point different-ly. Why should a superior not have the power to grant dispensation to a monk so that he may return to a secular life and marry, when he becomes aware of the flaming and restless temptation of the flesh welling up in him? If he cannot grant dispensation from the vow of chastity, how can he grant it from the others? And if from the others, why not also from the vow of chastity, especially when the necessity here is greater than in the other cases?

Consequently, vows have been divided into *substantialia* and *accidentalia*. That is, some vows are remissible, others are irremissible. They have determined that there are three irremissible vows: poverty, chastity, and obedience. All the others, together with the whole rule and order, they call remissible. What a wicked rogue is the devil and full of a thousandfold cunning! If we ask for the reasons for such distinctions and the authority to do so, they can only reply that they do so by their own authority without any reason or purpose. For when they saw how impossible it was that they vowed to observe a rule which they simply could not keep, they thought, well, what shall we do? All these vows have been taken and are not being kept? If all monks are worthy of damnation, not one of them is in the blessed state, even though all orders and rules are clearly impossible and foolish. We shall deal with this situation in the following way: we will exclude three vows and call them irremissible; whoever does not keep them, shall be damned. The others will be called remissible and do not carry the penalty of damnation in case of non-observance.

That is what happened, and that is what they all believe, practice, and teach. But just a moment, dear sirs, there is something we want to discuss with you, concerning this matter.

If you truly have the authority to introduce remissible and irremissible vows, you also have the power to condemn people or to pronounce them blessed. Tell me, how can I be certain that your distinction is right and pleasing to God? Who will quieten and assure my conscience, when it is hard pressed by this commandment: *vovete et reddite*? Do you imagine that all I need is to know that you have made this distinction or that you will indicate those things that need not be observed? No, your distinctions and dispensations will never satisfy me when I have to face the storm: *vovete et reddite*. For I did not simply vow to keep the irremissible parts: I vowed to observe the whole rule, both its remissible and irremissible sections. The Supreme Judge will not permit me to change his word and say, *Omnia vovete, aliqua reddite*, but he will rather say: *quodcunque voveris, redde*, and again: *redde vota tua*. Accordingly this separation of three vows from the rest is erroneous, it leads people astray, it is a device invented by human arrogance; alternately, all vows must be equally remissible, for they have been equally vowed and are demanded by the same commandment. It must be equally possible to keep them or to refrain from keeping them. What will you say to that, dear sirs? You will say: It is impossible and ridiculous that monastic life should be regulated in this way. Very true, and fools we are, for we take our vows, and do not know what those vows imply. Then we try to solve our problem, and we distinguish between the possible and the impossible, to keep and not to keep, remissible and irremissible, as we think fit, but the Supreme Judge will not permit that. He will not allow us to bend his commandments, now this way, now that way, to suit ourselves.

You learned this from the pope, for he, too, takes this commandment of God, *vovete et reddite*, and stretches it in whatever direction it pleases him. He is prepared to give dispensation from all vows except from those of chastity and from those of pilgrimages to Rome, St. James, and Jerusalem. Accordingly, God's commandment is to be understood as follows: Vow chastity, and pilgrimages to St. James, Rome, and Jerusalem, and keep these vows. Any other vow you are not obliged to keep. Behold, in this way God's commandment is subject to the pope's authority; he determines what is to be kept and what need not be kept. O you cursed abomination, how presumptuous and blasphemous is your arrogance against your God! But what is the pope's reason and purpose in all this? None other than that chastity and pilgrimages are a wonderful thing, and the other matters are insignificant. Behold him, that stupid fool and blasphemer, who relaxes God's commandment when it commands a small thing and teaches us to keep it when it demands big things, rather rigidly and in complete opposition to Christ, Matthew 5[:19]: "Whoever then relaxes one of the least of these commandments and teaches men so, shall be called least in the kingdom of heaven," like the pope. What is least you need not keep; we relax the commandment: *vovete et reddite*

264

in all that is least. His children, the clergy, speak as their father teaches them: *vovete et reddite* the three irremissible vows, but *vovete et non reddite* the remissible ones. Now tell me whether the ecclesiastical estate is not the devil's own realm and business, founded on plain lies and blasphemy against God.

No, what is demanded in God's commandments, whether it is small or great, must be observed. We must not judge importance according to works, but by the commandment. You must not determine whether the work is great or small, whether it must be observed or relaxed, but only whether it is commanded. If it is commanded, there can be no relaxation, no matter what the situation may be, for Christ says: "Not an iota, not a dot, will pass from the law" [Matt. 5:18]; it must all be accomplished. However the pope and his disciples do not only remove the iotas and the dots from this commandment, *vovete et reddite*, but even the letters, the text, the meaning, everything. The clergy cannot deny that they vow all the remissible or accidental vows and they are all included in the word *vovete*. For they always refer to *vota*, vows, even though they make them remissible. Therefore they cannot deny that they are in duty bound to observe them and that they also cannot escape the word *reddite*. Otherwise you could well harbor an enmity in your heart against your neighbor and say you are not bound to love him. It fully suffices that you do not kill him and so keep the greater part of the Fifth Commandment and leave the smaller part. Likewise we might just as well divide all of God's commandments into great and small ones or into remissible and irremissible works and say: We are not bound to observe the small or remissible ones. God forbid, even though the pope and the universities thus hold and teach, and the clerics unfortunately follow them.

What, then, shall we do about this? If those in holy orders must keep all their vows and rules as irremissible, who of them will be saved? Will you condemn them all? I am not prepared to condemn a single one of them and would rather that all of them either leave the monasteries or have had the opportunity to practice the religious life in some other way. But they must surely all be condemned, if they arbitrarily tear apart and stretch the word of God. For that reason I have prolonged this debate that I might plainly make my point, that either all vows must be remissible or all must be irremissible; they must be completely equal, one like the other. Thus if any one of them may be relaxed for a purpose with a good conscience, so also chastity and any other may and shall be relaxed if there is compelling need and reason. I hope I have shut the mouths of my opponents so that they must keep silent and have no way to answer me. Since we see publicly that in the case of impossibility vows are relaxed, even for those in holy orders, and God does not demand that they keep them, I would like it determined that no vow may be taken before God in any other way, or administered in any other manner, than with the reservation and intention: provided it is possible and the superior permits it. Then we will be able to give all young monks and nuns wives and husbands and secularize them if they feel that this is what they must have and if they find it impossible to observe their vows with a good conscience and in a way pleasing to God and in keeping with his will. So we will return the monasteries to their ancient, initial, original form and life and let them be Christian schools in which boys and girls are taught discipline, honor, and the faith, remaining there voluntarily till their death, or as long as they like, for God has never regarded them in any other way, or desired them to be otherwise.

To continue, we must cross swords with them once more, so that we may see how confused and groundless this religious life is. Let me assume now that their dream about the three irremissible vows, namely poverty, chastity, and obedience, is true. There are two kinds of poverty, spiritual and physical. Of spiritual poverty Christ says, Matthew 5[:3]: "Blessed are the poor in spirit," by which he means that we should be detached, and ready to do without all possessions, with no desire for them in our hearts, even though we have and exercise control over many riches, like Abraham, Isaac, Jacob, and all good Christians. This poverty is vowed in baptism and is common to all Christians; the vow is not taken by those in the ecclesiastical estate, for their vow presupposes Christian, evangelical poverty, which all have in common. Physical poverty means that we have no external possessions. This is impossible, and Christ has neither commanded nor observed it himself, for man cannot live on this earth without food and clothes. So they have interpreted physical poverty to mean that we have nothing that belongs to us. This kind of poverty was found among the apostles and described by Luke in Acts 4[:32]. Christ also practiced it, for the purse which Judas had, was the common possession of all the apostles. Thus John 15 [12:6] does not say that Judas had Christ's purse, but that he had the purse and was in charge of what was put into it. These words prove that the purse was the common property of all. Otherwise he would have said: He had Christ's purse and was in charge of what was given to Christ. Note that St. Bonaventure was a cardinal, Pope Eugene was St. Bernard's disciple, and many religious became bishops and popes. Tell me now, what became of their vow of poverty? Yet they are saints. If that vow had not been remissible and voluntary in the eyes of God, they would certainly stand condemned as those who had failed to keep their vow till death. Popes, cardinals, and bishops always have their own possessions and use them as they please, which is altogether contrary to the vow of poverty. Thus in the eyes of all the office of pope or cardinal or bishop is considered as virtually secular in contrast to the estate of the religious.

If now you reply that they practiced obedience and were elevated to an office of greater perfection and were not in charge of their own possessions, but of those of the church—my dear man, be careful what you say. Is that not mere verbiage? Do you think you can silence me with that? Not so, my dear brother. First, whatever ideas you may have about obedience, the keeping of vows is obedience to God and God's commandment; in this we may not obey anyone else, not even an angel, as St. Paul says in Galatians 1[:8] and Peter in Acts 5[:29]: "We must obey God rather than men." If they have departed from obedience to God for the sake of obedience to the pope, they have departed from heaven and have gone to hell. No, you cannot treat God's commandments and obedience to him in such an off-handed way. Otherwise, I too could say that you may give up the vow of chastity for the sake of the pope and transgress all of God's commandments, for if you can transgress one of God's commandments for the sake of men, then you can transgress them all. Second, even if the office of cardinal and pope and bishop were an estate of perfection, they would still not be permitted to transgress God's commandments. No estate

can ever be considered as free from obedience to God's commandments, least of all an estate of perfection; that is quite erroneous
and plain deception. Perfection is never against God's commandments; on the contrary, it is entirely bound by God's commandments and breaks none, but keeps them all. You see how big those
people's lies and swindle are, so that they do not know what they
say or of what they speak, when they elevate perfection beyond
God's commandment and thereby try to annul God's commandment. Since the offices of pope, cardinal, and bishop have assumed
sovereign authority, the most imperfect of all, we will not be able
to save these saints, unless we assert that in the eyes of God all
vows are only temporary and can be altered at will, in the same
way as we see the vow of poverty being varied. Why should not
the vow of chastity lend itself to a similar change when there is
compelling need and reason, inasmuch as it is in no way more than
the vow of poverty?

But if we grant that these saints have entered the state of
perfection and have thus been elevated beyond the vow of poverty, then you will have to concede that the estate of matrimony is
an estate of perfection comparable with the estate of chastity or
impossible chastity, as St. Paul says in I Corinthians 7[:9]: "It is
better to marry than to be aflame with desire." It is always better
for a man to lie with his wedded wife than to have seminal discharges, or to burn with sexual desire, or to have sexual intercourse
with an unmarried woman. Therefore, let all who observe a life of
unchaste chastity and are bound to an imperfect, involuntary estate of chastity, depart from all this and enter the perfect estate of
matrimony. Or do you oppose this? Your excuses on behalf of the
estate of perfection are also invalid.

Third, how can you be so daring as to claim that the vow of
poverty has not been broken because they are not in charge of
their own possessions but rather those of the church? If that were
really so, they would not be more than a secular domestic servant
or bailiff, would they? Why then do you not consider them members of the clergy as well, if they are not in charge of their own
possessions. Nothing but idle tales! In fact, the contention is not
true. The bishops do have possessions of their own; in comparison
with the clergy who are bound to the vow of poverty, their life is

considered to be totally different in a thousand ways. In short, no excuses are possible here. If we want to keep our saints, we will have to assert that the vow of poverty should not extend beyond what the superior determines or sound reason demands.

But there is no need to roam about in our argument; it is clear that a man in the ecclesiastical estate vows no more than childlike servile poverty, which consists in having no possessions of his own, in being subject to authority, and in accepting whatever is given to him. However, as soon as he comes to power, supervises others, and distributes goods, he is not bound to the vow of poverty until such time as he is dismissed and again is subject to a superior. For as far as the holding, use, control, and distribution of possessions are concerned, what difference is there between such a ruler and a secular manager or bailiff? They are false words, as St. Peter says [II Peter 2:3]. Whatever one may call it, it is basically a secular profession, work, and estate. God does not accept the vows in any other sense than as voluntary and remissible, otherwise no monastery would have a superior. Necessity compels us to maintain monasteries as places where the young can be schooled and their bodies exercised.

Likewise obedience cannot and may not be understood in any other way than as childlike servile obedience, since the words of the vow clearly demand obedience to the abbot or prior. But if one becomes himself a bishop or a superior, what of the vow of obedience? We are required to be obedient to him; he, however, need not obey. Will you once more offer your lame excuse that such a man is elevated to a higher obedience or retains the willingness in his heart to return to the life of obedience? All this has already been considered. For we read, *vovete et reddite*, and no gloss can survive those words, for God will not allow us to destroy his commandments for the sake of a higher or middle or lower obedience. It is clear, then, that those in holy orders vow a subjection of the body and not of the heart. The willing subjection of the heart to everyone is common to all Christians, as St. Paul says in Romans 12[:16]: "Have respect for one another and let each have the other as his superior." If that is so, monasteries may not have superiors, nor may there be bishops, otherwise the obedience that was vowed will cease with the vow. You see now how aptly these two vows have been called irremissible, and how they operate with fables and fictitious words. God, however, allows his saints to take their vows and live their religious lives in this way. Patient with their foolishness, he will not acknowledge the irremissible vows as you will have gathered from this whole argument; they are contrary to Christian liberty and good order. However, the evil spirit must and shall have his game with unbelievers and his folly must be evident in their deeds, as St. Paul teaches.

That leaves us with the solitary vow of chastity; it is the only one that they insist is absolute and irremissible; yet of all vows it surely ought to be the most flexible and remissible. In the case of all other vows they say: *vovete et non reddite*; in this case they are as hard as steel, quite unbending and say: *vovete et reddite*. Is this not a horrible perversity? The evil one has done so, that he might more powerfully keep souls in the bondage of unchastity and catch them where they are weakest and easily held. He knew very well that the other vows could be more easily observed. That is why he did not insist on them, but concentrated entirely on this impossible one, in order to establish his tyranny more securely. O Lord God, behold the deception and tomfoolery with which he ensnares those who are in holy orders!

Therefore nothing in this religious life has firm foundation, nothing is certain, nothing is consistent; it is erratic and is observed without both scriptural basis and reason. The absence of a scriptural basis, even like numerous fundamental errors and lies, would in itself be sufficient reason to leave it all and run away. In addition all this is so powerfully condemned by Christ (Matthew 24[:23 ff.]), Paul (II Timothy 3[:2 ff.]), and Peter (II Peter 2[:1 ff.]), that even though you had made ten vows, you would be bound to abandon them or to take another, new and voluntary one, as was pointed out above, because you would see that those vows are the devil's doing and were made against the will of God. They have one counter-argument; some of the sacred fathers lived the religious life. They should feel uneasy, however, for in reply, we point to the word of Christ that even the elect will be deceived by them, in the same way as the magi here were led astray by Herod. And there are many similar examples: the three young men, Hananiah, Azariah, and Mishael remained in the fiery, burning furnace in

270

Babylon [Dan. 3:19 ff.], Naaman of Syria alone remained faithful to God in the temple of the idol [II Kings 5:1 ff.], Joseph remained faithful in Egypt [Gen. 39:7 ff.]. What more can I say? St. Agnes remained chaste in a brothel;[29] the martyrs did not deny their faith in the dungeons, and there are Christians who constantly remain faithful in the flesh, in the world, and in the midst of devils. Should he not have been able to preserve Francis, Bernard, and others like them in the midst of error, and deliver them, even though they erred at times? There is hardly a great saint whom he permitted to live without blame; he let Moses and Aaron and Miriam, David, Solomon, Hezekiah, and many others stumble, so that no one might put his trust in the exemplary lives of the saints or in works not based on the Scriptures. But we in our clumsy way, blindly rush for anything we see or hear about saints, and what we generally hit upon is the very thing in which they were human and had their weaknesses and erred. So error becomes a fundamental truth for us, and we build on the leaning wall, of which Psalm 62[:3–4] speaks: "How you set upon the man! You will shatter yourselves as on a leaning wall and upon a tottering fence. But they planned to thrust him down. They take pleasure in falsehood. They bless with their mouth, but in their hearts they curse," etc.

Even if everything else were well with the ecclesiastical estate, the abuse of the mass would be sufficient reason to flee and run away at its very mention.[30] In my opinion this abuse of the solemn sacrament must be held up against this estate as the most wicked, the most destructive, and the most horrible that has occurred on this earth; of all evils it will be the greatest and last. They change the mass into a sacrifice and a good work which they sell to people and on which they levy every conceivable toll. Oh what a terrible perversion, what angry judgment it deserves! Would to God that all private masses were abolished, then we could hope that God might be a little more gracious to us. But in our blindness we think we might commit a serious sin if we abolished the mass, and so we

---

[29] Luther is referring to a legend found in the *Legenda aurea*; cf. WA 6, 461 and WA 8, 602.

[30] Cf. Luther's *On the Abrogation of the Private Mass* (*De abroganda missa privata* [1521]), WA 8, 411–76. This Latin treatise was immediately translated into German: *Vom Misbrauch der Messe* (1521). This latter is available in an English translation: *The Misuse of the Mass*, LW 36, 133–230.

have the audacity to propitiate and serve God with such horrible abuse, so that there is no end to his wrath and, as Psalm 109[:7] proclaims, "all our prayers are counted as nothing but sin." There should be only one mass each day celebrated as a communion, as a sacrament for the whole congregation. Indeed, only one mass a week would be even better. But there is nothing we can do about it, the practice is too deeply ingrained.

I have digressed with the best of intentions. Let him who will, take my advice. I am not at all concerned if the clergy will be angry with me and shout abusive language. I would rather they are angry, and not Christ, for I myself am bound to give advice to miserable consciences and souls, to help them, and to impart to everyone a little of that which God has given me. I do not want to burden myself with guilt for shirking my duty. I am not answerable for him who refuses to accept my advice; let him look to himself. My faithful service and advice cannot help him; if I could do more, I would. Let him who will, enter holy orders and remain in them. But let him who would have eternal life, see to it that he becomes a Christian, and let those who would be priests, be priests.

Perhaps the chaste hearts and holy priests of God who take no pleasure in anything but what they themselves say or write, will open their mouths at this and say: What a burden the cowl is for that monk! All he wants is a woman! Let them heap their slander and mischief upon me, those chaste hearts and great saints. Let them keep their hearts of iron and stone, let them puff themselves up, as long as you do not deny that you are human, a person of flesh and blood. For the rest let God judge between these angelic, staunch heroes and you, a sick and despised sinner! I should like to think that I have reached a point in life where by the grace of God I will remain as I am, although I am not yet over the hill and dare not compare myself with those chaste hearts. Indeed it would be a pity if I did, and I pray that God in his mercy may save me from that. For if you knew them as they really are, those men who pretend such great chastity and make such a public show of their self-discipline—and what it is that St. Paul means when he says in Ephesians 5[:12]: "For it is a shame even to speak of the things that they do in secret,"—then you would consider that their highly

272

praised celibacy was not even worth a prostitute wiping her shoes on it. Everything is topsy-turvy, that the chaste are the unchaste, and appearances deceive. Dear boy, do not be at all ashamed that you desire a girl, or that a girl longs for a boy, but see to it that it leads to marriage, and not fornication. Then there is nothing disgraceful about it—as little as eating and drinking is a disgrace.[31] Celibacy is supposed to be a virtue, but it is a veritable miracle of God, just as if a person did not eat or drink. It is beyond the capacity of a healthy body, not to mention the incapability of sinful and depraved human nature. There are not many virgins to whom God granted a long life; rather hurriedly he whisked them out of this world, like Cecilia, Agnes, Lucia, Agatha, and others like them. I know full well how noble that treasure is, but also how difficult it is to preserve for any length of time. If in every town, there were five boys and five girls, all twenty years of age, completely pure, with no experience of natural discharge, then I would be right in saying that the state of Christianity was better than in the days of the apostles and martyrs. O Lord God, I believe that unchastity would not have become so prevalent and spread in such a terrible way, if it had not been for this rule and vow of chastity. What a Sodom and Gomorrah the devil has created through these rules and vows! How vulgar has he made this odd chastity, causing unspeakable anguish. No brothel stimulant is as dangerous as these rules and vows invented by the devil.

Furthermore, I say that those boys and girls who entered an order before they felt the stirrings of flesh and blood, that is, those who are fifteen or sixteen or twenty years of age, should be immediately released, if they so desire. Their vow after all is useless, just as if a child had taken it. Consecration is valueless in this case, nor does it matter whether he is a priest, a deacon, or has entered some other holy order. Those consecrations are frauds and have no validity in the eyes of God. But enough of that, we must again pick up our subject at the point where we left off.

When the magi left Herod and turned to go to Bethlehem, the star again appeared and they were very glad. Such is always the case when the heart returns to the knowledge of the pure truth of

---

31 Luther's views on marriage and celibacy at this time are also presented in *The Estate of Marriage* (1522), *LW* 45, 17–49.

the gospel after being led astray in error. Then it is quickly rid of Herod and realizes how sure and bright the way of truth is in comparison with the glamor which the Herodists display, and the heart is glad. For the gospel is a comforting doctrine which leads us from human arrogance to a trust in nothing but the grace of God, as Psalm 4[:6–7] says: "Lift up the light of thy countenance upon us, O Lord! Therewith thou has put joy in my heart." All those who walk in their own strength and put their trust in human doctrines lead a hard and anxious life, and in the end it is all in vain. Which heart should not be glad upon realizing that the pope's dominion is nothing but work and a burdening of consciences which deceives the whole world with its external glamor? It is the nature of the divine light and truth to comfort consciences, cheer the heart, and establish a free spirit, in the same way as human doctrines naturally depress consciences, torture the heart, and extinguish the spirit.

Moreover, the star goes before them and does not leave them until it brings them to Christ. It goes no further and comes to rest over the place where the child is. The light of the sacred gospel does the same thing, for it is like a bright lamp in the darkness, as St. Peter calls it, II Peter 1[:19], which goes before us and leads us as long as we cling to it with a firm faith. It will not leave us until it brings us to Christ and the truth. It will not go further, for it teaches nothing but Christ. Thus the nature and work of the gospel are signified by this guiding star. The magi signify all the faithful. In the same way as the star led them physically to Christ and they followed it physically, so the gospel spiritually guides the hearts of men in this world. Faithful hearts see it and follow it with joy until they come to Christ. Hence St. Paul boasts in I Corinthians 2[:2], "I decided to know nothing among you except Jesus Christ and him only as crucified"; in Colossians 2[:8] he forbids us to follow any doctrine which does not teach Christ. What else can this mean but that this star points to Christ alone and to nothing else, and goes no farther? Hence all doctrine of men is condemned by this allegory; only the one, simple, pure light of the gospel shall be proclaimed to Christians, and we are to follow nothing but that same star. Therefore this word condemns the pope, the bishops, the priests and monks, and all their realm and doctrines; it requires us to avoid them as the tyranny of Herod.

This verse also shuts the mouth of the papists and Herodists and properly castigates their lies when deliberately and outrageously they teach not only that we should assume the presence of the Christian church and faith among them but also that he who does not hear them shall be regarded as one who does not hear the Christian church. They presume to be that sign and star which leads to Christ and truth, but that is false and a lie. If you would know where Christ and the truth are to be found, learn it from this story. Do not look to the pope, to the bishops' hats; do not seek it in the universities and monasteries, do not be deceived by the fact that they preach, pray, and sing much and conduct frequent masses; do not be impressed that they occupy the seat of the apostles and point to the authority of their ecclesiastical office. All this can deceive, and, in fact, does unceasingly deceive. They err and teach error. There is no other sign by which you can know where Christ and his church may be found than this one sure sign, this star, the holy gospel; every other sign is false and fails. Where the gospel is preached, there this star shines brightly, there without a doubt Christ is present, there you will assuredly find the church, whether it be in Turkey, in Russia, in Bohemia, or anywhere else. It is impossible that God's word should be proclaimed and God, Christ, and the Holy Spirit not be present. Likewise it is impossible that God, Christ, the Holy Spirit, the church, or anything blessed should be present where God's word is not proclaimed, even if they were to perform every imaginable miracle; nothing but the Herodists and the devil's realm can be present there. It has always been clear that the pope and the clergy do not proclaim God's word, but are merely concerned about doctrines of men.

> "They went into the house and found the child with Mary his mother and fell down and worshipped him" [Matt. 2:11].

This house is the Christian church, the assembly of all believers on earth, in which alone you find Christ and his mother. Only in the Christian church are they to be found who are pregnant and fruitful by the Holy Spirit, give Christian birth, and lead a Christian life. Nothing outside of this house, however beautiful its light, however great its wisdom, can be the abode of Christ and his mother, that is, there is no Christian life there, for this is possible only in faith and by the Holy Spirit. Therefore when the pope, a bishop, or whoever it may be, demands that you should look to them if you would see the church, think of this Gospel and look to the star and be assured that if that star does not rest above it, it is surely not the house in which you will find Christ and his mother. In other words, you will certainly not find the Christian church in any place over which the gospel does not hold sway and shine. This star will never fail you; without it you will never find the house which you hope to find. The star leads to this house and rests above it. The gospel leads you into the church, rests above it, and steadfastly remains there and allows no persecution to move it. It resounds and shines freely in every place, to the dismay of all its enemies, as we see it fulfilled in the apostles, martyrs and all saints, and daily still see it at work, wherever it is proclaimed.

"And they opened their treasures and offered him gold, and frankincense and myrrh" [Matt. 2:11].

All material sacrifices in the law of Moses, wherever they were made, signify the spiritual sacrifices of which Hebrews 12 [13:15] speaks: "Through him let us continually offer up the sacrifice of praise to God, that is, the fruit of lips that acknowledge his name." And Hosea 14[:1–2] says: "Return, O Israel, to the Lord your God, for you have stumbled because of your iniquity. Take with you words, and return to God, and say to him, 'Take away from us all iniquity and accept that which is good (that is, banish the evil that you have brought upon us by your hand and take with your hand the good that you give us) and we will render to you the calves of our lips,'" that is: praise and thanksgiving, for these are the proper calves which we are to offer to you. Of these Psalm 51[:18–19] says: "Lord, do good to Zion in thy good pleasure that the walls of Jerusalem may be rebuilt, then wilt thou accept the sacrifices, then calves will be offered on thy altar." Likewise Psalm 50 [cf. vv. 7–14]: "Hear, O Israel, I am your God, I do not reprove you for your sacrifices. What sacrifice will you bring to me? Do I eat the flesh of bulls or drink the blood of goats? For the world is mine, all

276

the birds of the air and every beast in the field, every offering you can render is continually before me. Offer to your God a sacrifice of praise and pay him the vows you have made. The sacrifice of praise honors me duly and that is the way to salvation." These texts clearly show that it must be a sacrifice of praise and thanksgiving, in order to be acceptable to God, certainly never an offering without praise and thanksgiving. If offered without praise and thanksgiving, he dislikes it and will not accept it, as he says, Isaiah 1[:11]: "What to me is your sacrifice? I have enough of your burnt offerings," etc.

There is nothing else we can give God, for he possesses everything and what we own, we have from him. We can give him nothing but praise and thanksgiving and honor. That is what Psalm 116[:12–13, 16–17] expresses: "What shall I render to God for all his bounty to me? I will lift up the cup of salvation and call on the name of God. Thou hast torn my bonds; therefore I will offer to thee the sacrifice of praise." Praise is simply confessing the good gifts which we have received from God, not ascribing them to ourselves but to him alone, and returning them to him. Such praise and witness may be made in two ways: first, to God alone, second, before men. Praise is really a work and fruit of faith, concerning which St. Paul teaches in Romans 10[:10, 9]: "For man believes with his heart and so is justified, but he confesses with his lips and so is saved. For if you confess with your lips that Jesus is Lord and believe in your heart that God raised him from the dead, you will be saved." St. Paul here seems to want to say: To believe in Christ secretly in your heart and to praise him in a private corner, is not true faith. You must confess openly with your lips before everyone what you believe in your heart. A confession may cost you your head, for the devil and men do not like to hear it and the cross is a necessary part of this confessing, for you see that the pope, the bishops, priests, and monks neither hear Christ's word nor tolerate it, so that the prophet truly says: "I will lift up the cup of salvation and call on the name of God" [Psalm 116:13], as if he wanted to say: If I praise and confess God, they will give me to drink of the cup of martyrdom. Come then, I will accept it in God's name and will not cease in my praise of God; that cup will not harm me but will be my healing and greatly help me to receive salvation. That is what Christ means when he says, Mark 8[:38]: "Whoever is ashamed of me and of my words in this sinful and adulterous generation, of him will the Son of man also be ashamed, when he comes in the glory of his Father with his holy angels."

Many exegetes have thought about these three gifts, some explaining them in one way, the others in another, but generally they are agreed that they represent three difficult confessions. Of these explanations we will choose those which seem best to us at present. The sacrifice of gold, it is said, signifies their confession that Christ is a king, the frankincense, that he is priest, the myrrh, that he died and was buried. These three aspects, it is said, apply to the humanity of Christ, but in such a way, that he is God and that all this happened to his humanity because of his divinity. First, then, Christian faith confesses and praises Christ as Lord and King over all things, according to the word in Psalm 8[:6]: "Thou hast made him lord over the works of thy hands and put all things under his feet," and Psalm 110[:1] says: "God has said to my lord: 'Sit at my right hand, till I make your enemies your footstool.'" This confession of true faith is the great, mighty, courageous, and fearless trust of all Christian believers in the face of everything that is against them, whether that is (as St. Paul says, Romans 8[:35, 39]) sword, or hunger, or cold, or any creature. Who will harm a Christian or terrify him, if he offers this gold, if he believes and confesses that his Lord Christ is also lord of death, hell, devils, and all creatures, and that all is in his hands, yea lies under his feet? He who has a gracious prince, fears nothing that is subject to that prince, but defies it, glories in his master's mercy and might, and testifies to it. How much more does a Christian glory in defiance of pain, torture, death, hell, and the devil! Confidently he says to them, what harm can you do to me? Are you not under the feet of my Lord? Defy me and devour me against his will! Behold, such a couragous heart is the fruit of this sacrifice of gold. How rare it has become in our day! Therefore when something terrifies or harms you it is most comforting that you speak up, confess Christ, and say: *Omnia subiecisti sub pedibus eius*, all things are under his feet, who can be against me?

Second, frankincense is used in worship according to the law of Moses that incense should be burned in the temple. This is the

278

privilege of the priestly office. So the sacrifice of frankincense is simply the confession that Christ is a priest who intercedes between God and us, as St. Paul says in Romans 8[:84]: He is our advocate and intercedes for us before God, which is of all things most necessary for us. For through his kingdom and with his priesthood he protects us from every sin and the wrath of God, and in our stead sacrifices himself to reconcile us with God so that through him we can face God with confidence and our conscience need not be terrified or fear his wrath and judgment, as Paul says, Romans 5[:1–2]: "Through him we are at peace with God and have access to his grace by faith." Now it is a much greater thing that he gives us security before God and pacifies our conscience, so that God and we ourselves are not at enmity with each other, than that he protects us from every harm that creatures may do to us, for guilt is greater than pain and sin is worse than death. Sin causes death, and if there were no sin, there would be no death, or at least it would not be harmful. Just as Christ is lord over sin and death and has the power to bestow grace and life to all who live in faith, so the sacrifice of gold and frankincense signifies the confession that he has these two offices and performs these two works. At the same time we give him thanks, as Paul does in I Corinthians 15[:55–57]: "O death, where is thy sting? The sting of death is sin, but the law is the power of sin. But thanks and praise be to God who has given us the victory over death and sin through our Lord Jesus Christ." That is truly the highest and most courageous trust, that a man can confront his sin, his evil conscience, and God's terrible wrath and judgment with this priest and say and confess with a firm faith: *Tu es sacerdos in eternum,* "You are a priest for ever" [Ps. 110:4]. But if you are a priest, then you are an advocate for the sins of all who confess you to be such a priest. As little then, as God's judgment, wrath, sin, and an evil conscience can condemn or terrify you, so little do they condemn or terrify me for whom you are such a priest. Behold, the true sacrifice of frankincense is undismayed in the face of every sin and the wrath of God, through Christ in faith.

Third, we use myrrh to anoint the dead body so that it may not decay in the grave. Hence Christ's death and resurrection are indicated here, for he is the only one who died, was buried, and did not suffer decay, but was raised again from the dead as Psalm 16[:10] says: "For thou wilt not leave my soul in hell, or let thy holy one see corruption." And his incorruptibility is attested to all by those who are preserved and kept by physical myrrh. Therefore the sacrifice of myrrh signifies the confession that Christ died but without being subject to corruption, that is, that death was conquered in life, that he never died according to his divinity and was raised again from the dead according to his humanity. To confess this, is of all three the most necessary, even though all three are necessary and should remain inseparable. For you should not think that if he became king and priest for you and has granted you such great benefits, this was achieved without price or with little cost or came to you by your merits. In him and through him your sin and death are overcome and you are granted grace and life, but it cost him much and was achieved with hard work and bitter sweat since he paid for it most dearly with his own blood and life. For it was not possible to overcome God's wrath, judgment, conscience, hell, death, and all evil things, and indeed to gain all benefits, unless God's righteousness received satisfaction, sin was given its due reward, and death was overcome by justice. Accordingly, St. Paul generally refers to the suffering and blood of Christ when he proclaims the grace of God in him, in order to indicate that all the benefits that are given to us through Christ, are granted only because of his ineffable merit and the price he paid. Thus in Romans 3[:25] he says: "God has put him forward as an expiation by his blood, to be received by faith." And in I Corinthians 2[:2]: "For I decided to know nothing among you except Jesus Christ and him crucified," etc. To sacrifice myrrh, then, is to confess the great price and work which it cost Christ to be our priest and king.

Behold, these are the three things by which we must praise and confess Christ and his three works which he has shown us and daily continues to show us till the last day. The order in which they occur is also fine, even though the evangelist begins with the gold as the greatest gift. For it would not be possible for him to be king over all things for our good, if he had not first reconciled God with us and quietened our conscience, so that he might rule and do his work within us in peace and quiet, as in his own kingdom. Therefore he also had to be our priest. But if he was to be priest and

280

reconcile us with God through his priestly office, he had to satisfy God's righteousness for us. But no other satisfaction was possible than that he offered himself and died and in his own person conquered sin together with death. Thus in dying he became priest and through his priesthood he received the kingdom. Hence he received myrrh before frankincense, and frankincense before gold. Nevertheless Scripture always speaks of the kingdom first, then of his priesthood, and then of his death, as Psalm 110[:1] also does when first it describes his kingdom thus: "God has said to my lord: 'Sit at my right hand, till I make your enemies your footstool,' " etc. And then it continues to speak of his priesthood as follows: "God has sworn and will not change his mind, 'You are a priest for ever after the order of Melchizedek'" [Ps. 110:4]. Finally, it speaks of his passion as follows: "He will drink from the brook on his way; therefore he will lift up his head" [Ps. 110:7]. Hence we could also say here: He will taste myrrh, therefore he will be a priest, therefore he will also be king, so that the one follows from the other, and the one is the cause of the other, and each in order points to the other.

These plain and simple explanations must suffice. I leave it to those who have more time to furnish a more learned exposition. As for us, we must above all take care that we do not separate any one of these three confessions from the other, but offer them together. That Isaiah merely speaks of the gold and frankincense in the Epistle [Isa. 60:6] and is silent about the myrrh, is perhaps due to the fact that Christ's kingdom and priesthood have always existed, ever since the foundation of the world, as Paul says in Hebrews 13[:8]: "Christ yesterday, and today and for ever." All saints have been saved from death and sin by him, through faith in him, but at that time the third part, his suffering, the myrrh, had not yet been accomplished; so it was fitting that the evangelist should mention it after fulfillment had taken place. The Herodists and papists, however, have not only torn these three sacrifices apart but have destroyed them in such an abominable way as to defy description. They do indeed retain the names, and with their lips that Christ died for kings and priests and for us, but they come with contradictory words, deny everything with their heart and with their whole life, condemning it all in a most horrible way. We should begin to let myrrh remind us of all this, because they teach that man can achieve worthiness and become receptive for the mercy of God by his own strength, by the natural ability of his reason and free will, without God's grace. What else is this, but the desire to satisfy the righteousness of God, to calm his wrath and judgment and give peace to the conscience through one's own works, without the blood and suffering of Christ? That amounts to nullifying Christ's blood and his whole passion, indeed his whole humanity and all his work, and to regarding them as superfluous and trampling them under foot. St. Paul speaks of this in Hebrews 6[:4–6]: "For it is impossible that they who committed apostasy should again be restored to repentance, since they again crucify the Son of God on their own account and hold him up to contempt." Without Christ there is nothing but wrath and neither grace nor repentance. The papists fail to teach that we ought to seek and find grace in him alone. Thus the sacrifice of myrrh is totally abolished.

And so the sacrifice of myrrh is meaningless. How can Christ be their priest and mediator if they are so good and pure that they do not need his blood and mediation, but rather act as their own mediators and come before God's presence on their own behalf and seek to obtain grace and life by their own natural powers? In this way they confess, and indeed teach, that our natural powers are pure and good; under such circumstances Christ cannot be their priest. Who would have thought that Christians would see the day when someone could teach or hear that which is horrible to contemplate? Everywhere we can observe how the universities and the pope and the clergy hold the same belief and claim that whoever teaches otherwise propounds heresy. How accurately St. Peter has described them when he says in II Peter 2[:1]: "False teachers will arise among you who will deny the Lord who has bought them." He does not say, they will deny Christ, but: "the Lord who has bought them," as if he wanted to say: They will confess Christ with their lips, but they will not acknowledge that he has bought them with his blood; they will redeem themselves, without his blood and by their own natural powers seek to obtain God's grace, when indeed Christ alone purchased it for us all by his blood. This they have in mind when they say that the grace of

God can be obtained without cost or price. And so they come along and want to obtain it by their own strength and will not have Christ's purchase. But where Christ is not acknowledged as a priest, he will much less be acknowledged as king, for in no way are they subject to him; they are their own lords, that is, the devil's own retinue, because they will not allow him to rule over them or to do his work in them alone. Yet he remains king, priest, and redeemer over all creatures, even if they refuse to thank him for it. Thus you know that now is the time when St. Peter denies Christ thrice. Would to God they heard the crowing of the cock, repented, realized their apostasy, wept bitterly, and departed from the house of Caiaphas, that is, from the hellish assembly of the pope, where the fire of love of the world is kindled and the pope's retinue are gathered around it to warm themselves; the love of God has altogether grown cold in them. Let that suffice concerning spiritual sacrifices. We continue:

"And receiving an answer in their sleep not to return to Herod they departed to their own country by another way" [Matt. 2:12].

That is the final conclusion, that we should avoid the doctrines of men and not again be ensnared by them once we have been freed, just as these magi who once they were rid of Herod did not again return to him. For the sake of the salvation of our souls (and lest we fall into the disfavor of God), I therefore declare that we should avoid the laws and teachings of the pope and all papists, especially since we have recognized the pure, evangelical truth. By their teachings they lead us away from God, so that we follow our own reason and works. Thereby God's work is hindered. Yet he would and should give to us all things, even as he works in us all things. Indeed, he wills that we should expect this of him. But the doctrines of men impel us to anticipate him in every work; we desire to seize the initiative and seek God; he may come later and watch us. Let me give you one example for this: Those who seem to be most able, teach our youth and tell them they should gladly pray and go to church, and live a chaste and pious life. But they do not tell the youth how they should go about it or where to find it, as if it were sufficient to have taught them to be pious. Likewise, if these young people should marry or enter holy orders, they think it

283

is sufficient for them to do so by themselves, they do not consult God or even acknowledge his presence. But after the step has been taken, then God is expected to come and see what they have done and to regard the matter with favor and approval. Truly, young people are brought up in such a way that a girl is ashamed to ask God for a boy, or the boy for a girl. They think it foolish to make such a request known to God and prefer to stumble blindly into it themselves. That is why marriages are so rarely successful. Should we not rather teach a girl in all seriousness to come into God's presence confidently saying: Behold God, I have reached the age where I can marry, be thou my Father and let me be thy child, grant me a good man, and by thy grace help me to enter the estate of matrimony. Or if it be thy will, grant me the gift of chastity. Likewise a young man should pray for a girl and not initiate the matter by himself, but ask God to make a beginning and lay the first stone. Such are the true children of God who take no first step in any matter, however trivial, unless they have first addressed themselves to God about it. In this way Christ remains our king and all our works are his works and well done. But the doctrines of men will not permit that; they stumble ahead blindly as if there were no God and all depended on them, if it is to be done well. Behold, from this example you may well learn how seductive and contrary to God are the doctrines of men.

There are three ways in which we can avoid the doctrines of men. First, they can be avoided by conscience but not outwardly, as for example, when I make confession of sins, pray, and fast in accordance with papal law, nor indeed in the belief that I am obliged to do so or that it is a sin if I were to refrain; rather, they can be avoided voluntarily, of my own accord, without obligation, so that I could just as well let go if I so desired. In this case the doctrines of men have prompted the deed, but the conscience is free and regards the doing of the deed to be the same as its omission; it sees no sin in omitting it and no merit in doing it, for it is not rendering obedience, but acting out of its own good pleasure. Such people are probably the best. Thus these magi are still in the land of Herod and travel under his dominion; but they take no notice of him, however, do not go to him, and do not render him obedience. Likewise, whoever lives his life actively under the dominion of the pope and observes his laws of his own free will, how and when and where and as long as he desires, will not be harmed by them. But that is a deep insight which few people have and which can be gained only through God's Spirit in the heart, just as these magi received it in a dream, secretly; indeed no one can persuade anyone with so many words, from the outside, to have this insight, if the heart will not of itself feel it, as something from heaven.

The second way to avoid the doctrines of men is to avoid them both in conscience and in deed, as those do, who trample them under foot and observe the very opposite with a secure and happy conscience. This way is most necessary and best for the sake of the weak consciences in order to lead them out of their narrow confines and to make them as perfect and free as those strong people of the first group. This cannot be done very well by word of mouth or with the conscience, but one must intervene and show the opposite by practical example, just as Christ did when he told his disciples not to wash their hands in opposition to the laws of the Pharisees, etc. Similarly it would be good if some disregarded the prescribed and definite times for confession of sins and prayers and fasting, to show by way of example that the papal laws are foolishness and deception, and would then do all these things voluntarily, at some other time.

The third way to avoid the doctrines of men is to avoid them in deed but not in conscience, as those do, who arrogantly disregard them and yet believe they do wrong not to observe them. Unfortunately such a conscience can be found in the average man everywhere. Because of such people St. Paul says that these are critical times. Such consciences sin without ceasing, whether they keep the laws or break them, and the pope, because of his laws, is the murderer of their souls and the cause of such danger and sin. If they observe them, they act against faith, which must be free from all doctrines of men. If they do not observe them, they act against their conscience, which harbors the belief that they must be observed. This group needs a good instruction in the freedom of Christian faith and in putting aside the false conscience. If they are unable to do so, we bear their weakness for a while (as St. Paul teaches in Romans 15[:1–6]), allowing them to follow their conscience and to act accordingly, because of faith, until they too grow up and become strong. The other way is to go home and not to return to Herod; for every beginning that one makes to be a good and pious person is generally initiated by doctrines of men and outward holiness. But one must go beyond this to a simple faith and not lapse back into works and discard faith. In this way we come back at last to our homeland, from which we set out, that is, to God, by whom we were created. So the end and the beginning are reunited, like a golden ring. May God grant us that for the sake of Christ, our king and priest, to whom be praise for ever and ever!

We shall break off here for a space so that the book will not grow too large or boring to read. I hope that in these twelve Epistles and Gospels the Christian life may have been so fully depicted that more than enough has been said to the Christian about what is necessary for salvation. Would to God that my exposition and that of all doctors might perish and each Christian himself make the Scriptures and God's pure word his norm. You can tell by my verbosity how immeasurably different God's words are in comparison with any human word, how no single man is able to fathom sufficiently any one word of God and expound it with many words. It is an infinite word and must be contemplated and grasped with a quiet mind, as Psalm 84 [85:8] says: "I will hear what God himself will speak within me." None but such a quiet, contemplative mind can grasp it. He who is able to achieve that without glossary and exposition, will find my glosses and those of everyone else unnecessary, in fact, merely a hindrance. And so, my dear Christians, get to it, get to it, and let my exposition and that of all the doctors be no more than a scaffold, an aid for the construction of the true building, so that we may ourselves grasp and taste the pure and simple word of God and abide by it; for there alone God dwells in Zion. Amen.

INDEXES

INDEX OF NAMES AND SUBJECTS

INDEX TO SCRIPTURE PASSAGES

76:11 — 260
78:31 — 113
78:39 — 81
80:3 — 129
82:6 — 157
83:6–8 — 115
85:8 — 286
89:4–5 — 30
89:47–48 — 142
91:1–7 — 97
91:4 — 98
103:7 — 131
105:18 — 119
107:9 — 85
107:10 — 119
109:7 — 272
109:17 — 99
110:1 — 278, 281
110:4 — 279, 281
110:7 — 281
111:3 — 96
112:3, 9 — 96
116:10 — 143
116:11 — 88, 248
116:12–13 — 277
116:14 — 251
116:16–17 — 277
119:171 — 36
132:11 — 30
133:1 — 34
140:4–5 — 137
147:19–20 — 131

Proverbs
3:5 — 182
8:22–32 — 44
13:10 — 27
24:16 — 86

Ecclesiastes
21:30 — 190

Isaiah
1:11 — 277
2:4 — 28
3:9 — 121
5:5–6 — 99
7:14 — 24

8:11–15 — 112
8:15 — 116
8:19–20 — 181
9:6 — 16
11:9 — 28
11:10 — 61
28:13 — 116
28;16 — 43, 106, 113
42:8 — 188
46:3 — 79
48:1 — 84
48:4 — 164
53:1 — 116
55:11 — 104
60:1 — 207
60:6 — 281
60:19 — 68

Jeremiah
3:3 — 121
5:2 — 84
23:24, 23 — 63
23:29 — 13
26:23 — 93
29:6 — 220
36:21–24 — 90
48:10 — 238

Daniel
1:6 — 192
3:19 ff. — 271
3:20 ff. — 192
8:19 — 142

Hosea
3:1 — 123
3:4–5 — 101
14:1–2 — 276

Micah
5:1 — 186
5:2 — 185, 187 f.
5:3–4 — 189

Habakkuk
1:13 — 257
2:4 — 114

Haggai
2:6, 21 — 7

Zechariah
11:11 — 90

Malachi
4:2 — 97

Matthew
1:21 — 157 f.
2:2 — 164
2:3 — 170
2:4–6 — 171
2:6 — 186
2:7–8 — 189
2:9–10 — 190
2:11 — 160, 194,
  275 f.
2:12 — 198, 283
3:11 — 74
3:16 — 65
4:7 — 200
5:3 — 25, 266
5:18 — 265
5:19 — 264
6:24 — 25
6:28–29 — 87
8:4 — 23
10:32–33 — 141
10:37 — 218
11:5 — 25
11:6 — 197
11:11 — 3
11:12 — 65
11:13 — 105
12:34 — 46
13:54–56 — 146
13:57 — 146
14:3–12 — 90
16:17 — 175, 194
16:18 — 113
16:24 — 234
17:3 — 21
17:24–27 — 7
17:27 — 215
18:15 — 225
20:25 — 214